The affluent worker: industrial attitudes and behaviour

JOHN H. GOLDTHORPE
Official Fellow, Nuffield College, Oxford

DAVID LOCKWOOD
Professor of Sociology, University of Essex

FRANK BECHHOFER
Lecturer in Sociology, University of Edinburgh

JENNIFER PLATT
Lecturer in Sociology, University of Sussex

CAMBRIDGE UNIVERSITY PRESS

Cambridge
London New York Melbourne

Published by the Syndics of the Cambridge University Press
The Pitt Building, Trumpington Street, Cambridge CB2 1RP
Bentley House, 200 Euston Road, London NW1 2DB
32 East 57th Street, New York, NY 10022, USA
296 Beaconsfield Parade, Middle Park, Melbourne 3206, Australia

Library of Congress catalogue card number: 68-21192

ISBN 0 521 07109 7 hard covers
ISBN 0 521 09466 6 paperback

First published 1968
Reprinted 1970 1972 1978

Printed in Great Britain at the
University Press, Cambridge

Contents

Contents

Preface

The research on which this monograph is based was financed by the Department of Applied Economics of the University of Cambridge, assisted in part by a grant from the Human Sciences Committee of the Department of Scientific and Industrial Research (now the Science Research Council). We thank both these bodies for their support.

The research was directed jointly by the two senior authors as Research Associates of the Department of Applied Economics, while the two junior authors were members of the Department's research staff. The following were also, at various times, engaged on the project: as research officer, Mr Michael Rose; as research assistants, Mrs D. Dutkiewicz, Miss P. Ralph and Mrs R. Crompton; and as interviewers, Messrs P. Batten, J. Dichmont, D. Goddard, P. Jenkins and R. Payne. We acknowledge their valuable collaboration and, in particular, that of Mr Rose during the period of the main interviewing programme. Our appreciation must also be expressed to the many members of the Department's computing and typing staff who have given assistance to the project at all stages.

In carrying out our work in the field, we received the co-operation of a large number of individuals and organisations. Our thanks are due, in particular, to the following: Messrs R. R. Hopkins, W. Butt and R. Hamilton of Vauxhall Motors Ltd; Mr R. Grant of The Skefko Ball Bearing Company Ltd; Messrs P. Lister and R. Northam of Laporte Chemicals Ltd; Mr A. J. Sjogren of the Amalgamated Engineering Union; and Mr W. J. Bird of the National Union of General and Municipal Workers. We are also, of course, yet further indebted to the five hundred or so men and women who, in total, afforded us over a thousand hours of their time in interviews—with quite remarkable tolerance and goodwill.

Finally, we must acknowledge the advice, information and other assistance that we have received from our academic colleagues both in Cambridge and elsewhere. Those who have helped are too numerous to mention individually but we hope that they will, collectively, accept our gratitude.

1. Introduction

The primary aim of this monograph is descriptive: to give some account of the attitudes and behaviour of a sample of 'affluent' manual workers in the context of their industrial employment. A secondary aim is theoretical: to examine how the attitudes and behaviour in question can best be explained and understood. The presentation of our findings begins in chapter 2 with a fairly detailed examination of our sample's experience of their industrial jobs and of the nature of their attachment to the organisations which employ them. On this basis, the argument is then advanced that among the men we studied a particular *orientation* to work—one of a markedly instrumental kind—is predominant. In chapters 3 to 6 this argument is developed in relation to material which covers the other main areas of our workers' industrial lives. At various points in these chapters we are also concerned with the explanatory usefulness—and limitations—in regard to our findings of certain current theoretical approaches in the field of industrial sociology. In chapter 7 we move on to the question of the social correlates and sources of the view of work which characterises our affluent workers, and which is reflected in their industrial attitudes and behaviour in a variety of ways. Our principal objective is to develop a number of explanatory hypotheses; but some empirical material—in part of a confirmatory nature—is also produced. Finally, chapter 8 briefly reviews what appear to us as the main implications of the monograph in both its descriptive and theoretical aspects.

The research on which this monograph is based was carried out as part of a more general study of the sociology of the affluent worker. The main objective of this study was to test empirically the widely accepted thesis of working-class *embourgeoisement*: the thesis that, as manual workers and their families achieve relatively high incomes and living standards, they assume a way of life which is more characteristically 'middle class' and become in fact progressively assimilated into middle-class society. This question of *embourgeoisement* is not a concern of the present work other than in an indirect way: it is hoped that this and other similar publications, dealing with issues somewhat apart from the central problem of the research, will preface, and facilitate, the writing of the final report. However, the fact that this monograph is, as it were, a by-product of an enquiry with a different focus[1] has always to be kept in mind in assessing the wider significance of its findings. Considerations relevant to the main purpose of the project have, of course, largely determined the way in which the workers to be studied were selected and also the design of the interviewing schedules, which were our chief research instruments.

In planning the field investigations which formed the major part of the research, our first concern was to find a *locale* for these which would be *as favourable as possible* for the validation of the *embourgeoisement* thesis. We had, from the outset, considerable doubts about the soundness of the arguments involved in this, at least in the crude form in which they were usually expressed. These doubts were set out in publications prior to the start of our research.[2] Thus, we felt it important that our test of the thesis should, if possible, be made a critical one in the following sense: that if, in the case we studied, a process of *embourgeoisement* was shown *not* to be in evidence, then it could be regarded as extremely unlikely that such a process was occurring to any significant extent in British society as a whole. This strategy of the critical case involved, therefore, an attempt, in the first place, to specify theoretically the ideal kind of *locale* for our purpose—that is, the social setting in which *embourgeoisement* would seem most probable; and then, secondly, a decision about the best 'real-life' approximation to this.

The problems which arose in this connection were numerous; but although the ways in which they were resolved are, of course, vital in relation to our project as a whole, they need not concern us here at any length.[3] It will be sufficient to say that our eventual choice fell on the town of Luton in south-west Bedfordshire, and that among the chief considerations favouring this were the following:

(i) Luton was a prosperous and growing industrial centre in an area of the country which had in recent years experienced general economic expansion.

---

[1] A further monograph, *The Affluent Worker: Political Attitudes and Behaviour* (Cambridge, 1968), has appeared as a companion piece to the present study, and the final report on the project as a whole, in which discussion of the thesis of *embourgeoisement* and related issues occupies a central place, is *The Affluent Worker in the Class Structure* (Cambridge, 1969).

[2] See David Lockwood, 'The "New Working Class"', *European Journal of Sociology*, vol. 1, no. 2 (1960), and John H. Goldthorpe and David Lockwood, 'Affluence and the British Class Structure', *Sociological Review*, vol. 11, no. 2 (July 1963).

[3] They are discussed at length in *The Affluent Worker in the Class Structure*, ch. 2. For an early attempt at specifying the major conditions favourable to *embourgeoisement*, see David Lockwood and John H. Goldthorpe, 'The Manual Worker: Affluence, Aspiration and Assimilation', paper presented to the Annual Conference of the British Sociological Association, 1962 (available from the Department of Applied Economics, University of Cambridge).

(ii) In consequence, the town's labour force contained a high proportion of geographically mobile workers—workers who, it might be supposed, had come to Luton in part at least in search of higher living standards.

(iii) Also in consequence of the town's rapid growth, a high proportion of its population lived in new housing areas which included a relatively large amount of private development.

(iv) At the same time, Luton was somewhat removed from the older industrial regions of the country and was thus not dominated by their traditions of industrial relations or of industrial life generally.

(v) Luton contained a number of industrial firms noted for their high wages, their advanced personnel and welfare policies, and their records of industrial peace.

Once this setting for the research had been chosen, our next step was to draw up the sample of affluent workers to be studied through an interviewing programme. It was decided that the best basis for doing this would be provided by the pay-rolls of three of Luton's leading firms, which accounted between them for about 30% of the total labour force of the town and its immediate environs. We wished that, in the same way as with the *locale* for the study, the interviewing sample should be subject to certain specifications designed to favour the *embourgeoisement* thesis; and in this respect the personnel statistics which the firms were able to supply were invaluable to us. A further advantage of basing the sample on a small number of establishments was that we could thus collect fairly detailed information on the conditions of work and work situations of all the individuals concerned. In particular, we wished to examine the effect on workers' attitudes and behaviour of different types of production system, and our choice of firms was in fact made so that three major types—small-batch, large-batch and mass, and process production—were represented.[1]

The three firms in question were: Vauxhall Motors Ltd, a totally owned subsidiary of General Motors Corporation, engaged in Luton in the manufacture of saloon cars, station wagons and vans; The Skefko Ball Bearing Company Ltd, a member of the international SKF Organisation,

---

[1] This reflected our concern to incorporate into our research a full investigation of the industrial lives of the workers we studied. Current discussion of the *embourgeoisement* issue revealed a very one-sided emphasis on the worker as consumer rather than producer. However, we did not believe that in this respect we had enough information to follow through the strategy of the critical case to the point of concentrating on one particular kind of technological environment as being probably that most conducive to *embourgeoisement*. Rather, we aimed at covering a number of the most important general types of industrial technology. In this we were guided by the classification of production systems made in Joan Woodward, *Management and Technology*, H.M.S.O. (London, 1958).

producing ball and roller bearings;[1] and Laporte Chemicals Ltd, a member of the Laporte Group of companies which at its Luton plant produces a range of ammonium, potassium, sodium and barium compounds.

Within these enterprises, we then decided to confine our attention to male employees who were working in shop-floor jobs and who were in addition: (i) between the ages of 21 and 46; (ii) married and living with their wives; (iii) *regularly* earning *at least* £17 per week gross (October 1962); and (iv) resident in Luton itself or in immediately adjacent housing areas.[2] Further, we decided that in the case of each plant we would concentrate on men performing types of work which were central to the main production systems that were in operation. In Vauxhall, thus, we defined our field of interest as covering men who were engaged in assembly-line work. In Skefko, we concentrated on machine operators involved in small- and large-batch production, together with machine setters and craftsmen who were concerned in one way or another with servicing machines. And in Laporte we aimed to take in all types of process worker and all craftsmen engaged on process maintenance.[3] In effect, therefore, the 'population' of our critical case was made up of workers in the above occupational categories who also met our criteria regarding age, marital status, earnings and residence. It should be recognised, then, that the decisions taken here in defining the workers to be studied are in some degree arbitrary, other than in relation to our concern with the *embourgeoisement* issue, and that this is true in particular of the numbers of men covered by the different occupational categories which were included.

In sampling our population for interviewing purposes, certain difficulties and complications arose which are explained in appendix B. However, the sample which was eventually obtained was one of 326 individuals. Of these, we were unable to contact 12 (3·7%), and 64 (19·6%) refused to participate. This left, therefore, 250 (76·7%) of the sample who agreed to be interviewed at their place of work. After these interviews had been carried out, we then asked all those we had seen if they would agree to a further interview, together with their wives, in their own

---

[1] Skefko have in fact two physically separate plants in Luton. These are, however, in many ways interdependent and, for our purposes, could reasonably be treated as one.

[2] This condition was relaxed slightly for Laporte workers so as to include three 'satellite' communities very close to Luton in which there was some concentration of Laporte employees.

[3] To be entirely consistent here we should have included two other types of worker from Vauxhall: men engaged in the manufacture (as opposed to assembly) of components and, as in the other plants, craftsmen. However, this would have been beyond the resources of the project, and we thus decided to concentrate on the assemblers as the most distinctive group.

TABLE I. *Distribution of final sample by firm and type of work*

Firm	Type of work	No. of workers interviewed	
Vauxhall	Assembly	86	
		—	86
Skefko	Machining	41	
	Machine-setting	23	
	Maintenance etc. (craftsmen)	45	
		—	109
Laporte	Process work	23	
	Process maintenance (craftsmen)	11	
		—	34
	TOTAL	229	

homes. Of the 250, 229 (91·6 % or 70·3 % of the original sample) consented to this, and these men—and their wives—were then taken as being the main subjects of our research.[1] The distribution of the 229 men between the three firms and the different types of work which we considered within each firm is shown in table I.[2]

For reasons which are given in appendix B, our sample is not in fact a random one. Nonetheless, there are good grounds—also noted in this appendix—for regarding it as being for the most part highly representative. The one main exception to this is that the number of assemblers included is a good deal too low, judged by the size of this occupational category relative to the others which the population comprises. This is of little consequence since, as we have already noted, the number of men in each category is itself largely arbitrary. What *is* important to realise in this connection is that, in using the interview material based on the sample, no great significance can attach to data relating to the sample *as a whole* where there is any marked variation in the pattern of response from one occupational group to another.[3] For this reason the discussion of our interview findings throughout this study is most frequently based upon comparisons and differences between occupational groups, and generalisations concerning the sample as a whole are introduced into the argument only where *all* groups display an essentially similar pattern.

In addition to this main sample, we also planned, for comparative purposes, a sample of lower-level (i.e. non-managerial) white-collar

[1] Interviewing took place between October 1962 and February 1964.
[2] Table A1 in appendix A (Additional tables) gives corresponding details of response rates.
[3] For, to the extent, of course, that such variation exists, the 'overall' pattern of response of the sample will be a function partly of the number of respondents in each group.

employees, drawn from the same three firms. Unfortunately, administrative and other difficulties prevented the inclusion of Vauxhall, and the sample had thus to be taken from the relevant grades in Skefko and Laporte. We again limited our attention to married men between the ages of 21 and 46, but in this case no minimum level of earnings was fixed and the requirement of residence in Luton was dropped. In all, 75 white-collar workers were approached[1] and of this number 54 (72%) agreed to our request for a single interview, at home and together with their wives.

Table 2 gives some indication of the relative economic positions of our affluent manual workers and the men in the white-collar sample in terms of age, income and number of dependent children. The data show that the white-collar workers tend to hold some advantage over the manual workers in that they have higher *family* incomes (more white-collar wives worked) and fewer dependent children (white-collar couples had smaller families at all age levels); in other words, the advantages appear to result from some more or less deliberate family 'policy'. On the other hand, considering the amount brought in weekly by the chief breadwinner, it is the manual sample who are better off.

Considered as a study in industrial sociology, it is certain that this monograph suffers from various shortcomings through its dependence upon research in which the industrial attitudes and behaviour of the subjects of the investigation were but one of several areas of interest. On almost every topic discussed in the pages which follow it is not difficult to think of further information which it would have been desirable to have but which our enquiry neglected. Furthermore, our research methods were not as rigorous as might have been possible in a more restricted project. For example, a study concerned with 'attitudes' should, ideally, have used more sophisticated methods of ordering and measuring these than we were able to apply across the variety of issues our interviews covered. And, similarly, to study 'behaviour' in the most satisfactory way would have called for more systematic observational studies, in addition to interviewing, than we were able to carry out.[2] Finally, there is, of course, the point that the workers we studied were—with the central objectives of our research in mind—a highly selected group. It is particularly important that this should be remembered wherever material concerning our sample is

[1] In Skefko, clerks, cost clerks and 'correspondents' (clerks dealing with orders); in Laporte, clerks and commercial assistants. All eligible men in these grades were included.

[2] In all three firms a good deal of observational work was in fact performed, but this was of an impressionistic kind rather than the detailed and quantitative study of the behaviour of individuals and groups which is possible, say, through 'activity sampling' techniques.

TABLE 2. *Age, income and number of dependent children: manual and white-collar samples*

	Manual sample (N = 229) percentage	White-collar sample (N = 54) percentage
Age		
21–30	23	28
31–40	49	41
41 +	28	31
	100	100
*Income**		
Husband: Under £18	47	61
£18–£23. 19s.	49	32
£24 and over	4	6
No information	1	1
	101	100
Family: Under £18	19	20
£18–£23. 19s.	56	39
£24–£29. 19s.	18	26
£30 and over	7	11
No information	1	4
	101	100
Dependent children†		
0	17	35
1	28	32
2	34	19
3	14	9
4+	7	6
	100	101

* Reported average weekly earnings, *net* of tax etc., i.e. 'take-home pay'.
† I.e. children under 15 plus children over 15 still in full-time education.

used as a basis for the discussion of general theoretical issues: the significance of the sample must always be taken as that of a special rather than of a typical case.[1]

[1] It would, however, be wrong to suppose that, in terms of their 'affluence' alone, the workers we studied represented very special groups *within* their firms' labour forces. All assemblers with two years' service at Vauxhall, and some with less, earned more than our £17 per week limit, and so did the large majority of the Skefko craftsmen and setters and of the Laporte craftsmen. With the machinists and the process workers, we would estimate that we were confined to the best-paid third. In accounting for the quite small numbers of these workers included in our sample, the limiting effects of our other specifications—regarding age and residence especially—must be borne in mind.

On the other hand, some compensating advantages of drawing our data from a wider study do exist; and, as far as possible, the monograph has been designed so as to exploit these. First, while our information on our respondents' attitudes and behaviour in the context of their employment may not always be as detailed or as precise as might be wished, it is nonetheless fairly extensive in its range. For example, in subsequent chapters we deal with data relating to the worker and his job, the worker and his work group, the worker and his firm, the worker and his union, and the worker and his economic future. The same range has not always been covered in other studies of industrial employees. Secondly, and more importantly, we also have a considerable amount of material at our disposal concerning our respondents' 'out-plant' lives. Because the perspectives of our research were much broader than those of most specifically 'industrial' studies, we know something about the men in our sample not only as industrial employees but also as husbands and fathers, as neighbours and friends, as individuals with certain life-histories and objectives and so on. We have, therefore, the opportunity of seeing their attitudes and behaviour as workers not in the context of the industrial enterprise alone but, rather, in the much wider context provided by family, community and class.

It is chiefly on account of these features of our data that we believe the present study can have some theoretical as well as descriptive interest. On the basis of our wide range of information about the men we studied, pertaining to both their working and non-working lives, it would seem possible to offer something of value towards the examination of questions such as the following: In what degree and in what ways are industrial attitudes and behaviour *patterned*—so that the nature of the worker's relationship, with say, his employing organisation is associated with the nature of his relationships with his workmates, his supervisor, or his union? To the extent that such patterning is in evidence, in what terms is this to be explained and understood? Is it to be seen, for example, as being determined primarily by features of the work situation itself—as being, say, the result of workers' experience of, and reaction to, the work-tasks and -roles which they are required to perform? Or is it rather the case that any such pattern may equally, or perhaps more basically, derive from a particular orientation which workers have taken towards employment—from the wants and expectations they have of it, and thus from the way in which they *define* their work situation rather than simply respond to this? If this latter alternative applies, what are the major determinants, external to the work situation, of the meaning which men give to their work and of the place

8

and function they accord to work within their lives as a whole? This study does not pretend to make any final statement on these questions. It does, however, offer data which enable them to be raised and, hopefully, to be answered at least in part in a specific case. And it is largely in this way that the material which is presented gains such wider significance as it may be said to possess.

Lastly, though, we would wish to suggest that the interest of the monograph at a purely descriptive level should not be underestimated. The workers we have studied, if not highly typical of the present, may well prove to be in many ways more typical of the future. This is a point to which we shall from time to time return in the course of later chapters as we compare the findings of our research with those of investigations carried out among less affluent workers living in older, more 'traditional', industrial communities. However, one likely objection to this claim of 'proto-typicality' may perhaps be anticipated at this stage: that is, that the workers in our sample are all employed in establishments using more or less 'conventional' methods of manufacture—whereas the industrial workers of the future must surely be thought of as working in plants with highly automated production systems. The important question here is, of course, what one means by 'the future'.[1] If one is taking the very long view, then it is no doubt reasonable to suppose the near universality of the automatic factory. But if, on the other hand, one restricts one's range to, say, the next few decades—as we would wish to do—then the idea of fully automated industry as the dominant type appears to be somewhat premature. The best assessments would seem to indicate that during this period, even in the most highly developed countries, the more advanced conventional methods of production—and notably mass production—will, on balance, decline little in importance, and that it may even be the case that the extent of their utilisation will increase more than that of automation itself.[2] Thus, we would argue, workers in jobs of the type with which we are concerned by no means represent figures of diminishing significance on the industrial scene; and the great interest which automation now excites should not be allowed to distract us from learning more about such workers, particularly in the condition new to them of relative prosperity.

[1] And also, perhaps, what one means by 'automation'. We use the term here in its strict sense to refer to production systems which involve an automatic and in some respects self-regulating chain of process. See L. Landon Goodman, *Man and Automation* (London, 1957), pp. 24–6.

[2] See, for example, Georges Friedmann, *Le Travail en Miettes*, 2nd ed. (Paris, 1964), pp. 14–22 and the statistical appendices; also Department of Scientific and Industrial Research, *Automation* (London, 1956).

2. The worker and his job

In the previous chapter, table 2 showed the distribution of our sample of 229 manual workers among the three firms on which the sample is based and in relation to types of work characteristic of the production systems of these firms. The different groups of workers represented in this table can also be classified into three main skill levels, as follows:

(i) *Highly skilled:* the craftsmen in Skefko and Laporte—toolmakers, millwrights and other maintenance men—who are all workers with apprenticeships or comparable training.

(ii) *Relatively skilled:* the setters in Skefko, who have not in general had any lengthy training but who have 'picked up' over time the particular skill which their present jobs require.[1]

(iii) *Semi-skilled:* the ordinary production workers in all three firms—assemblers, machinists and process workers—who are performing jobs which usually call for only very short training periods of a few hours or days.[2]

In considering the relationship between the worker and his job[3] it will be useful to combine this classification by skill with that based on type of work performed. By so doing the sample may be divided into five 'occupational groups' in the manner shown in table 3. Our findings reveal that for the workers in these five groups, industrial employment offers significantly different patterns of satisfaction and deprivation, and further that these men differ too in the stance they take towards work and in the meanings they give to it.[4] At the same time, though, our data also indicate that these

---

[1] One foreman in Skefko remarked that a good machinist, after having watched his setter working for several years, could almost do a set-up himself without any training at all. Generally, though, it was thought that new setters needed to work under supervision for a month or more before they were proficient.

[2] The main exception to this arose in the case of nineteen of the machinists (Skefko) who had been trained to do some of the setting for their own machines.

[3] The term 'job' is commonly used with two quite different meanings, the distinction between which is of some importance to the content of this chapter: 'job' may refer either to the worker's immediate work-task and work-role or, more broadly, to his employment in a particular firm. In writing—as in interviewing—we have found that the only practical solution is to use the term in both senses and to make explicit which is intended in any particular case other than where the context leaves no doubt or where the ambiguity is unimportant or convenient.

[4] The bringing together of the craftsmen from two different firms is to be justified on this basis.

TABLE 3. *Classification of manual sample into five occupational groups*

Group	Firm(s)	No. in sample	
1. Craftsmen (highly skilled)	Skefko	45	
	Laporte	11	
		—	56
2. Setters (relatively skilled)	Skefko	23	
3. Process workers ⎤ all	Laporte	23	
4. Machinists ⎬ semi-	Skefko	41	
5. Assemblers ⎦ skilled	Vauxhall	86	
		—	150
TOTAL		229	

differences are capable of being understood as variations on a theme; that notwithstanding differences in skill and job content, our affluent workers for the most part share in a relatively distinctive orientation towards work, and one which, it may be suggested, is not unconnected with their affluent condition.

The difficulties involved in assessing the degree of workers' satisfaction with their jobs are by now fairly well recognised among industrial sociologists. The evidence of a number of studies reveals that the large majority of workers, if asked how they like their jobs, tend to give generally favourable answers; or, if asked to rate the level of their satisfaction on some sort of scale, tend to make choices which fall in the positive range. Results of this kind have in fact been several times achieved in cases where other evidence has indicated fairly clearly that the workers in question experienced quite severe deprivations in performing their jobs.[1] Part of the explanation of this is probably that, as Blauner has suggested, a worker will find it difficult to admit he dislikes his job without thereby threatening his self-respect. For, in our kind of society, a man's work tends to be a more important determinant of his self-image than most other of his social activities. Thus, there is considerable psychological pressure upon the individual to say that he finds his job acceptable: to say otherwise may well be tantamount to admitting that he does not find *himself* acceptable.[2] In particular, one would add, this will tend to be so where economic

[1] See for example the review of research presented by Robert Blauner, 'Work Satisfaction and Industrial Trends in Modern Society', in W. Galenson and S. M. Lipset (eds.), *Labor and Trade Unionism* (New York, 1960).

[2] Blauner, 'Work Satisfaction and Industrial Trends', pp. 341, 354–6.

conditions permit a relatively wide range of job choice and offer definite inducements to occupational mobility.

Furthermore, under such conditions, the very fact that men remain in particular jobs may generally be taken to imply *some* degree of satisfaction with them, relative to other jobs which are in the market. It may be reasonably assumed that the jobs which are retained meet some, at least, of the wants and expectations which employees have in regard to work, and that there are no other jobs known to be available which offer sufficiently greater rewards to make a move worth while. In this case, then, the finding that a high proportion of workers assess their jobs more or less positively can be regarded as neither a surprising nor a very illuminating one.

In our interviews, we deliberately avoided any direct questions on job satisfaction of the type which have become conventional. Rather, we approached the matter obliquely, and, initially, through two questions which invited our respondents to *compare* their present job with (*a*) others they had held previously in the same firm and (*b*) others which might be regarded as potentially open to them in their present employment.[1]

We asked first: 'Do you prefer the job you're doing now to others you have done in [name of firm]?' The pattern of response which this question produced across our five occupational groups is shown in table 4.

In the case of the craftsmen, only a smallish minority had worked in other jobs in the same firm and thus the data for this group are of limited value. This, however, does not affect the most salient feature of the table as a whole: the very high job satisfaction, as revealed by our question, on the part of the setters. Twenty out of the twenty-one men in this group who had held some other job in Skefko reported that they preferred their present work, as compared with between a half and two-thirds of the men in the other groups. The explanation of this, in general terms at least, is fairly obvious: these setters were all men who had been upgraded to their present jobs from the ranks of the ordinary machinists. Thus, they differed from the large majority in all the other groups in that they had experienced some quite significant occupational advancement *within* their firm. The process workers and assemblers, like the rank-and-file machinists, had almost all come into semi-skilled work when taking up their present employment and had remained in broadly similar jobs at this level; similarly, the craftsmen had mostly been in skilled jobs throughout their employment and in fact from completing the apprenticeship which had

---

[1] I.e. it was made clear that at this point we were using 'job' in the narrower of the two senses indicated on page 10, n. 3, above. This usage is thus retained throughout our discussion of the results of these two questions.

TABLE 4. *Preference for present job in comparison with other jobs previously held in same firm*

	Craftsmen (N = 12)	Setters (N = 21)	Process workers (N = 21)	Machinists (N = 29)	Assemblers (N = 70)	All (N = 153)*
			Percentage			
Prefer present job	58	95	52	66	66	67
Do not prefer present job (i.e. preferred a previous job in same firm)	33	0	38	31	19	22
Other, D.K.	8	5	10	3	16†	10
TOTALS	99	100	100	100	101	99

* Men who had always worked in their present job are excluded.
† Comprises eleven men who stated that in Vauxhall 'all jobs are the same'.

specifically qualified them for this type of work. Only the setters had achieved a 'break-through' from their initial occupational level to a clearly higher one.

In more detail, however, the setters' high level of satisfaction can best be understood in terms of the reasons they themselves gave for preferring their present jobs. One factor was, of course, pay; setters' earnings were generally higher than those of ordinary machinists.[1] But reasons relating to pay were far from being those most frequently given. Much more important were reasons concerning the actual nature of the job itself—the greater opportunity it gave for using skills and for acting autonomously, and the greater variety and interest in work-tasks which it afforded. The following are typical of the replies given by setters when asked why they preferred being in this kind of work:

'As setter you have to use your mind more and it [the job] is more responsible. You feel as if you *are* somebody.'

'Being a setter draws more skill out of you. There's nothing to it being an operator. [As a setter] you have to use your brains more; there are little snags to get round.'

'You're left alone—there's only myself on the job. You go along nicely on your own.'

'As a setter, I've more opportunity to work on my own initiative, and figure things out for myself. I'm not tied to a machine all day long.'

'There's nothing monotonous about it. Most machining is cut up so much that it's all repetition. My present work is all varied.'

[1] See table A2 in appendix A.

TABLE 5. *Reasons given for preferring present job to other jobs previously held in same firm*

Class of reason	Craftsmen (N = 12)	Setters (N = 21)	Process workers (N = 21)	Machinists (N = 29)	Assemblers (N = 70)	All (N = 153)
			Times mentioned			
A. Reasons relating to intrinsic rewards:						
Greater opportunity for use of skill	3	11	4	10	10	38
Greater variety in work tasks	3	4	5	8	14	34
Greater autonomy, room for initiative	2	4	5	6	16	33
Greater intrinsic interest (not further specified)	0	5	1	1	8	15
TOTALS	8	24	15	25	48	120
B. Reasons relating to physical and social environment:						
Better physical conditions	3	0	3	3	13	22
Better supervision, 'shop atmosphere'	0	0	2	3	5	10
TOTALS	3	0	5	6	18	32
C. Reasons relating to extrinsic rewards and considerations, convenience etc.:						
Better pay	0	4	2	10	3	19
Habituation to present job	0	0	0	1	9	10
Other	0	3	4	3	9	19
TOTALS	0	7	6	14	21	48
ALL REASONS	11	31	26	45	87	200
Reasons in class A as percentage of all reasons	73	77	58	56	55	60
Reasons in class B as percentage of all reasons	27	0	19	13	21	16
Reasons in class C as percentage of all reasons	0	23	23	31	24	24
TOTALS	100	100	100	100	100	100

Table 5 provides a classification of the reasons given by *all* those in our sample who preferred their present job to previous ones in the same firm. It can be seen that, as might be expected, the setters, along with the craftsmen, more frequently offered reasons which referred to the intrinsic rewards of their jobs than did the semi-skilled workers. At the same time it should be noted that, even with the latter, reasons of this kind would still

TABLE 6. *Preference for some other shop-floor job in comparison with present one*

	Craftsmen (N = 56)	Setters (N = 23)	Process workers (N = 23)	Machinists (N = 41)	Assemblers (N = 86)	All (N = 229)
			Percentage			
Would prefer some other shop-floor job	16	9	9	29	62	34
Prefer present job	84	87	74	64	36	62
Other, D.K.	0	4	17	7	2	4
TOTALS	100	100	100	100	100	100

appear to be more important than any other, and account for more than half of all reasons given.

Our second question followed on immediately from the first. We asked: 'Are there any other shop-floor jobs in [name of firm] which you would rather do than your own?' If respondents answered 'Yes' to this, we then asked which job or jobs they had in mind and why they thought they would prefer these. The nature of the response to the first part of the question is shown in table 6. Again it can be seen that there is one outstanding feature: the assemblers appear on this basis to be by far the *least* satisfied group; that is to say, clearly more of the assemblers than of any other group— two-thirds, in fact—would prefer some other shop-floor job to the one they hold at present. The replies of the assemblers to the second and third parts of the question make clear why this is so. Overwhelmingly, the kind of job change that assemblers would like turns out to be one which would take them off the 'track' altogether and into such jobs as inspection, testing, rectification and maintenance.[1] And among the reasons given for favouring such a change, ones relating to the content of work-tasks are clearly the most important. The following is an illustrative selection, the preferred type of job to which the comment is related being shown in italics.

rectifying
'You learn more about a car. You can see it whole. You know every part independently and how they fit together.'

testing
'There's more to it. You look for snags and sort them out. You have to pull the engine down and so forth. There's more skill to it.'

[1] One or other of these jobs was mentioned by more than half of the assemblers who said they would prefer some other job to their own. By contrast, only 1 in 10 mentioned other assembly jobs and then invariably ones which were not track-paced or were easier-paced than their present jobs, or were near the end of the line (and were thus felt to be more interesting).

inspecting

'Foremen and management rather look down on the production worker. They have to appreciate what an inspector does.'

inspecting

'There's more to it. You get the variety in jobs. You're left to look for things. There's the chance to move around more.'

maintenance

'It's a better grade of job. There's more scope to use your initiative. There are different jobs every day. It's not so repetitive, not so boring, as assembly work.'

Table 7 shows the extent to which reasons of this kind predominated in the replies of the assemblers in comparison with those of such other semi-skilled men—process workers and machinists—as would also have preferred some other shop-floor job. It is evident that insofar as process workers and machinists did wish to have a different kind of job, their reasons for this were less concentrated than were those of the assemblers on job content and intrinsic rewards. But again, as with the previous question, it is equally clear that such considerations have to be recognised as being of fairly widespread importance in determining workers' job preferences, at least within the range of opportunities provided by employment within a given enterprise.[1] Furthermore, it may also be observed, taking the two questions together, that a particularly strong emphasis on the actual nature of their work-tasks is associated *both* with the setters' very high level of job satisfaction, as indicated by the first question, *and* with the assemblers' notably low level of satisfaction, as indicated by the second. In other words, there is evidence here that among the workers we studied it was this immediate relationship between men and their jobs which was the aspect of their work most capable of producing either some feeling of personal fulfilment or, on the other hand, some clear sense of deprivation.[2]

This conclusion is one that is supported further by the data we obtained from three more direct questions in our interviews concerning respondents' immediate experience of their work-tasks and -roles. Moreover, since these questions were broadly comparable to ones asked in other investigations of

[1] The reasons given by the 9 craftsmen and 2 setters who would have preferred some other shop-floor job are not included in table 7 because of the smallness of the numbers. But here again reasons relating to intrinsic rewards were by far the most prominent, accounting for 11 out of the 15 reasons given by the 11 men together.

[2] To this extent, then, our findings are in accord with the views of writers such as Georges Friedmann, who have insisted upon the fundamental importance of the content of work-tasks to job satisfaction, and go clearly against the idea that many factory workers are simply 'happy robots'. See G. Friedmann, *Où va le Travail Humain?* (Paris, 1953), and *Le Travail en Miettes* (Paris, 1964).

TABLE 7. *Reasons given for preferring some other shop-floor job to present job: process workers and machinists compared with assemblers*

Class of reason	Process workers and Machinists (N = 14)	Assemblers (N = 53)
	Times mentioned	
A. Reasons relating to intrinsic rewards:		
Greater variety in work-tasks	5	20
Greater opportunity for use of skill	2	18
Great intrinsic interest (not further specified)	3	13
Greater autonomy, room for initiative	0	11
TOTALS	10	62
B. Reasons relating to physical and social environment:		
Better physical conditions	2	4
Better supervision, 'shop atmosphere'	1	1
TOTALS	3	5
C. Reasons relating to extrinsic rewards and considerations, convenience etc.:		
Better pay	3	6
Other	4	8
TOTALS	7	14
ALL REASONS	20	81
Reasons in class A as percentage of all reasons	50	77
Reasons in class B as percentage of all reasons	15	6
Reasons in class C as percentage of all reasons	35	17
TOTALS	100	100

job attitudes, the results produced enable us to form some idea of the nature of this experience relative to that of other industrial workers. The questions were: 'Do you find your present job monotonous?'; 'Do you find you can think about other things while doing your job?'; and 'Do you ever find the pace of the job too fast?'.[1] In framing these three questions, we had in mind the contention of Friedmann and others that modern factory work is essentially characterised by its *lack of variety*, its *fragmentation* and its *speed*. Table 8 shows the response which was obtained from our five occupational groups.

[1] In the case of the machinists, the only group who were on piecework, we asked: 'For a man wanting to make a decent wage, do you think the pace of the job is ever too fast?'

TABLE 8. *Experience of work-tasks and roles*

		Craftsmen (N = 56)	Setters (N = 23)	Process workers (N = 23)	Machinists (N = 41)	Assemblers (N = 86)	All (N = 229)
				Percentage			
Find job monotonous	Yes	14	13	22	46	67	41
	No	70	78	70	49	26	50
	Other, D.K.	16	9	9	5	7	9
	TOTALS	100	100	101	100	100	100
Can think about other things while doing job	Yes	55	35	65	78	86	70
	No	39	61	35	20	13	28
	Other, D.K.	5	4	0	2	1	3
	TOTALS	99	100	100	100	100	101
Find pace of job too fast	Yes	11	26	22	54	36	31
	No	84	74	74	42	64	67
	Other, D.K.	5	0	4	5	0	3
	TOTALS	100	100	100	101	100	101

The replies we received to the question on monotony reveal that, as might be expected, monotony is experienced more among the semi-skilled men than among the craftsmen and setters, and most of all among the assemblers. This pattern thus reinforces the indication from previous data that monotony is a definite source of job dissatisfaction, and indeed it proves to be the case that within the sample as a whole a highly significant association exists between experiencing monotony and having a preference for some other shop-floor job.[1] Furthermore, it should be noted that the proportion of men among both the assemblers and the machinists who report that their jobs are monotonous appears to be definitely high in comparison with the findings of other studies. The data brought together by Wyatt and Marriott for Great Britain and by Blauner for the United States provide us with useful standards in this respect.[2]

[1] $\chi^2 = 25\cdot2$; 1 df; $p < 0\cdot001$.

[2] In the British studies, the most comparable data relate to a sample of 400 semi-skilled factory workers and show that the proportion of men who said they found their jobs 'very boring' or 'boring' (as opposed to 'very interesting', 'interesting' or 'neither boring nor interesting') ranged from 30% in the case of machine-feeders and 27% in the case of men on conveyor-assembly work to 8% with men on lathe work. See S. Wyatt & R. Marriott, *A Study of Attitudes to Factory Work*, Medical Research Council, Special Report Series, no. 292 (London, H.M.S.O., 1956), appendix B, pp. 110 and 111. Cf. also the data given on pp. 19–22 of this report. Of the American data, the most extensive are those from the *Fortune*–Roper survey covering almost 3,000 'blue-collar' factory employees. Of the unskilled and low-skilled men,

The replies to our second question reveal that many men who did not complain that their work was monotonous nonetheless found that they could think about other things while doing their jobs; that is to say, their work did not absorb their full attention. In all groups other than the setters this was in fact the experience of the majority; and it is particularly notable that only 39% of the most skilled men—the craftsmen—claimed that their work required their total mental commitment. This experience of unabsorbing jobs may also be regarded as being, for most individuals, a further form of deprivation in work, and it, too, is found to be clearly associated with a preference for having some other kind of job.[1] Moreover, in this case again, comparisons with other findings would suggest that, with the exception of the setters, a notably high proportion of our sample were conscious of the unfulfilling nature of the work-tasks they were required to perform.[2]

Finally, the response to our question on the pace of work indicated that, among the workers we studied, this was in fact another important variable bearing on job satisfaction. Although finding the pace of work too fast was not significantly associated with experiencing monotony or with being able to think about other things, it again *was* associated with having a preference for a different shop-floor job.[3] And, once more, the available comparative data imply that, at least among the less skilled men in our sample, the number who felt that they had to work too fast was relatively high, even though it was only with the machinists that this was reported by a majority.[4]

In sum, then, two points emerge: first, that among our affluent workers

the overall proportion reporting that they found their jobs 'mostly' or 'completely' 'dull and monotonous' (as opposed to 'interesting', 'mostly' or 'nearly all of the time') was 34%. In the case of such workers in the automobile industry, which appeared to be that most likely to create monotonous work, the corresponding figure was 53%. See R. Blauner, *Alienation and Freedom: the Factory Worker and his Industry* (Chicago, 1964), pp. 116–17 and appendix B, table 42.

[1] $\chi^2 = 18.8$; 1 df; $p < 0.001$. Only in a handful of cases did men regard positively the lack of attention which their jobs required or, for that matter, view negatively the need for full attention in jobs where this need arose. And both of these reactions were largely confined to men in particularly fragmented or routine jobs in which the ability to 'daydream' was seen as a relative compensation, or the need for constant 'surface' attention was felt to be an added strain in the absence of any associated satisfaction.

[2] The most comparable data are again from the *Fortune*-Roper survey. Respondents were asked: 'Can you do the work on the job and keep your mind on other things most of the time, or not?' The highest proportion of affirmative answers from any industry was 54%, and only in three industries out of the 16 covered were such answers given by a majority of workers. See Blauner, *Alienation and Freedom*, appendix B, table 41.

[3] $\chi^2 = 5.1$; 1 df; $p < 0.025$.

[4] Wyatt and Marriott report that in a study of 557 semi-skilled workers in car assembly plants and 419 in rolling mills, only 10% of the men in the former type of work and 6% of those in the latter commented unfavourably about the speed of their work. *A Study of Attitudes to*

generally, the experience of monotony, of unabsorbing work and of an excessive pace of work were all apparent sources of deprivation and of job dissatisfaction; and, second, that, at least with some groups in the sample, such experience would seem to be more than usually widespread, in the light of more extensive studies of factory employees. In other words, it could be said that, among our affluent workers, the performance of work-tasks was accompanied by various, and in some groups fairly generalised, psychological or physical stresses.

One other set of data from our interviews proves relevant to the present discussion, and particularly in clarifying further the variations in job experience and attitudes which exist between our five occupational groups. At the end of the section of the interview which dealt with the respondent's present job, we asked: 'If there was one thing about your job here you could change, what would it be?' Through the extremely 'open' form of this question, we aimed to bring out the nature of those dissatisfactions with their work-tasks and work-roles which had greatest salience in our respondents' minds. The results which were achieved are summarised in table 9. The kinds of change which were most often suggested have been arranged in the first column so as to show the way in which, from group to group, different aspects of the job appeared to cause the greatest concern.[1]

Among the craftsmen it can be seen that 36 (or 60%) of a total of 60 changes suggested had to do with the organisation of work, with supervision, or with tools, equipment and machines. And, typically, the opportunity was taken to express strong criticism of the existing situation in these respects. The following are illustrative of the replies our question received.

'One change I'd like to make? The supervision without a doubt! They're an inept crowd. And you can't offer an opinion of your own. In your apprenticeship you're taught to be independent—how to design your own work. Here...they won't accept that anyone on the floor is capable of that. They've no faith in the chaps under them.'

'I'd like to have the work allocated and then be free to get on with it without immediate supervision. There are too many people around here who want to know the lot.' [Meaning supervisors.]

Factory Work, pp. 34–7. In the *Fortune*-Roper survey, respondents were asked whether their job made them work too fast *most of the time*—unfortunately a clearly stronger form of words than that used in our question. The highest proportion of affirmative answers was 35%— from workers in the automobile industry. See Blauner, *Alienation and Freedom*, appendix B, table 33.

[1] In doing this, account was taken not only of which particular changes were most frequently desired in any group, but also of which desired changes appeared, in the light of comments made, to be associated with basically the same problem or difficulty.

TABLE 9. *Desired changes in present job*

Kind of change	Craftsmen (N = 56)	Setters (N = 23)	Process workers (N = 23)	Machinists (N = 41)	Assemblers (N = 86)	All (N = 229)
	Times mentioned					
Better physical conditions	5	5	5	10	8	33
More convenient hours	4	8	1	3	4	20
Easier pace of work	0	0	0	0	9	9
More job changes, job enlargement	3	0 } 15	0	1	12 } 39	16
Different organisation of work	9	7	3	3	18	40
Better supervisory, personnel methods	18 } 36	0	3	8	3	32
Better tools, equipment, machines	9	1	2	4 } 23	1	17
Different method of payment	5	0	0	11	0	16
Other	7	1	4	7	13	32
TOTALS	60	22	18	47	68	215
No. having no desired change	4	3	9	3	27	46
Percentage of no. in group	7	13	39	7	31	

* Although the question asked about 'one thing' which could be changed, a number of respondents mentioned two kinds of change they would wish for, and in these cases both have been included in the table.

'I'd like to see them get rid of the idea that if Harry organised it like that forty years ago, *you*'ve got to now. I like to use my own initiative.'

'I'd like to change the ways they have of doing things. Their methods are outdated—and so are the tools...But if you make a suggestion to the management of the shop—who've been here and nowhere else—it's a joke!'

'I'd be happier if they had some new machines. There are a lot round here that are only fit for scrap.'

It could be said, then, that the main emphasis in the craftsmen's replies was, in effect, on changes which would, in their view, lead to greater efficiency, and which would at the same time increase their own involvement in, and control over, the work processes with which they were concerned.

Again, with the setters, the organisation of work also appears as a favourite theme. But in this case the main emphasis was less on changes which would increase efficiency than on ones which would make the setter's own job a little less demanding. This is related to the other main issue of concern—more convenient hours. Changes suggested in these two respects account for 15 (68%) of the 22 changes which the setters suggested in all.[1] Typical comments were as follows.

'They should make it easier to have spares and so on at hand—the things you need. Often you can't get hold of them.'

'I'd like to see a more even flow of work. It'd be good for us and for the operators.'

'I'd like more chance to get on day work. Shift work is too tiring.'

'Day-work hours were cut but not shift-work. We got more money as compensation but I would like to see home a little bit more.'

Among the semi-skilled men, the process workers were distinctive in being the one group which had no particularly clear focus of dissatisfaction. Improvements in physical conditions were more frequently suggested by this group than by any other, but perhaps more significant is the fact that the process workers also had the highest proportion of men who reported no desired change at all. With the machinists and assemblers, on the other hand, fairly marked—but differing—patterns of dissatisfaction are revealed.

Of the changes suggested by the machinists, 23 (or 49%) of the total concerned supervision or tools, equipment and machines. Examination of these suggestions in detail indicates that difficulties arising from piece-rates were most frequently at the root of the discontent. In this case, the quality of supervision or of technology tended to be a cause of complaint not because, as with the craftsmen, it was seen as preventing efficiency and good workmanship, but rather because of the way in which, it was felt, piece-rate earnings could be adversely affected. Foremen or setters might be less than just in the way they allocated 'good' and 'bad' work,[2] and supervisory or technical failures could lead to hold-ups for which men on piece-rates might not receive adequate compensation. The following are illustrative of the comments made by machinists in these respects.

'They should do away with piece-work—it's been done at Vauxhall. They would still get a fair whack of work and a man wouldn't be racing against the clock the whole while. Every ten to fifteen minutes, you look at the clock.'

---

[1] This pattern of response is consistent with the results of a further specific question we asked on our interviewees' immediate experience of their jobs: 'Do you find your present job physically tiring?' 65% of the setters said that they did, as compared with 25% of the craftsmen, 26% of the process workers, 49% of the machinists and 45% of the assemblers.

[2] I.e. work with piece-rates generally regarded as favourable ('loose') or as unfavourable ('tight') to the operative.

'I'd like to see more fairness on the shop floor. Foremen should have less authority. Some people are victimised by the foreman...It [giving out piece-work] ought to be done by a group of persons.'

'I'd like to change the way the firm's run—the administration—the way work is handed out. It's badly organised and unfair.'

'They should replace the machinery. It's not doing enough work and we suffer.'

With the assemblers, the emphasis was an entirely different one. Con-sistently with the reasons they gave for preferring some other shop-floor job, the changes most frequently desired by the men in this group were ones whereby their actual work-tasks would be made somewhat more rewarding or, at least, less monotonous and constraining. Thirty-nine (or 57%) of all the changes suggested related to an easier pace of work, to more variation in jobs and to job enlargement, or to other organisational changes, most of which were envisaged as leading to these same ends. Typical replies were as follows.

'I wish they'd make the track longer at my station so I could go a bit slower or get further in hand if I wanted to.'[1]

'There should be better organisation to stop jobs bunching on the line. They should be spread out more.'[2]

'Every man should move down a job occasionally, then you'd know every job really well. You could have a move every fortnight or week.'

'I'd like to have more to the job—as there used to be before the time for it was cut down.'

'They should make the jobs bigger. There'd be less monotony then.'

Considered together with the previous data, the response to this last question enables us, we believe, to form now a fairly clear idea of the main themes and variations in job experience and job attitudes among the five occupational groups which our sample comprises. We can sum up briefly as follows:

On the evidence presented, the most satisfied workers are clearly the setters. They are most positive towards the jobs they presently hold in their firm and, although their work is taxing and many would welcome some lessening of its physical demands, the effort they are required to make would appear to be largely experienced by them as a cost that is associa-ted with some more basic reward, rather than as any ultimate form of

---

[1] I.e. be able to work for longer at above the average pace required simply to keep up with the track and so gain more time in which to take a rest subsequently.

[2] Assemblers might be responsible for performing operations which were necessary only on some types of engine or body: if the types on which they had to work were not fairly regularly spaced as they came down the line, the pace of work required could become excessive.

23

deprivation.[1] Compared with workers in other groups, setters were more likely to speak of inherently rewarding aspects of their work and less likely to complain of inherent frustrations.

Next after the setters, in terms of immediate job satisfaction, we must place the craftsmen. Very few of the latter would wish to have any other shop-floor job and few appear to experience any very marked degree of stress in the actual execution of their work-tasks. On the other hand, though, less than half find their work totally absorbing, and there is a good deal of discontent and frustration over standards of supervision, work organisation and technical efficiency.

With the semi-skilled workers, the balance of rewards and costs is in general less favourable than with the more skilled men; and the greatest deprivations of all are undoubtedly experienced by the assemblers. Almost two-thirds of the men in this group would like to move to another shop-floor job, largely in order to escape from the monotony, 'meaninglessness' and constraints of their present tasks. Their dissatisfaction with their jobs stems from basic, inherent features of assembly-line work—repetitiveness, fragmentation, mechanical pacing. The machinists, too, seem generally to gain little direct reward from their jobs, even though two-thirds say they would not prefer any other kind of job at shop-floor level. Moreover, more than half these men claim that they have to work at too fast a pace in order to earn a decent wage, and piece-work appears to be a fairly frequent source of other grievances—with supervision and with tools, equipment and machines.

Finally, we have the process workers—a somewhat colourless group. Their jobs, it would seem, neither entail any very severe costs nor offer any great possibility of intrinsic rewards. Process workers appear to experience less deprivation in their work than do assemblers or machinists and they have no particularly marked dissatisfactions. Yet at the same time the data indicate, on almost all counts, that this group falls clearly below the level of job satisfaction enjoyed by the craftsmen or setters.[2]

[1] Baldamus has equated effort in work with the sum of the deprivations experienced by the worker, and regards such satisfactions as may be associated with effort as 'only apparent satisfactions, which are actually derived from deprivation'. However, although often appropriate, this approach would appear to neglect the possibility that with some kinds of industrial work it may rather be the case that quite 'real' satisfactions are gained and that, to reverse Baldamus's argument, it is the effort—or deprivation—which is now only 'relative' and which in fact 'derives from' the satisfaction. See W. Baldamus, *Efficiency and Effort* (London, 1961).

[2] In the case of the process workers, the idea of 'negative satisfaction' suggested by Frisch-Gauthier would appear particularly appropriate. See Jacqueline Frisch-Gauthier, 'Moral et Satisfaction au Travail' in Georges Friedmann and Pierre Naville (eds.), *Traité de Sociologie du Travail*, vol. 2 (Paris, 1962).

Overall, therefore, it could not be claimed that our affluent workers derived any very high degree of satisfaction immediately from the work-tasks and -roles which they performed. There are, as we have seen, some significant variations in this respect within our sample. Nevertheless, the general impression produced by our data is that with the majority of the semi-skilled men, at least, their work was largely experienced and regarded as an expenditure of effort made with the aim and expectation of extrinsic rather than intrinsic returns: in other words, the meaning which was given to work was essentially that of *labour*. From this point of view, the relatively high job satisfaction of the setters is then to be understood as a result of their having been promoted from the ranks of the semi-skilled—whose expectations regarding work they presumably once shared—into jobs which are more directly rewarding as well as being better paid. And, on the other hand, the degree of dissatisfaction revealed by the craftsmen— centring on social and technical aspects of their work—may be related to the fact that these men have expectations which are generally greater than those of the workers in the other groups; expectations, that is, which take for granted fairly high economic returns and which are also concerned with the degree to which the individual is allowed to exercise his skills in an autonomous way.

So far we have been concerned with assessing workers' experience of, and attitudes towards, their jobs in the sense of their actual work-tasks and -roles. However, also relevant to the question of satisfaction in work is the nature of workers' *attachment* to their jobs in the wider sense of their present employment. How do variations in the pattern of satisfaction and deprivation which men experience immediately from their work relate to variations in the strength and quality of this attachment? A number of questions in our interview schedule enable us to investigate this further problem.

To begin with, each worker in the sample was asked: 'Have you ever thought of leaving your present job at [name of firm]?' Those who answered 'Yes' to this were then asked: 'Have you done anything about it?' Table 10 shows the results which these questions produced.

From these data, two main points emerge. In the first place, it is clear that, contrary to what might have been expected, it is by no means those groups whose work-tasks and -roles appeared least rewarding whose members had thought most often or most seriously about leaving. For example, the strength of the semi-skilled workers' attachment to their present employment seems little different from that of the setters. Secondly, on the evidence in question, the attachment of our respondents

TABLE 10. *Possibility of leaving present employment*

	Craftsmen (N = 56)	Setters (N = 23)	Process workers (N = 23)	Machinists (N = 41)	Assemblers (N = 86)	All (N = 229)
			Percentage			
Have never thought of leaving	30	52	65	56	63	53
Have thought of leaving but has taken no action	20	22	9	15	17	17
Have thought of leaving and has taken some action*	50	26	26	29	20	30
TOTALS	100	100	100	100	100	100

* Chiefly, asking workers in other firms about employment possibilities; following up jobs advertised in newspapers; and approaching other employers.

to their firms could, in general, be regarded as being fairly stable[1]—despite the indication from our previous findings that, for the most part, their work afforded them no high degree of immediate satisfaction. Only among the craftsmen have a majority ever thought of leaving, and while half of this group report having taken the matter further, the proportion of such 'potential' leavers in the other groups in no case amounts to as much as a third.

Those men who said that they had thought of leaving were also asked why this was. Table 11 classifies the reasons they gave, and these prove to be broadly consistent with what was established earlier about the main sources of dissatisfaction from group to group. Nevertheless, the point remains that at group level no connection is evident between what we know of the typical nature of work-tasks and the apparent strength of job attachment. Moreover, there is no indication from our data that at the individual level, either, any association exists between actually experiencing unrewarding work and having thought of leaving. For example, those men who reported that their work was monotonous, or that it did not absorb their full attention, or that the pace of work was sometimes too fast were not significantly more likely than others in the sample to have considered the possibility of taking employment with some other firm.

[1] It would have been desirable to have a further measure of the strength of workers' attachment to their present employment through the labour turnover rates, or better, the 'quit' and 'stability' rates, for each of our occupational groups. Unfortunately personnel data were not available from which we could compute rates broken down in this way.

TABLE 11. *Reasons given for having thought of leaving present firm*

Class of reason	Craftsmen (N = 39)	Setters (N = 11)	Process workers (N = 8)	Machinists (N = 18)	Assemblers (N = 32)	All (N = 108)
			Times mentioned			
Nature of work (lack of variety, scope for skill, etc.)	4	3	2	6	18	33
Unsatisfactory management, supervision or 'shop atmosphere'	13	2	3	2	2	22
Poor physical conditions	4	1	1	3	4	13
Poor promotion chances	5	1	2	2	2	12
Level of pay	5	1	0	2	0	8
Wants wider job experience	7	0	0	1	0	8
Wants to start own business	2	1	2	0	2	7
Poor security	1	1	1	2	0	5
Other	13	3	3	5	7	31
ALL REASONS	54	13	14	23	35	139

In view of these findings, the question of the *quality* of the job attachment of the men in our several occupational groups becomes one of even greater interest. The implication is that some notable differences in this respect will be found from one group to another, but that at the same time the form of attachment most typical of the sample as a whole will be of a distinctive kind; that is, one which is not incompatible with a relatively low degree of direct satisfaction from work-tasks and -roles. Data which confirm that this is the case are provided by the answers we received to a further question which we put to all our respondents, whether or not they said they had thought of leaving. We asked: 'What is it, then, that keeps you here [i.e. in your present employment]?' The replies that were made are classified in table 12.

From this table, it can be seen that, overall, the *level of pay* was the item which was by far the most frequently mentioned, accounting in fact for more than a third of all reasons given. Although, then, appreciable variations exist from group to group, it could be said that the 'cash nexus' was certainly more important than any other tie in binding the workers we studied to their current employers. This is brought out more clearly still in table 13, which shows the proportion in each group who referred to the

TABLE 12. *Reasons given for staying at present firm*

Class of reason	Craftsmen (N = 56)	Setters (N = 23)	Process workers (N = 23)	Machinists (N = 41)	Assemblers (N = 86)	All (N = 229)
	Times mentioned					
Level of pay (nothing else mentioned)	4	2	2	7	26	41
Level of pay (mentioned with other reasons)	34	11	9	20	39	113
Level of pay (total)	38	13	11	27	65	154
Good security	23	14	8	17	24	86
Fair employer, good industrial relations, good management	8	4	6	8	19	45
Nature of work	15	8	6	9	6	44
Lives near factory	13	2	1	9	5	30
Good physical conditions	8	1	2	1	4	16
Good workmates	3	2	2	1	6	14
Too old to move	3	1	2	2	4	12
Good fringe benefits, welfare provisions	1	0	0	0	9	10
Other	6	2	4	4	9	25
ALL REASONS	118	47	42	78	151	436
Reasons relating to level of pay as percentage of all reasons given	32	28	26	35	43	35

level of pay as one, or as the only, reason for staying in their present work. Apart from the overall pattern, the most notable features are the extreme importance of pay to the assemblers, in comparison particularly with the setters and process workers, and the fact that almost a third of the assemblers say that it is the pay *alone* that keeps them in their present jobs. Characteristic comments were ones such as the following.

'What is it that keeps me here? Money and again money—nothing else!'

'It's money every time. I sell my labour to the highest bidder—and around here, that's Vauxhall.'

'Basically, it's the money. Really, I would like an open-air job—but there isn't the money in those.'

'You sell your labour where you can get most. I couldn't better myself...That's what you go to work for.'

28

TABLE 13. *Level of pay as a reason for staying in present employment*

	Craftsmen (N = 56)	Setters (N = 23)	Process workers (N = 23)	Machinists (N = 41)	Assemblers (N = 86)	All (N = 229)
	Percentage					
Level of pay given as only reason for staying	7	9	9	17	31	18
Level of pay given as one reason for staying (with at least one other)	61	48	39	49	45	49
Level of pay not mentioned as reason for staying	32	44	52	34	24	33
TOTALS	100	101	100	100	100	100

Three other factors in job attachment also figure with some prominence in table 12: first, good security and then, some way behind, a fair employer etc. and the nature of work. The percentages in each occupational group mentioning these further items as reasons for staying in their present employment are shown in table 14. The primary significance of these data is that they emphasise again the importance of the economic basis of our affluent workers' attachment to their jobs, in that men in all groups mention security next most frequently to the level of pay as a reason for 'staying put'. And, moreover, it should be noted that typically with our respondents, 'security' seemed to be thought of far more in relation to long-run income maximisation than to the minimum requirement of having a job of some kind. At the same time, though, the data in question are also of interest in indicating the still distinctive patterns of job attachment which exist between the different occupational groups within the overall similarity which has been observed.

With the setters, for example, the importance of pay is relatively low compared with other groups, but these workers place notably high importance on their security and on the nature of their work. In contrast to this, the main factor binding the assemblers to their present jobs, after pay and security, would seem to be their appreciation of Vauxhall as an employer— the nature of their work having probably a negative rather than positive value so far as job attachment is concerned.[1] Then again, in the case of

[1] As can be seen from tables 11 and 14, 18 assemblers out of 32 (56%) gave the nature of their work as a reason for having thought of leaving, whereas this item was mentioned by only 6 out of the total of 86 (7%) as a reason for staying in their present employment. A survey

29

TABLE 14. *Security, a fair employer etc., and nature of work as reasons for staying in present employment*

	Craftsmen (N = 56)	Setters (N = 23)	Process workers (N = 23)	Machinists (N = 41)	Assemblers (N = 86)	All (N = 229)
			Percentage			
Security given as reason for staying	41	61	35	42	43	38
Fair employer etc. given as reason for staying	14	17	26	20	34	20
Nature of work given as reason for staying	27	35	26	22	7	19

process workers—the group with the lowest proportion of men who have thought of leaving—both pay and security are mentioned less often than in any other group, and there would seem to be no other particularly important source of job attachment. However, against this must be set the fact, noted previously, that this is the group with no very marked job *dis*satisfaction and with the highest proportion of men who could think of no change they would like to make in their present job. Once more, then, it would seem that the process workers are in a 'neutral' position—that they are attached to their present employment less because of things positively valued than because of the absence of severe work deprivations and grievances which could lead to thoughts of quitting. Finally, the craftsmen and machinists are much alike in that both give relatively strong emphasis to pay and security but have no other markedly powerful ties with their jobs. The important differences between these two groups is that with the machinists—as with the assemblers—a primarily economic nexus appears to be a fairly effective one, whereas with the craftsmen it does not. In the latter case, one would suggest, a high level of economic return is often not in itself entirely sufficient to offset the relatively low estimation which the craftsmen place on their firms' standards of technical efficiency and shop management.[1] Moreover, it should be remembered that the craftsmen

conducted by Vauxhall over the year 1963 revealed that of all those leaving their Luton labour force, 41% were in their first six months of employment. Difficulties in adapting to what were termed 'the realities of mass production work' appeared to be the main reason for this high loss rate among newcomers.

[1] Table 11 shows that a third of the craftsmen who said they had thought of leaving gave a reason for this relating to their dissatisfaction with management, supervision, or 'shop atmosphere'.

TABLE 15. *Previous work experience: classification of majority of previous occupations*

Occupational category*	Craftsmen (N = 56)	Setters (N = 23)	Process workers (N = 23)	Machinists (N = 41)	Assemblers (N = 86)	All (N = 229)
			Percentage			
1. Professional, managerial, white-collar	0	0	0	0	4	1
2. Self-employed	0	0	0	2	1	1
3. Supervisory, inspectional, minor official and service	2	0	0	0	5	2
4. Skilled manual (apprenticeship or equivalent)	79	9	13	10	13	28
5. Skilled manual (other)	11	35	13	10	16	15
6. Semi-skilled manual	2	57	44	42	38	32
7. Unskilled manual	4	0	17	12	5	7
8. Unclassifiable†	4	0	13	24	19	14
TOTALS	102	101	100	100	101	100

* For full details of the occupational classification used throughout the research, see appendix C.
† Chiefly because of the extreme variety of previous employment.

would have far better chances than the semi-skilled men of being able to match their present high earnings elsewhere—just as they would have much better chances than the setters of finding other work at the same skill level.

From the foregoing, then, one very definite result emerges: that job satisfaction in terms of workers' experience of their immediate work-tasks and -roles cannot be associated in any direct way with job satisfaction in terms of workers' attachment to their present employment. The degree of this attachment is clearly determined by a number of factors of which the nature of work-tasks and -roles is but one—and, as in the case of the workers in question, one which may be of no overwhelming importance. Thus, work which offers relatively high intrinsic rewards may not in fact form the basis of a powerful tie between the worker and his employment because of countervailing dissatisfactions and grievances; and, conversely, work which by its very nature entails severe deprivations for those who perform it may

31

TABLE 16. *Previous work experience: classification of highest occupational level attained**

Occupational category	Craftsmen (N = 56)†	Setters (N = 23)	Process workers (N = 23)	Machinists (N = 41)	Assemblers (N = 86)	All (N = 229)
			Percentage			
1. Professional, managerial, white-collar	7	9	0	12	7	7
2. Self-employed	5	9	17	15	7	9
3. Supervisory, inspectional, minor official and service	7	17	0	20	28	18
4. Skilled manual (apprenticeship or equivalent)	64	13	13	10	16	26
5. Skilled manual (other)	9	26	17	15	23	18
6. Semi-skilled manual 7. Unskilled manual	5	26	52	29	19	21
TOTALS	97	100	99	101	100	99

* Jobs lasting less than one year were not counted.
† One craftsmen was unclassifiable through having had no previous job.

nonetheless offer extrinsic—that is, economic—rewards which are such as to attach workers fairly firmly to the employer who offers this work.

Furthermore, in regard to this latter situation there is one point which calls for some emphasis. It cannot simply be assumed that workers whose attachment to their present jobs is very largely economic have in effect little alternative to making do with this, as it were, 'inferior' form of job satisfaction—that they are constrained to take jobs of the kind in question because they lack the ability or skills to secure employment which would offer them some more desirable balance of intrinsic and extrinsic returns. Such an assumption would certainly *not* be a generally valid one for the semi-skilled workers in the sample we studied. From further of our interview data, it can be demonstrated that the machinists and assemblers, the men for whom the cash nexus is most important, are in fact quite varied in their levels and types of skill and in their previous work histories —somewhat more so, if anything, than the men in the other occupational groups. Table 15 shows for all five groups the kind of work in which their members were *chiefly* engaged before taking the jobs they now hold, and table 16 the percentage in each group who *at some time* were engaged at a higher occupational level than their present one.

From the data presented, it can be seen that the previous work experience of over 20% of the machinists and of almost 40% of the assemblers was *chiefly* in more skilled manual work than that which they now perform or in nonmanual occupations; and further, that less than 30% of the machinists and less than 20% of the assemblers have thus far been *confined* in their working lives to unskilled or semi-skilled jobs. Moreover, we have also information which suggests that of these latter men a sizable proportion had previously been employed mostly in jobs of a kind which does not entail the rigours and stresses of work in mass-production industry—for example, in jobs in small-scale industry, in agriculture, and in distributive and other services.[1]

What these findings would imply, therefore, is that a majority of the machinists and assemblers have in fact entered their present employment not for want of any real alternative, but rather as the result of some more or less calculated decision; that they have in effect *chosen* to abandon employments which could offer them some greater degree of intrinsic reward in favour of work which enables them to achieve a higher level of economic return. In more technical terms it could be said that a decision has been made to give more weight to the *instrumental* at the expense of the *expressive* aspects of work.[2]

Such an interpretation can, moreover, be supported by the results obtained from a question which we put to each of our respondents after he had recounted his work history. We asked: 'Did you like any of your other jobs more than the one you have now?' Those answering 'Yes' were then also asked to explain why this was. Table 17 shows the proportion in each occupational group who said that they had liked a previous job more, and table 18 classifies the reasons which were given for such preferences.

From these data it can be seen that 66% of the machinists and 59% of

---

[1] This was the case with approximately 40% of both the machinists and the assemblers in question.

[2] Findings leading to a similar conclusion are also reported in Walker and Guest's study of auto-assembly workers; see Charles R. Walker and Robert H. Guest, *The Man on the Assembly Line* (Cambridge, Mass., 1952). In her sample of redundant motor industry workers in the Midlands (1956), which contained men of a variety of occupations and skills, Kahn found that 44% stated that they had joined their firms in the first place in part at least because of the level of pay, and this was the only reason given by 26%. No other reason was mentioned with anything approaching this frequency. Reasons relating to the nature of the work itself—interest, skill, etc.—were among those least often referred to. At the same time, though, 91% of the sample said that they would have wanted to remain with their firm if they had not been made redundant. See Hilda Kahn, *Repercussions of Redundancy* (London, 1964), pp. 47–52.

TABLE 17. *Preference for some previous employment in comparison with present employment*

	Craftsmen (N = 56)	Setters (N = 23)	Process workers (N = 23)	Machinists (N = 41)	Assemblers (N = 86)	All (N = 229)
			Percentage			
Preferred some previous employment	48	44	44	66	59	55
Did not prefer any previous employment	46	44	52	32	33	39
Other, D.K.	4	13	4	2	8	6
D.N.A. (no previous employment)	2	0	0	0	0	1
TOTALS	100	101	100	100	100	101

the assemblers, as against some 45 % of those in the other groups, preferred a previous job to their present one, and that they did so largely because of the greater direct satisfactions which it had offered and, to a lesser degree, because of its more favourable physical or social environment. Reasons relating to *ex*trinsic attractions account for only 1 in 10 of all reasons given.[1]

Comments made by the machinists and assemblers frequently revealed that a dilemma had been recognised between taking a more directly rewarding job and one which would afford a relatively high level of earnings, and that while the decision had been made for the latter, it had often not been an easy one. The following extracts from interviews are illustrative in this respect.

'I liked the hat trade all right—it was interesting. But it hadn't picked up after the war. I was older and I wanted a job with good pay and security.'

'When I came out of the R.A.F. the wife wanted income rather than an interesting job for me. I was pushed into the highest-paid work—which in Luton means Vauxhall.'

'I liked being a waiter. It's a single man's job, of course—you've got to go with the crowd to make money. It was clean and I didn't mind the hours. Meeting people—that was the great thing.'

[1] Too much should perhaps not be made in itself of this preponderance of reasons referring to intrinsic rewards and environmental conditions since these are the aspects of work which are most closely associated with the idea of 'liking a job': extrinsic rewards are more relevant to the idea of 'keeping a job'—as we have seen. What is really significant is that 6 out of 10 of the machinists and assemblers had held previous jobs which they found more 'likable' than their present ones, even if not so attractive when extrinsic rewards were taken into account.

TABLE 18. *Reasons given for preferring some previous job (i.e. employment) to present job*

Class of reason	Craftsmen, Setters and Process workers (N = 54)	Machinists and Assemblers (N = 84)	All (N = 138)*
	Times mentioned		
A. Reasons relating to intrinsic rewards			
Greater variety in work tasks	14	30	44
Greater autonomy, room for initiative	16	19	35
Greater scope for, variety in, human contacts in work	4	14	18
Greater opportunity for use of skill	10	7	17
Greater intrinsic interest (not further specified)	4	12	16
Greater sense of importance, responsibility	4	5	9
TOTALS	52	87	139
B. Reasons relating to physical and social environment			
Better physical conditions	5	29	34
Better supervision, 'shop atmosphere'	13	4	17
TOTALS	18	33	51
C. Reasons relating to extrinsic rewards and considerations, convenience, etc.†			
Better pay	4	3	7
Better promotion chances	4	1	5
More security	0	3	3
Other	7	7	14
TOTALS	15	14	29
ALL REASONS	85	134	219
Reasons in class A as percentage of all reasons	61	65	64
Reasons in class B as percentage of all reasons	21	25	23
Reasons in class C as percentage of all reasons	18	10	13
TOTALS	100	100	100

* In addition to the 125 respondents definitely stating that they preferred a previous job, 13 others (7 from the craftsmen, setters and process workers and 6 from the machinists and assemblers) who gave answers which in the end were indeterminate also advanced reasons for such a preference.

† E.g. living near to place of work.

'I liked it at the tobacco company best. Being smaller, it was one big family—in a big company you're just a part. There was less money there, though.'

'I preferred being in service [as a footman]. It was a clean life and you were mixing with a much better class of people—they were brought up better. But the money wasn't so good.'

The main conclusion which we would wish to draw from the foregoing discussion is, then, the following: that the question of *satisfaction from* work cannot in the end be usefully considered except in relation to the more basic question of what we would term *orientation towards* work. Until one knows something of the way in which workers order their wants and expectations relative to their employment—until one knows what *meaning* work has for them—one is not in a position to understand what overall assessment of their job satisfaction may most appropriately be made in their case.[1] In seeking to become 'affluent workers', the machinists and assemblers in our sample have, no doubt with varying degrees of self-awareness, given primacy to extrinsic satisfaction from work, and have therefore chosen jobs of a kind which would enable them to come near to maximising the economic returns from their labour. In consequence of this, they frequently experience deprivation in their present employment in relation to some, at least, of those aspects of work which they have devalued. And in this sense, as we have shown, they could clearly be said to have low job satisfaction. But, on the other hand, their relatively high degree of attachment to their present employment, and the explanations they give of this attachment, indicate that their major wants and expectations relative to work—the kinds of satisfactions which in their case have priority—are in fact being generally met.

In the case of the other occupational groups in the sample, the emphasis on extrinsic rewards, while evidently still quite marked, could be said to be somewhat less decisive. The process workers might be thought to be in a way more fortunate than the other semi-skilled men in that they have found work which, though relatively highly paid, is apparently not so stressful as that of the machine shop or 'track'; and, as we have seen, their job attachment is comparable to that of the machinists and assemblers, while their dissatisfaction with their work-tasks and -roles appears appreciably less. At the same time, however, it should be noted that, as can be

The argument that any worthwhile attempt to assess workers' levels of job satisfaction must take into account their levels of expectation was first elaborated by Nancy Morse, *Satisfactions in the White-Collar Job* (Michigan, 1953). However, our approach seeks to go beyond that of Morse in stressing not only the *level* of expectations but also the *variable direction* of these in relation to different work orientations. For an attempt to develop Morse's argument along similar lines, see Frisch-Gauthier, 'Moral et Satisfaction au Travail'.

seen from table A2, process workers are clearly under-represented at the higher earnings levels within our sample. The remark of one process worker might well apply to the position of the group as a whole: 'Of course, you could make more at Vauxhall,' he commented, 'but life here is just that much easier.'

Among the setters and craftsmen, a concern with other than economic considerations is yet more apparent—but with very differing outcomes so far as satisfaction in work is concerned. With the setters, the fact of their promotion from the ranks of the machinists appears to be crucial. This upgrading has meant not only a higher rate of pay but, at the same time, more opportunity for these men to satisfy expressive needs—to use skills, exercise initiative and so on—in a way which their previous jobs did not permit; and the intrinsic rewards which are thus afforded by their work have been shown to be one of the more important factors in attaching the setters to their present employment. The craftsmen, on the other hand, while gaining some direct reward from the nature of their work-tasks, appear frequently to experience frustration in other non-economic aspects of their jobs; notably in regard to their desire for autonomy and responsibility and for the conditions they believe essential for 'good workmanship'.[1] And this frustration would seem to be at the root of their critical attitude and often uncertain commitment to their employers. Thus, whereas the setters, of all the occupational groups, appear to find the widest range of satisfactions—intrinsic and extrinsic—in their work, the craftsmen, one could say, are most obviously the group with important wants and expectations relative to work which are left inadequately fulfilled.

An appreciation of differences in orientation to work has to be regarded as basic to any useful analysis of patterns of job satisfaction among the workers we studied. Nevertheless, while this is so, it is important that the attention which must be given to such differences should not be allowed to obscure one further highly significant fact to which our data also point: that notwithstanding the variations in orientation to work which have been outlined, the *instrumental* aspect of employment is very strongly emphasised by

[1] It should be noted that those craftsmen who expressed a preference for some previous employment very largely referred to jobs they had held which in one way or another were of a clearly less routinised character than their present ones; e.g. maintenance jobs in smaller firms in which they 'had to do everything' and 'plan things out alone', or toolmaking jobs in which they worked closely with development engineers. What this indicates, then, is that even *within* skilled work, some appreciable differences still exist in the balance of intrinsic and extrinsic rewards which different employments offer. Large-scale firms tend to pay higher rates, but in such firms even skilled work is likely to be relatively specialised and bureaucratically administered—as was the case in Skefko and Laporte.

all groups of workers within our sample. In all groups, as we have seen, considerations of pay and security appear most powerful in binding men to their present jobs; and tables 17 and 18 indicate that workers in other groups differ only in degree from the machinists and assemblers in having left previous, and otherwise preferred, employments largely for reasons of economic advantage.

It may perhaps be thought that we are here underlining the obvious—since in our type of society economic activity virtually *implies* instrumental activity and can only exceptionally have chiefly expressive functions. However, there are two arguments which might be advanced for believing that among the men we studied a *markedly* instrumental orientation to work is to be found:

(i) that as manual wage-workers, quite regardless of their affluent condition, all those in the sample are in effect engaged in selling their labour power, by the hour or 'piece', in a market situation; they are thus, more than men in, say, professional, administrative or managerial positions, particularly *constrained* to regard work primarily as a means to an end, and to be primarily concerned with its economic return.

(ii) that while important variations may exist in the extent to which non-economic rewards from work are subordinated, workers in all groups within our sample tend to be particularly *motivated* to increase their power as consumers and their domestic standard of living, rather than their satisfaction as producers and the degree of their self-fulfilment in work.

In developing the first of these arguments, the comparison which can most appropriately be drawn is that between our affluent workers and salaried, white-collar employees; in developing the second, that between our affluent workers and manual wage workers of a more 'traditional' kind. Such comparisons will in fact be repeatedly made, on an empirical basis, throughout the remainder of the monograph. But, in conclusion of the present chapter, it may be useful from the point of view of analytical clarity if we set out in 'ideal-type' form three contrasting orientations to work which may be associated with the affluent worker, the salaried employee, and the traditional worker respectively. These orientations can be labelled: (A) instrumental, (B) bureaucratic, and (C) solidaristic.

(A) *Instrumental orientation*

(i) The primary meaning of work is as a means to an end, or ends, external to the work situation; that is, work is regarded as a means of acquiring the income necessary to support a valued way of life of which work itself is not an integral part. Work is therefore experienced as mere 'labour' in the sense of an expenditure of effort which is made for extrinsic rather than for intrinsic rewards. Workers act as 'economic men', seeking to minimise effort and maximise economic returns; but the latter concern is the dominant one.

(ii) Consistently with this, workers' involvement in the organisation which employs them is primarily a *calculative* one;[1] it will be maintained for so long as the economic return for effort is seen as the best available, but for no other reason. Thus, involvement is of low intensity, and in terms of affect is neutral or 'mild' rather than being either highly positive or negative.

(iii) Since work is defined essentially as a mandatory and instrumental activity, rather than as an activity valued for itself, the ego-involvement of workers in their jobs—in either the narrower or wider sense of the term— is weak. Their jobs do not form part of their central life interests;[2] work is not for them a source of emotionally significant experiences or social relationships; it is not a source of self-realisation.

(iv) Consequently, workers' lives are sharply dichotomised between work and non-work. Work experiences and relationships are not likely to be carried over into 'out-plant' life, and workers are unlikely to participate in 'social' activities associated with work—e.g. in works clubs and societies or in other than what are seen as economically urgent or essential trade union activities.

(B) *Bureaucratic orientation*

(i) The primary meaning of work is as service to an organisation in return for steadily increasing income and social status and for long-term security—that is, in return for a career. Economic rewards are regarded not as payment for particular amounts of work done or of labour expended,

---

[1] We take this concept of 'calculative involvement', along with those of 'alienative' and 'moral' involvement, from Amitai Etzioni, *A Comparative Analysis of Complex Organizations* (Glencoe, 1961).

[2] See Robert Dubin, 'Industrial Workers' Worlds: a study of the "Central Life Interests" of Industrial Workers', *Social Problems*, vol. 3 (January 1956). In a later work Dubin has suggested a typological distinction between 'community oriented' employees, for whom work is not a central life interest, and 'work oriented' employees, for whom it is; see *The World of Work* (Englewood Cliffs, 1958), ch. 14. We do not take over this terminology for two reasons: first, because for some individuals the community may be no more of a central life interest than is work; and, second, because workers whom Dubin would regard as not work-oriented have nonetheless a quite distinctive orientation towards work—i.e. an instrumental orientation—as Dubin himself has shown. To indicate the direction of central life interests, we prefer to think of employees as being work-*centred* as opposed to non-work-centred, and within this latter category to distinguish between individuals and groups as being community-centred, leisure-centred, family-centred, etc.

but rather as the emoluments appropriate to a particular grade and function or to a certain length of service.[1]

(ii) Arising from this, the involvement of workers with their organisation contains definite moral elements rather than deriving from a purely market relationship. It entails, to paraphrase Max Weber, an acceptance of a specific obligation of faithful administration in return for a relatively secure and privileged existence. It is unlikely, thus, that in this case involvement can be neutral: it will tend normally to be positive, where moral expectations are being faithfully met, or perhaps strongly negative, if it is felt that commitments or a moral kind are not being honoured.

(iii) Since, in this case, work is associated with progressive economic and status advancement in the form of a career, it inevitably plays an important part in determining the worker's conception of himself and of his future; his 'position' and 'prospects' are significant sources of his social identity. Thus, in this sense, ego-involvement in work is strong. Work represents a central life interest, in so far as the individual's career is crucial to his 'life-fate'.

(iv) Consequently, workers' lives cannot be sharply dichotomised into work and non-work. Their organisation and their colleagues may, or may not, continue to form the basis of their social life outside of work; but self concepts and social aspirations formed through work necessarily carry over into non-work activities and relationships; and the same is also likely to be true of organisational status.

(c) *Solidaristic orientation*

(i) In this case, while work, as always, has an economic meaning, it is experienced not simply as a means to an end but also as a group activity; the group being either the immediate work group or 'shop', or possibly— say, in a small firm—the entire enterprise. Economic returns from work are thus likely to be sacrificed where 'maximising' behaviour would offend group norms and threaten group solidarity: for example, workers may limit earnings under a financial incentive scheme in accordance with group output norms, or stay 'loyal' to 'their' firm when higher wages could be had elsewhere.

(ii) Where the group with which workers identify is the enterprise, then their involvement with their work organisation is obviously of a moral

[1] See Max Weber, 'Bureaucracy' in H. H. Gerth and C. Wright Mills (eds.), *From Max Weber: Essays in Sociology* (London, 1948), pp. 198–204. It should be noted that in modern society not all white-collar workers will tend to approximate this ideal type; many are in effect members of white-collar labour forces rather than having the position of bureaucratic officials.

and positive kind. Alternatively, though, where identification is only with the work group or shop, then the nature of involvement with the organisation is likely to be to some extent alienative; that is, workers are likely to be in some degree negatively oriented towards the organisation and to see their group as a source of power against their employer.

(iii) Consistently with either of these possibilities, ego-involvement in work is strong; the social relationships and shared activities of work are found emotionally rewarding. Work thus represents a central life interest in that, in addition to its instrumental significance, it is also of some major importance in satisfying workers' expressive and affective needs.

(iv) Consequently, it is likely that work experiences and relationships will help form the basis of workers' out-plant social existence—that there will be some distinctive occupational culture and occupational community[1] involving relatively high participation in work-linked formal or informal associations. Thus, in this case, work and non-work are intimately related; work in fact implies a whole way of life.[2]

We would emphasise that these three orientations to work are not intended to stand in *total* contrast to each other: the point that *all* work activity, in industrial society at least, tends to have a basically instrumental component is fully accepted. It might thus be best to consider only (A) as forming an 'ideal type' in the strict sense, and to regard (B) and (C) as referring to deviations from an instrumental orientation in a 'bureaucratic' and 'solidaristic' direction respectively—just as other deviations are conceivable, as, for example, in a 'professional' direction.[3] The purpose of the constructs we have set out is to help us keep our discussion of differences in attitudes and behaviour *within* our sample of affluent workers in some broader perspective, and to prevent us from neglecting the more basic similarities which, as it were, underlie these differences.

In each of the four chapters which follow, our ultimate argument will be that, in considering the attitudes and behaviour of the workers we studied

[1] Or perhaps, where identification is with the enterprise, a *Betriebsgemeinschaft* or 'plant community'.
[2] See Blauner, 'Work Satisfaction and Industrial Trends', pp. 350–2; also, on the idea of an occupational community, S. M. Lipset, M. A. Trow and J. S. Coleman, *Union Democracy* (Glencoe, 1956), chs. 5, 6, 7. The existence of an occupational community may itself lead to further limitations on economic rationality, as, for example, where the prevalence of a traditional standard of living leads to the amount of labour offered by a labour force being likely to *decline* once some critical level of pay is attained. On the sociological implications of this phenomenon of the 'backward sloping supply curve', see Max Weber, *The Protestant Ethic and the Spirit of Capitalism* (London, 1947), pp. 58–60.
[3] See Talcott Parsons, 'The Motivation of Economic Activities', in *Essays in Sociological Theory* (revised ed.) (Glencoe, 1954), pp. 62–5 esp.

—in relation to their work groups, their firms, their unions and their own economic future—themes and variations alike can best be explained in terms of the degree to which, in the different occupational groups, an instrumental orientation to work is approximated. At the same time, we shall also argue, on the basis of such comparative material as is available, that the ways in which our affluent workers differ from white-collar employees and from more traditional workers are, in the main, ones which the contrast between an instrumental and a bureaucratic or a solidaristic orientation to work makes most readily intelligible.

3. The worker and his work group

From the time when the Hawthorne Studies made their first impact down to the mid 1950s, it would probably be true to say that the major focus of interest within industrial sociology was on the primary work group. Certainly, by far the greatest research effort in the field was that directed towards investigating the influence on workers' attitudes and behaviour of the structure and quality of interpersonal relationships at shop-floor level.[1] As an early result of this research, attempts at understanding the industrial worker in individualistic terms, whether as a manifestation of 'economic man' or as a 'bio-psychological organism' were shown to be seriously inadequate. The findings of a large number of studies carried out by exponents of the 'human relations' approach revealed that group values and related group norms could largely determine workers' responses to many different features of their work situation—to work-tasks, physical conditions, payments systems, work rules, and so on.

On this basis, then, a leading concern, from a practical point of view, was that of devising ways in which these group values and norms—and thus worker attitudes and behaviour—could best be brought into alignment with managerial objectives and policy, rather than being in conflict with these. In this connection, major emphasis came to be placed on the role of the first-line supervisor as the person who represented and embodied management within the system of shop-floor social relations. Thus, a further series of research studies was instigated, aimed at determining the effectiveness of different 'styles' of supervision in creating solidary work groups, oriented towards co-operation with management and encouraging in their members high morale and motivation in relation to managerial goals.[2]

This preoccupation with the work group and the first-line supervisor, as the characteristic feature of the 'human relations' phase of industrial sociology, was frequently the subject of critical comment. Probably the most basic objection was that in the light of research data neither the cohesiveness

[1] Cf. J.-R. Tréanton and J.-D. Reynaud, 'La Sociologie Industrielle, 1951–62', *Current Sociology*, vol. XII, no. 2 (1963–4).
[2] For surveys of this research see M. S. Viteles, *Motivation and Morale in Industry* (New York, 1953); M. Argyle *et al.*, 'The Measurement of Supervisory Methods', *Human Relations*, vol. 10, no. 4 (1957); and R. Likert, 'A Motivation Approach to a Modified Theory of Organization and Management' in M. Haire (ed.), *Modern Organization Theory* (New York, 1959).

nor the conduct of work groups appeared to be so subject to managerial control as 'human relations' theory would imply. However, only towards the end of the last decade did criticism of this kind lead to the formulation, in any explicit way, of an alternative approach; one which is still being elaborated.

Briefly, and simplifying a good deal, this new approach starts from the claim that exponents of 'human relations' methods have failed to see certain important limitations to both their theory and their practice. Specifically, they have tended to neglect the extent to which work relationships may be structured *independently* of particular persons and independently, too, of the level of 'social skills' or of 'interpersonal competence' which supervisors or other 'leaders' may display. The social relationships of the workplace, it has been argued, are not created in 'free space', but are rather significantly influenced by the way in which the actual processes of production are designed and organised; that is, by the way in which work-tasks are specified and work-roles defined, and by the way in which these tasks and roles are related to each other and co-ordinated. In other words it is urged that in seeking to understand social relations on the shop floor, the *type of productive technology* which is in operation—the set of means chosen by the enterprise in order to achieve its business objectives—must be taken as an essential starting point. Any given form of technology has to be seen as imposing at a minimum certain constraints on the structuring of work relationships and probably as forcing these into certain more or less specific patterns rather than others. While in some situations technical arrangements may compel a high degree of interdependence and thus of co-operation between men on the shop floor, in other situations any sustained form of interaction in work processes may be technologically precluded. Or, again, in some cases relations between workers and their supervisors may be structured in ways which greatly favour a 'give and take' approach or which encourage supervisors to adopt a largely *laissez faire* position; but in other cases these relations may be so structured that recurrent conflict is made virtually unavoidable—regardless of the attributes of workers or of supervisors as persons.[1]

[1] For contributions to this approach, each with its distinctive emphases and elaborations, see the following: W. H. Scott, A. H. Halsey, J. A. Banks and T. Lipton, *Technical Change and Industrial Relations* (Liverpool, 1956), pp. 16–21 esp.; L. R. Sayles, *Behavior of Industrial Work Groups* (New York, 1958), chs. 6 and 7 esp.; Joan Woodward, *Management and Technology* (H.M.S.O., London, 1958); 'Industrial Behaviour—Is there a science?', *New Society* (8 October 1964); F. E. Emery and E. L. Trist, 'Socio-Technical Systems', in *Management Sciences: Models and Techniques*, vol. II (London, 1960); John H. Goldthorpe, 'Technical Organisation as a factor in Supervisor–Worker Conflict', *British Journal of Sociology*, vol. x, no. 3 (1959), and 'La Conception des Conflits du Travail dans l'Enseignement des Relations Humaines', *Sociologie du Travail*, no. 3 (1961).

With this approach, then, the work group can no longer be regarded as providing the major focus either for sociological analysis or for direct managerial action. The degree to which solidary work groups can form, or be maintained, is itself seen as being primarily dependent upon technology. And in attempting to explain patterns of behaviour and related attitudes on the part of workers, the emphasis is no longer placed on the influence of inter-*personal* relationships within the group, but rather on the influence of the particular roles which individuals are required to fulfil within the prevailing system of technical organisation. The idea of role-determined behaviour becomes analytically crucial, being symptomatic of a radically sociological reaction against the inherent 'psychologism' of the 'human relations' phase.[1]

In planning our investigation of the industrial lives of our affluent workers, we were guided to an important extent by the approach we have just outlined. For example, as described in chapter 1, our sample was deliberately based on three firms with widely differing production systems. At the same time we tended to be critical of this approach for two closely related reasons: first, because of its neglect of the way in which workers' own definitions of the work situation (their work-roles included) may significantly determine their attitudes and behaviour in this situation, to some extent independently of its 'objective' features; and, secondly, because of the limitation which is implied in seeking to explain industrial attitudes and behaviour entirely from the point of view of the functioning of the enterprise and in thus ignoring the possibility of explanation from the point of view of the actors themselves, considered not only as workers but also in their various other social roles as members of families, communities, social classes and so on. As will be seen in this and succeeding chapters, our findings can in certain respects be shown to reinforce these criticisms and to point to the need for the approach in question to be complemented by a mode of analysis which begins not with differences in technology but rather with some appreciation of differences in orientations to work on the lines attempted at the end of chapter 2.

However, at least as a starting point here, the technological environments of each of the five occupational groups within our sample must be brought under examination; and, in particular, in terms of their implications for the development of work groups of a solidary kind. In the observational studies which we made in our three firms, we gave special attention to this

[1] This shows particularly clearly in Woodward, 'Industrial Behaviour: Is there a science?', and also in Goldthorpe, 'La Conception des Conflits du Travail'.

matter, and a substantial amount of relevant information was collected. This information is presented in summarised and classified form in table 19. It will be seen that in some cases sub-divisions have been made within occupational groups in order to give a more accurate picture.

The most significant fact which emerges from this table is that there is *no* occupational group, or sub-group, where conditions prevail which are entirely favourable for the creation of solidary work groups. The closest approximation to such conditions is with the toolmakers, but these are workers who operate on an almost entirely individual and independent basis: thus, while in the toolmakers' shops some kind of group life was observable, it would be truer to say that these group relations were *permitted* by the form of technical organisation than that they were directly encouraged by it.[1] Certain of the machinists—among the heavy grinders and the turret-lathe operators—also had some possibility of developing primary group structures, and again these could in a few cases be seen to exist. But once more the degree of group cohesiveness for the most part was limited through the lack of any interaction in work processes and in addition by the distance separating machines and by the fairly frequent redeployment of operatives from one machine to another.[2]

[1] Toolmakers were seen to move around from their benches a good deal to chat to fellow workers and sometimes to discuss with them the work on which they were engaged. It was also fairly clear that the toolmakers were conscious of forming a (superior) status group within the factory labour force, and that associated with this were certain norms of dress and appearance —for example, white coats, neatly knotted ties, and well-groomed hair. But, on the other hand, group norms and relationships seemed to be involved relatively little in the toolmakers' actual work activities.

[2] In the case of both the heavy grinders and turret-lathe operators, management was anxious to establish the practice that men should move quite often. Heavy grinders might be moved as often as once a week. With the turret-lathe operators, changes occurred less frequently but about half the men in the departments we studied, who had no good reason for staying on the same machine, were likely to be moved every few weeks.

It is interesting to note, as a possible indication of the lack of group solidarity among the machinists generally, that so far as we could ascertain there were no well-enforced group norms of output or earnings. In the case of the automatic-lathe operators there was virtually no scope for control of output once the machines were running; most men had a 'target' for the day but would exceed this if their machine proved capable of it. The heavy grinders and turret-lathe operators had far more autonomy in this respect but acted in several different ways. About half of those we interviewed had an earnings norm, a 'bogey' for the day, which they did not usually exceed; once they were in sight of this—once they 'had the job in the bag'— they slowed down their rate of working. A further third, however, had a 'bogey' of this kind which they used simply as a basis for calculating at what rate they would have to work on any given job in order to 'make out'; if they found they could exceed this rate, then they would do so. The remaining men some days adopted one system, some days the other, depending chiefly, it appeared, on whether they thought the rate for the jobs they were given were 'tight' or 'loose'. Overall it could not be said that among these workers what Lupton has called 'the will to control' was very strong—although, one would suggest, for reasons different from those given by Lupton in his 'Wye' case: see T. Lupton, *On the Shop Floor* (London, 1963).

TABLE 19. *Aspects of technical organisation affecting the formation of solidary work groups*

Occupational group	Positive and facilitating factors			Negative and impeding factors		
	Degree of interdependence with others in same occupational group	Degree of control over work process	Degree of freedom of movement	Spatial constraints on informal group relations	Other constraints on informal group relations e.g. noise demands of machines etc.	Frequency of deployment involving changes in work location
Craftsmen:						
Toolmakers	low	high	high	low	low	low
Millwrights and other maintenance	low	high	high	high	low	high
Setters	low	high	high	high	low	variable to low
Process workers	variable to low	low	variable to high	variable to high	low	low
Machinists:						
Heavy grinders	low	medium	medium	medium	low	medium
Turret-lathe operators	low	medium	medium	variable to low	low	medium
Automatic-lathe operators	low	low	low	high	high	low
Assemblers	high	low	variable to low	high	variable to low	high

47

With all other occupational groups or sub-groups, the occurrence of primary group interaction was largely *prevented* by technological barriers of some kind or other. In the case of the millwrights and other maintenance men there was the fact that they spent only a small part of their working day in their shops and for most of the time were scattered about the plant wherever their services happened to be required. The setters, similarly, were not often found together as a group, their most regular social contacts being with the machinists whose 'set-ups' they carried out. But since any one setter would be responsible for anything from four to up to a dozen machines, the operatives of which might often change, even these relationships were rarely of a developed group character.

Spatial constraints were again the major barrier with the process workers and the assemblers, although in different ways. In the former case most men were quite widely dispersed about the plant, in ones and twos, and came together rather infrequently in spite of their fairly considerable freedom of movement.[1] In the latter case, men were strung out for the most part along the assembly lines and, while this encouraged interaction between individuals and their immediate neighbours on the line, the development of *group* relations was largely precluded; that is to say, individuals were prevented from sharing in *common* networks of social relationships, set off from others by more or less distinct boundaries.[2] Finally, with the automatic-lathe operators, group formation was inhibited not only by spatial factors but also by the machines themselves. In this case, individuals were almost totally subordinated to their machines—which were set quite widely apart—and could leave them for only very short periods. Moreover, because of the noise level in the shop, any sustained conversation required considerable effort.

Our findings, therefore, would strongly support the argument that the 'human relations' emphasis on the primary work group is somewhat misguided if only because in modern industry technological constraints often remove the possibility of such groups existing. However, while we believe this argument to be valid, we can also bring forward evidence to indicate

---

[1] Blauner appears to assume that *team* production is a general feature of work in chemical plants. On this and several other points our findings in Laporte diverge from his characterisation. See his *Alienation and Freedom*, pp. 146–8.

[2] cf. Walker and Guest, *The Man on the Assembly Line*, ch. 5; Frank J. Jasinski, 'Technological Delimitation of Reciprocal Relationships', *Human Organization*, vol. 15, no. 2 (1956), and Peter M. Blau and W. Richard Scott, *Formal Organisations* (London, 1963), pp. 88–9. In some few cases—e.g. where the lines 'snake'—clusters of assemblers are to be found. But even here conditions are far from ideal for the development of cohesive groups: these men do not choose each other but are brought together—and may be soon dispersed—by the operation of the line itself.

in turn that the technological environment *alone* constitutes a clearly inadequate basis on which to explain the nature of shop-floor relations among the workers we studied. This evidence derives from a number of questions included in our interviewing schedule with which we sought to complement the results of our observational efforts.

To begin with, we asked our respondents: 'In your job how much do you talk to your workmates? Would you say a good deal, just now and then, or hardly at all?' We then asked: 'When do you talk to them? Is it mainly during work or during breaks?' The replies we received to these two questions are brought together in table 20. From this it can be seen that more than half of the setters and of the assemblers report that they talk to their workmates 'a good deal', whereas at the other extreme this is reported by less than a quarter of the process workers. The craftsmen and machinists are in an intermediate position, but more than a quarter of the latter group—a higher proportion than in any other—say that they talk to their mates 'hardly at all'. As the note to the table indicates, the majority of these men were automatic-lathe operators, and here, as with the process workers, technological constraints to which we have already referred were clearly at work. In a similar way, and again as we have already implied, aspects of technical organisation can also serve to explain the relatively high level of talking on the part of the setters and assemblers. The setters are brought into fairly frequent contact with machinists, and the assemblers with the men adjacent to them on the line.[1] Moreover, in this latter case, talking seems often to have been regarded as an essential means of counteracting the stresses and tedium of the job itself. As one assembler put it: 'You've got to lark around with the mates a bit just to break the monotony'; or, in the words of another: 'If you didn't talk, you'd go stark raving mad!'

In sum it could be said that the content of table 20 appears consistent with, and is in large part made intelligible by, the content of table 19, and the discussion of this in previous paragraphs.[2] To this extent the 'technological implications' approach may be regarded as still validated.[3]

However, the replies which we received to a further question complicate

---

[1] Assemblers working on 'trim' lines were significantly more likely to report talking to their mates 'a good deal' than were those on 'engine' or 'body' lines.

[2] It should not be thought that in the case of the setters and assemblers a discrepancy exists between the 'high' spatial constraints on informal group relations (table 19) and the relatively high level of talking between workmates (table 20). These data are not incompatible because, as noted, setters are able to talk to a variety of *machinists* rather than to other setters and, while assemblers can talk to each other, they are rarely able to form groups.

[3] The general effect of technical organisation on the level of talking is indicated by the association, apparent from table 20, between talking 'a good deal' and being able to talk while working. $\chi^2 = 28 \cdot 6$; 1 df; $p < 0 \cdot 001$.

TABLE 20. *Reported frequency of talking to workmates and occasions when this mainly takes place*

Respondent talks to workmates	Occasions when talking mainly takes place	Craftsmen (N = 56)	Setters (N = 23)	Process workers (N = 23)	Machinists (N = 41)	Assemblers (N = 86)	All (N = 229)
		Percentage					
'Good deal'	Work, or work and breaks equally	32	52	22	27	52	40
	Breaks	7	9	0	5	8	7
	TOTALS	39	61	22	32	60	47
'Now and then'	Work, or work and breaks equally	36	22	35	20	16	24
	Breaks	16	17	9	20	13	15
	TOTALS	52	39	44	40	29	39
'Hardly at all'	Work, or work and breaks equally	2	0	4	10*	0	3
	Breaks	5	0	17	17*	7	9
	TOTALS	7	0	21	27	7	12
Other		2	0	13	2	4	4
TOTALS		100	100	100	101	100	102

* The twelve workers involved here include eight out of the eighteen automatic-lathe operators in this occupational group.

the situation considerably. In order to gain some idea of the degree of workers' affective involvement with their mates, as distinct from their frequency of interaction, we asked the men we interviewed: 'How would you feel if you were moved to another job in the factory, more or less like the one you do now, but away from the men who work near to you? Would you feel very upset, fairly upset, not much bothered, or not bothered at all?' The pattern of response produced by this question is shown in table 21.

From this table, three points of particular significance emerge. First, it is indicated that a relatively high level of verbal interaction among workers is not necessarily associated with strong feelings of personal attachment. This is brought out most clearly in the case of the setters. Although more than half of this group reported talking to their workmates 'a good deal', only a quarter would be 'very upset' or 'fairly upset' if moved away from the men near to whom they presently work. It is true that, as we have noted,

TABLE 21. *Feelings about being moved away from present workmates*

| | Craftsmen | | | Machinists | | | | | Assemblers | All |
Respondent would feel	Tool-makers (N = 19)	Mill-wrights* (N = 37)	All (N = 56)	Setters (N = 23)	Process workers (N = 23)	Autos operators (N = 18)	Others† (N = 23)	All (N = 41)	(N = 86)	(N = 220)
					Percentage					
'Very upset'	0	0	0	4	0	11	4	7	5	4
'Fairly upset'	5	16	13	22	13	44	26	34	27	23
'Not much bothered'	37	27	30	30	35	17	35	27	35	32
'Not bothered at all'	58	41	46	44	26	28	30	29	33	36
Other, D.K., D.N.A.	0	16	11	0	26‡	0	4	2	1	5
TOTALS	100	100	100	100	100	100	99	99	101	100

* And other maintenance men.

† I.e. turret-lathe operators and heavy grinders.

‡ In the case of the six men involved here the question did not apply since the men worked largely in isolation.

51

the great majority of the setters' contacts are likely to be with men in another occupational category—that is, machinists. But even in the case of the assemblers, where a man's workmates were almost invariably other assemblers and where the amount of talking was also high, still only a third of the group replied that they would find a move an upsetting experience.[1]

This leads us on to the second point, which is of more general importance; that is, that on the basis of table 21, it would appear that the workers in our sample *as a whole* have a notably *low* degree of affective involvement with their workmates, and that they do not for the most part derive any very highly valued 'social' satisfactions from the existing face-to-face relationships of their workplace. Only in one group—the machinists—were there less than 60% who stated that they would be 'not much bothered' or 'not bothered at all' at the prospect of a move to another part of the factory; and only 8 men out of the total of 229 would go so far as to say that they would be 'very upset' by a change of this nature. Thus, we have here evidence which would seem to confirm the view put forward earlier on the basis of table 19 that among the workers we studied participation in work relationships of a solidary kind was unlikely to be typical.

However—and this is the third point—table 21 also suggests rather strongly that this apparent lack of close attachments between workmates *cannot* be adequately explained *simply* in terms of technological constraints. Most strikingly, it turns out that the greatest indifference of all towards a move away from present workmates is shown by the toolmakers; that is, by the sub-group with the technological environment which, following table 19, is the most favourable for primary group formation. In fact, only 1 out of the 19 toolmakers stated that to have to make a move would be upsetting to him. Moreover, it is also interesting to note, on the other hand, —though the numbers are small—that clearly the highest percentages in the 'very upset' and 'fairly upset' categories are found to occur in the case of the automatic-lathe operators; that is, with the workers for whom sustained interaction would appear, because of technical factors, to be most difficult.[2]

Our conclusion here must be, therefore, that while technical organisa-

---

[1] No significant association exists within any group in the sample nor in the sample overall between reporting talking 'a good deal' to one's workmates and feeling that one would be 'upset' if moved away from them.

[2] Our data are insufficient to enable us to offer any reliable explanation of this intriguing—though minor—deviation from the general pattern of 'non-involvement' with workmates. One suggestion would be that working conditions which are *particularly* adverse to informal group relations will, paradoxically, generate motivations to overcome the barriers that exist, provided that the set of individuals concerned in the situation is relatively stable. As table 19 indicates, 'autos' operators were not frequently redeployed.

tion is likely to exert an important influence on the patterns and frequency of interaction among workers on the shop floor, and while it can clearly inhibit the formation of genuine work groups, it is nonetheless of much reduced significance as an actual determinant of the *quality* of work relationships, in the sense of the value and meanings which workers give to them. Men may set a relatively low value on close and stable relationships with their workmates even under conditions which would in no way prevent the development of solidary groups; conversely, even where men are dispersed and isolated in their work, a desire to retain contacts with particular fellow workers, however limited these contacts may be, can still persist. Industrial behaviour, within technologically advanced enterprises at least, may well be role-determined to a significant extent; but it must always be recognised that similar work-roles can be evaluated and interpreted in quite widely differing ways by those who are required to act them out.

In the case of our sample, the generally low degree of affective involvement between workmates must be explained both in terms of the data presented in table 19—technological barriers to primary group formation—*and* from the point of view of these workers' own definitions of their work situation. We would claim here the necessity of reverting to the hypothesis advanced previously that the characteristic orientation to work among the men we studied is one of a predominantly instrumental kind. On the basis of the ideal type of this orientation, set out at the end of the last chapter, it would be predicted that to the extent that work is defined as a mandatory form of activity and as one engaged in simply as a means to an end, the workplace will not be regarded as a *milieu* appropriate or favourable to the development of highly rewarding primary relationships, that is, as a *milieu* in which the worker's expressive or affective needs are likely to be met. Thus, given that among the affluent workers we studied economic considerations have predominantly determined their choice of job, or at any rate are now the main factor binding them to their present employment, it is not surprising that, in general, they show no great concern over maintaining stable relationships with any particular set of workmates. So far as work goes, emotionally significant experiences and 'significant others' tend neither to be looked for nor, thus, to be greatly missed in their absence. The following comments, made in answer to our question about the possibility of being moved, are illustrative of the attitudes in point.

'How would I feel about being moved? It wouldn't bother me much. You're here to earn your living.'

'I wouldn't be bothered at all. The job comes first. Work's what I come here to do.'

'I wouldn't be much bothered. I'm not an individualist or snobbish but you must look after number one—by that I mean myself, my wife and children. I would be glad to move anywhere to keep my present job.'

A marked contrast in attitudes and behaviour can, then, be seen between our affluent workers and at least some types of more 'traditional' worker. As is now becoming realised, the extent to which solidary work groups are to be found, in factory industry at any rate, has almost certainly been exaggerated by sociologists in the past;[1] but, nonetheless, an appreciable number of studies, notably of miners and steelworkers, leave no doubt that what we have termed a 'solidaristic' orientation to work is more than merely a figment of either 'human relations' or 'leftist' ideology. In the case of miners the constant presence of physical danger is conducive both to a high degree of ego-involvement in work and at the same time to a strong awareness on the part of the individual of his responsibility for, and dependence upon, his workmates. Miners tend to attach great importance to working as members of established groups of known and tried companions.[2] In the case of steelworkers, methods of production requiring closely co-ordinated crew operations have led to the development of strong traditions of group cohesiveness and stability; and here again there is ample evidence that the integrity of the work group is highly valued and that threats to it will be forcefully resisted.[3] For example, it is significant that recent studies made of technical change in both the coal-mining and steel industries have shown, in highly comparable ways, how new production systems which enable integrated work groups to remain in existence give rise to far greater job satisfaction and to fewer conflicts than do systems which entail individual working or the frequent redeployment of men.[4]

In comparison with workers of the kind in question, therefore, the instrumental orientation of our affluent workers is thrown into sharp relief. However, we feel it important to add here that a comparison made between the workers we have studied and *other factory workers*, who differed only in being somewhat less affluent, might well be far less striking and

---

[1] See, for example, Etzioni, *A Comparative Analysis of Complex Organizations*, pp. 165–71.

[2] See, for example, A. W. Gouldner, *Patterns of Industrial Bureaucracy* (London, 1954), pp. 129–34; Eugene A. Friedmann and Robert J. Havighurst, *The Meaning of Work and Retirement* (Chicago, 1954), pp. 62–5; N. Dennis, F. Henriques and C. Slaughter, *Coal is Our Life* (London, 1956), pp. 44–5, 79–80.

[3] See, for example, C. R. Walker, *Steeltown* (New York, 1950), pp. 63–89; and W. H. Scott et al., *Technical Change and Industrial Relations*, pp. 126–8.

[4] For coal-mining see A. T. M. Wilson, 'Some aspects of Social Process', *Journal of Social Issues*, vol. 7, no. 5 (1951); E. L. Trist and K. W. Bamforth, 'Some Social and Psychological Consequences of the Longwall Method of Coal-getting', *Human Relations*, vol. 4, no. 1 (1951); and E. L. Trist, J. W. Higgin, H. Murray and A. B. Pollock, *Organizational Choice* (London, 1963). For steel, see Scott et al., *Technical Change and Industrial Relations*.

very much a matter of degree. To the extent that the men in our sample are distinctive in having made through their choice of employment a more or less deliberate decision to give high income primacy over other possible returns from work, we would still expect them to show the closest approximation to a purely instrumental pattern of attitudes and behaviour. But it may well be that a lack of concern for maintaining solidary relationships with workmates is becoming generalised among employees in large-scale manufacturing industry, and thus that our findings represent one instance of the 'prototypicality' of our sample which we suggested in chapter 1.

So far we hope to have established that very few, if any, of the workers in our sample participate in work groups of a solidary kind, and that a substantial majority show a low degree of affective involvement with their immediate workmates. We have argued that these findings are in part to be explained in terms of technological constraints on primary group formation, but that the explanation cannot be complete without reference also to the orientation to work which, we have suggested, is characteristic of the workers in question. In the next part of this chapter we seek to strengthen this argument further by examining the extent to which work relations among the men in our sample formed the basis for friendships outside the factory. If it were the case that our affluent workers did feel a strong need for closer, more solidary ties with their workmates but were prevented from fulfilling this need simply because of an unfavourable technological environment, then it might be expected that they would seek to circumvent in-plant barriers by cultivating out-plant association. Our data indicate that association of this kind is not at a high level and thus provide additional evidence that among the men we studied work is generally defined in an instrumental way.

Following the questions which dealt with relations with workmates on the shop floor, we asked our respondents: 'How many of the men who work near to you would you call close friends?' The replies we received to this question are given in table 22. From this it can be seen that from a third to a half of those in all occupational groups except the process workers stated that they would regard *none* of their workmates as being close friends, while in the latter group this proportion was substantially higher.[1] Too much cannot be read into these findings in themselves, particularly since the real meaning of the answers given to a question of the

[1] The fact that 6 out of the 23 process workers were virtually isolated in the plant, as indicated in note ‡ to table 21, is relevant here; their nearest fellow workers were generally

TABLE 22. *Number of workmates regarded as 'close friends'*

Number stated	Craftsmen (N = 56)	Setters (N = 23)	Process workers (N = 23)	Machinists (N = 41)	Assemblers (N = 86)	All (N = 229)
	Percentage					
None	41	44	70	51	37	45
1 or 2	38	26	4	27	21	25
More than 2	21	30	26	22	42	31
TOTALS	100	100	100	100	100	101

kind we put will depend greatly on the ideas which respondents have of what a 'close friend' is. However, when we consider the further information which we collected with this latter point in mind, the weakness of the relational links between our workers' in-plant and out-plant lives becomes more, rather than less, apparent.

In the cases of those men who said that they had at least one close friend among their immediate workmates, we went on to ask: 'When do you see him/them outside of the factory?' The answers we received were then classified according to four different levels of association as is shown in table 23. In this way it is revealed that as often as not workmates who had been claimed as close friends were seen outside of work only in semi-casual or purely casual ways or not at all. Thus, among the craftsmen and setters in the sample, only two-fifths proved to have workmates whom they regarded as close friends *and* whom they either visited at home or accompanied on arranged outings; and with the semi-skilled men, this proportion fell lower still—averaging out for the three groups together at exactly one fifth. In other words, taking the sample as a whole, only around one in four of our affluent workers could be said to have a 'close friend' among his mates in the sense of someone with whom he would actually plan to meet for out-of-work social activities.

Two arguments might well be advanced for questioning whether these findings necessarily give further support for the view that among the workers we studied an instrumental orientation to work is predominant. It could, for instance, be held that the findings might simply reflect the effects of out-plant as well as of in-plant limitations on the development of

well out of speaking range. All six reported no 'close friends'. Again our findings diverge from those of Blauner, who sees the chemical process worker as being *more* likely than most other types of factory employee to be integrated into a work team. See his *Alienation and Freedom*, pp. 146–8.

TABLE 23. *Level of out-plant association with workmates regarded as 'close-friends'*

Level of association reported*	Craftsmen (N = 56)	Setters (N = 23)	Process workers (N = 23)	Machinists (N = 41)	Assemblers (N = 86)	All (N = 229)
			Percentage			
Visiting at home	21 ⎱ 41	22 ⎱ 39	0 ⎱ 4	10 ⎱ 22	19 ⎱ 24	16 ⎱ 27
Arranged outings	20 ⎰	17 ⎰	4 ⎰	12 ⎰	5 ⎰	11 ⎰
Semi-casual meetings†	7	13	13	10	14	11
Purely casual meetings‡ or no associations at all	11	4	13	17	26	17
No workmates regarded as 'close friends'	41	44	70	51	37	45
TOTALS	100	100	100	100	101	100

* Only the highest level recorded, in connection with *any* close friend, is counted—highest being judged in terms of the categories below.

† I.e. meetings at public houses, clubs, sports grounds and other places which both men frequented.

‡ I.e. chance meetings in the street, shops, etc.

close personal ties among the men in question—the effects, that is, of residential dispersion as well as of technical organisation; if this were so the data would tell us little about values and attitudes. Alternatively it could be claimed that, according to working-class norms, friendship does not have to involve visiting and arranged outings but is capable of being sustained entirely through what we have termed semi-casual meetings in public houses, clubs, at football matches and so on. Both these arguments are pertinent ones; but both can be controverted by other material on which we can draw.

In the first place we have information on the extent to which our respondents lived in close proximity to the workmates whom they counted as close friends; and on this basis it can be shown that no significant relationship exists between residential proximity and the level of out-plant association which was reported.[1]

[1] We asked those respondents who claimed at least one 'close friend' among their workmates: 'Do any of them/does he live near you—say, within ten minutes' walk?' Of the 62 men who had reported visiting with their friend(s) or going on arranged outings together, 31 came from the 55 men who said they had at least one friend living within ten minutes' walk and 31 from the 72 men who said they had none. Thus of the 65 men whose out-plant relations with their workmate friends were at most semi-casual, 24 were in the former group and 41 in the latter. These data are far from showing any statistically significant association between having workmate friends who live nearby and seeing such friends outside of work in an organised way.

In the second place we can reject the argument that we are seeking to impose alien ideas of friendship upon our sample since we have evidence that a sizable proportion of our affluent workers *do* have friends, other than workmates, with whom visiting fairly regularly takes place. This evidence is worth considering here in some further detail.

The material comes from the interviews we carried out with our respondents in their own homes, along with their wives, and in which we asked a series of questions on friends and leisure activities. One of these questions went as follows: 'We've been talking about your friends and your spare-time activities—how about having other couples round, say for a meal, or just for the evening; how often would you say you do this on average?' In the case of those couples who said that they did sometimes entertain in this way, we then also asked: 'Who is it you have round—are they friends, relatives, or who?' Information produced by these questions is given in table 24. From this it can be seen, first, that in each occupational group between a third and two-thirds of our affluent workers reported entertaining other couples in their homes at least once a month on average; but, secondly, that of *all* couples who were mentioned as being entertained in this way, only a small minority were couples involving workmates, even including here workmates of wives and all ex-workmates. Kin, as might be expected, were clearly the most frequent guests, but apart from kin, friends other than workmates were mentioned twice as often as the latter by the more skilled men in the sample and four times more often by the semi-skilled workers.[1] From these data it is then clear that men who saw little of their 'workmate' friends outside the factory, other than in a more or less casual way, might well associate with friends of a different kind in a quite different style.[2]

Finally, in this connection it is perhaps worth noting that in discussing the relationship between their work and non-work lives, the men we interviewed quite frequently used a phrase which had clearly the status of a maxim or piece of folk wisdom. 'Mates', they said, 'are not friends.'[3] And,

[1] Overall, as table 24 shows, 11 % of the couples mentioned involved a workmate; this compares with 12 % who were neighbours—loosely defined as persons living within ten minutes' walk of the respondents—and 20 % who were 'other friends', that is, neither workmates nor neighbours. See further *The Affluent Worker in the Class Structure*, ch. 4.

[2] Of the 167 men in the sample who saw no workmate friend outside of work other than semi-casually, 86 (52 %) had 'couples round' at least once a month on average. The corresponding figure for the remaining 62 men is 38 (61 %). Apart from the absence of workmates in the former case, the character of the couples entertained is not significantly different.

[3] This was said even by men who only a few minutes before had claimed one or more 'close friends' among their workmates. Sometimes they went on to explain that these were 'not friends *really*'.

TABLE 24. *Extent and details of home entertaining of other couples by manual workers and their wives*

	Craftsmen (N = 56)	Setters (N = 23)	Process workers (N = 23)	Machinists (N = 41)	Assemblers (N = 86)	All (N = 229)
Percentage reporting 'having couples round' at least once a month on average	68	35	39	49	57	54
Total number of couples mentioned as being regularly entertained at home	159	53	27	87	209	535
Percentage of above who were kin	54	49	74	55	61	57
Percentage of above where man or wife was a workmate*	13	23	7	9	7	11
Percentage of above who were neighbours or other friends	34	28	18	36	32	32
Number of couples mentioned per couple interviewed	2·8	2·3	1·2	2·1	2·4	2·3
Number of couples mentioned per couple interviewed where man or wife was a workmate	0·3	0·5	0·1	0·2	0·2	0·2

* 'Workmate' here includes past as well as present workmates of both husband and wife interviewed. It excludes any workmate who was also kin or with whom acquaintance *originated* outside of work—e.g. as neighbours; but the numbers in these cases are negligible.

like an earlier investigator of Luton industry who makes the same observation,[1] we would understand this remark as carrying normative as well as factual meaning. The following more extended comments, taken from our interview schedules, may serve to illustrate the point.

'With workmates—it's like the army. You're friends but as soon as you're away from work, you forgot them. It's the best way.'

'I wouldn't encourage having close friends at work. It wouldn't come off. At Kent's [another Luton firm] there was a mate I used to exchange Sunday teas with—but it didn't work out. We saw too much of each other. There wasn't anything to talk about.'

'Workmates are only friends insofar as work is concerned; it doesn't extend outside. I prefer it that way. I'd have a drink with them but I wouldn't make a habit of meeting with them socially if that could be avoided. My attitude is "Away from work, let's forget it."'

We may assert then not only that very few of the workers in our sample participate in solidary work groups, but also that few again base their

[1] F. Zweig, *The Worker in an Affluent Society* (London, 1961), pp. 117–18.

social life outside the factory to any important extent upon association with their fellow workers. Particularly with the semi-skilled men, workmates, including those who are regarded as 'close friends', have very little significance outside work. Relations with workmates seem, in this case, typically to take the character of a fairly superficial shop-floor *camaraderie*, the chief function of which, perhaps, is to provide diversion and possibilities of tension release within an often highly taxing work situation.

With the craftsmen and setters it occurs more frequently, but by no means generally, that one or two workmates are 'close friends' in the sense of persons with whom organised forms of association outside work do take place. This pattern can be interpreted as implying some solidaristic element in work orientation even if in an attenuated form. However, it has still to be remembered here that these workmate friends are likely to be only one kind among several, and that they can scarcely be regarded, in the light of our evidence, as being at the centre of the individual's social world. Something of a dichotomy still remains, even with the more skilled men, between their in-plant and out-plant lives in that largely different sets of social relationships are involved; this we see as being highly consistent with our view that in *all* occupational groups within our sample work is predominantly defined in an instrumental way.[1]

In this respect we can regard our findings as being once more in marked contrast with the quite numerous accounts of other industrial workers whose traditionally solidaristic orientations are reflected in their creation of distinctive occupational cultures and communities. Again, miners and steelworkers would offer obvious examples here;[2] but to these could be added further studies relating to dockers, railwaymen, trawlermen, textile workers and printers.[3] In all these cases, it has been shown how work may

---

[1] For a similar line of analysis, see S. R. Parker, 'Type of Work, Friendship Pattern and Leisure', *Human Relations*, vol. 17, no. 3 (August 1964); and 'Work and Non-Work in Three Occupations', *Sociological Review*, vol. 13, no. 1 (1965). It may be noted here that even if we consider our respondents' patterns of association in their out-of-work lives as a whole, so as to include semi-casual, informal contacts, we still find that workmates do not figure very prominently. E.g. in the 'home' interviews we asked: 'Who would you say are the two or three people [excluding spouse and children] that you most often spend your spare time with?' From the answers received, it emerged that, overall, of the persons mentioned by the husbands, only 23% were workmates compared with 32% who were kin and 46% neighbours or other friends. Not all respondents were able to name three or even two persons, and the number of workmates mentioned per man was as low as 0·4. No significant variations existed in any of these respects from one occupational group to another.

[2] See Gouldner, *Patterns of Industrial Bureaucracy*, pp. 134–6; Dennis et al., *Coal is our Life*, pp. 79–82 and ch. 4; and Walker, *Steeltown*, ch. IV.

[3] See, for example, on dockers, University of Liverpool, Department of Social Science, *The Dock Worker* (Liverpool, 1954), ch. III; on railwaymen, W. F. Cottrell, *The Railroader* (Palo Alto, 1940); on trawlermen, G. Horobin, 'Community and Occupation in the Hull Fishing

provide the foundation for an entire way of life. Outside the work place, workmates remain preferred companions; work is a central life interest, constituting a perennial topic of conversation; and, perhaps most significantly, the occupational group is the crucial reference group for all its members, setting standards of behaviour, forming opinions, creating social identity. One has here situations which are qualitatively different from that existing among the workers we have studied. The distinctive feature in this latter case is the extent to which the experiences and relationships of the factory are 'insulated' from other aspects of workers' existence—the extent of the separation which occurs, psychologically and socially, between work and non-work.

It is worth emphasising again that the workers with whom we are here comparing our sample are not, for the most part, men employed in large-scale manufacturing industry, and thus that it would be wrong to seek to explain the differences observed simply and specifically in terms of the 'affluence' of the workers we studied. Findings such as those we have produced might well be approximated in studies made of many other groups of factory workers with lower income levels, and we would indeed think this probable.[1] However the one further comparison which we have the means to make in conclusion of this section, is that between our affluent manual workers and the sample of white-collar employees which we took from Skefko and Laporte. Its main significance is the indication given that the workers we studied, while obviously lacking solidaristic patterns of association with their workmates, are at the same time also clearly differentiated in this respect from nonmanual workers of similar economic standing.[2]

Table 25 shows, first, that men in the white-collar sample were less likely than those in the manual sample to have fellow workers whom they regarded as 'close friends', but that in the case of colleagues who *were* so

Industry', *British Journal of Sociology*, vol. III, no. 4 (1957), J. Tunstall, *The Fishermen* (London, 1962), and P. Duncan, 'Conflict and Co-operation among Trawlermen', *British Journal of Industrial Relations*, vol. I, no. 3 (1963); on textile workers, Blauner, *Alienation and Freedom*, ch. 4; and on printers, Lipset *et al.*, *Union Democracy*, chs. 5, 6 and 7, A. J. M. Sykes, 'Trade Union Workshop Organisation in the Printing Industry', *Human Relations*, vol. 13, no. 1, 1960, and I. C. Cannon, *The Social Situation of the Skilled Worker*, unpublished Ph.D. thesis, University of London (1961), and 'Ideology and Occupation', paper presented to the Sixth World Congress of Sociology (Evian, 1966).

[1] Several cases have already been reported in the United States and Great Britain of *relatively* highly paid factory workers who have little contact with workmates in their out-plant life. See Blauner, 'Work Satisfaction and Industrial Trends in Modern Society'; C. Argyris, 'The Organization: What Makes it Healthy?', *Harvard Business Review*, vol. XXXVII, no. 5 (1958); Zweig, *The Worker in an Affluent Society*, pp. 117–18; and P. Willmott, *The Evolution of a Community* (London, 1963), pp. 63–8.

[2] Since no systematic differences were found in the pattern of response of white-collar employees from Skefko and Laporte, the two groups are considered together throughout the monograph.

TABLE 25. *Out-plant association with fellow workers: comparison of manual and white-collar samples*

Reported 'close friends' among fellow workers*	White collar (N = 54)	Craftsmen and Setters (N = 79)	Semi-skilled (N = 150)	All manual (N = 229)
Percentage reporting:				
None	61	42	46	45
1 or 2	26	34	20	25
More than 2	13	24	34	31
TOTALS	100	100	100	101
Percentage having 'close friends' with whom visiting and/or outings take place	28	41	20	25
Percentage *of those having* 'close friends' who associate with them through visiting and outings	72	70	37	49
Percentage reporting 'having couples round' at least once a month on average	76	57	52	54
Percentage of total number of couples mentioned in which man or wife was a fellow worker†	13	15	8	11

* In the case of the white-collar sample the actual question asked was: 'How many of the men who work near to you (say in your office or department) would you call close friends?'
† Or ex-fellow-worker.

regarded, association with these friends outside work was far more likely to be of an organised rather than of a more or less casual kind. On this point the difference arises almost entirely between the white-collar employees and the semi-skilled manual workers. However while the craftsmen and setters always tend to be closer to the white-collar pattern, a further, and more general, difference can be seen in that white-collar couples appear more regularly to entertain fellow workers and their spouses in their homes. As table 25 shows, the amount of entertaining in this style is a good deal higher overall in the white-collar sample; yet at the same time the relative importance of fellow workers, as opposed to guests of a different kind, varies relatively little between the two samples.

Among the white-collar workers, then, 'friendship', with fellow workers at least, is a more selective and probably also a more deliberately cultivated kind of relationship than among our affluent manual workers. Consistently with our idea of a 'bureaucratic' orientation towards work, colleagues are not particularly favoured as friends nor readily recognised as such; but where it does occur that friends are made at work, then there are no particular difficulties in the way of extending and developing the friendship outside work. This, we would argue, is not the case with the manual workers, or at least not with the semi-skilled men. Their characteristic orientation towards work and their definition of the work situation do not favour this as a source of social relationships which are valued and preserved 'for their own sake'.

Finally, in this chapter, we must say something about one further aspect of primary relationships within the work situation which we have so far neglected; that is, relations between workers and their immediate supervisors. We noted earlier that this has been a matter of central concern to industrial sociologists of the 'human relations' school because they believe that supervisory 'style' is a key determinant of worker motivation and morale. Typically it has been argued by exponents of this approach that supervisors who are 'employee-oriented' and who maintain a high level of informal interaction with the men in their charge will in this way create 'positive sentiment' among their men and encourage worker attitudes and norms of behaviour of a kind favourable to managerial objectives.[1] The basic assumption underlying this view is that workers generally experience a strongly felt need for personal recognition and approval from their superiors and that where this need is met a positive response on the part of workers will be forthcoming. The supervisor, as the man who largely embodies management so far as the rank and file are concerned, thus occupies a crucial position, and one in which a high premium will attach to his possessing the 'right' personal attributes and also a trained ability in the handling of interpersonal relations.

It should be added here that several more sophisticated writers have appreciated the difficulties which supervisors are likely to meet in attempting to follow approved 'human relations' practice under the technological conditions of mass-production work and, in particular, of assembly-line work. Nevertheless, it has still been generally supposed that even in these unfavourable circumstances supervisory behaviour aimed at meeting workers' expressive and affective needs is of major importance in creating a 'sound' shop-floor relationship and in encouraging workers to identify with their organisation. Moreover, a certain amount of evidence has been produced, chiefly in the United States, which can be used to lend support

[1] See, for example, N. R. F. Maier, *Psychology in Industry* (Boston, 1955), ch. 6, 'Supervisory Leadership'.

to this point of view. Most notably, Walker, Guest, and Turner, in their studies of supervisor–worker relations in American car assembly plants, have collected data of various kinds which show that where a high rate of informal interaction occurs between foremen and their subordinates, men tend to be more favourably disposed towards supervision (and also, it seems, towards the company) than where the rate of such interaction is low. Indeed, these authors have suggested that in cases where work-tasks are intrinsically unrewarding, this positive connection between interaction and sentiment may prove to be a particularly strong one.[1]

Our findings do not align themselves with this 'human relations' theory. Indeed, they throw considerable doubt upon the basic supposition that industrial workers will *in general* attach high value to contact with their superiors of an informal and personalised kind. Rather, our data would support the argument that workers such as the majority of those in our sample, who have to a greater or lesser degree an instrumental orientation towards their employment, will not tend to regard their supervisors, any more than they do their workmates, as representing highly significant 'others'.

To begin with, we asked our respondents: 'How do you get on with your foreman? Would you say you got on very well, pretty well, not so well, or very badly?' The pattern of response to this question across our five occupational groups is shown in table 26. From this it is apparent that, to a surprisingly large extent, our affluent workers were quite favourably disposed towards their immediate supervisors. Unfavourable attitudes, moreover, tended to be concentrated among the craftsmen and, to a lesser degree, the machinists.[2] The former group account for half of those who reported a negative relationship with their foreman, and the two groups together for virtually three-quarters.

However, when one comes to examine the reasons which were offered for the prevailing positive relationships, what emerges is not at all what would be expected from a 'human relations' point of view. As is shown in table 27, reasons referring to *in*frequent interaction with foremen are the kind which occur more than any other. Around half the reasons given were of this nature, against a third which referred to foremen's personal attributes or social skills. The following *verbatim* comments illustrate the majority view.

[1] A. N. Turner, 'Interaction and Sentiment in the Foreman-Worker Relationship', *Human Organization*, vol. 14, no. 1 (1955); C. R. Walker, R. H. Guest and A. N. Turner, *The Foreman on the Assembly Line* (Cambridge, Mass., 1956); A. N. Turner, 'Foreman, Job and Company', *Human Relations*, vol. x, no. 2 (1957).
[2] Compare chapter 2, pp. 20–1 above.

TABLE 26. *Assessment of relationship with foreman*

Respondent gets on with foreman	Craftsmen (N = 56)	Setters (N = 23)	Process workers (N = 23)	Machinists (N = 41)	Assemblers (N = 86)	All (N = 229)
			Percentage			
'Very well'	23	44	65	32	40	37
'Pretty well'	52	48	22	49	55	49
'Not so well'⎱ 'Very badly' ⎰	25	9	4	15	5	12
Other, D.K.	0	0	9	5	1	2
TOTALS	100	101	100	101	101	100

'Why do I get on with my foreman pretty well? He leaves us alone—that's reason enough, isn't it?'

'I only see the foreman now and then—for example, for my pay each week or when there's a bit of trouble. I like it that way.'

'We get on pretty well because he doesn't bother me—and that's important in my job [toolmaking]. You're left on your own and you do your job. It gives you confidence to know you can do it.'

'We get on very well because I never really see him. If you do the job he doesn't bother you. The track's the boss, not the foreman.'

'Why do we get on pretty well? Well, I'm on piece-work and I don't think he's very interested one way or the other. If you don't do the work you just carry the can.'

As the last two comments imply, technological and economic constraints upon the workers were sometimes seen as making supervision largely unnecessary and removing much of the basis for any legitimate interference on the part of the foreman. But more generally it seems that the main meaning which supervision had for the workers in question was one related to their necessary compliance to managerial authority and the loss of autonomy this entailed. Given this definition of the situation, it would follow that the less experience these workers had of supervision, the more favourably they would tend to regard it.[1]

[1] For comparable findings see Argyris, 'The Organisation: What makes it Healthy?', and 'Understanding Human Behaviour in Organizations: One Viewpoint' in Haire, *Modern Organization Theory*. It should be noted that in the studies by Turner and others, referred to above, a sizable minority of workers were found who went against the general pattern in having positive attitudes towards their foremen because they were left alone, or in displaying negative attitudes associated with the feeling that their foremen interfered with them too

TABLE 27. *Reasons given for getting on with foreman 'very well' or 'pretty well'*

Class of reason	Craftsmen (N = 42)	Setters (N = 21)	Process workers (N = 20)	Machinists (N = 33)	Assemblers (N = 81)	All (N = 207)
			Times mentioned			
A. Reasons relating to infrequent interaction with foreman:						
Is left alone, undisturbed by foreman	8	8	6	13	26	61
Works well and gives foreman no cause to interfere, speak to him, etc.	3	3	5	4	7	22
Rarely sees foreman	11	1	1	0	4	17
TOTALS	22	12	12	17	37	100
B. Reasons relating to foreman's personal attributes or social skills	5	8	8	12	31	64
C. Other reasons	4	3	0	8	5	20
ALL REASONS*	31	23	20	37	73	184
Reasons in class A as percentage of all reasons	71	52	60	46	51	54
Reasons in class B as percentage of all reasons	16	35	40	32	42	35
Reasons in class C as percentage of all reasons	13	13	0	22	7	11
TOTALS	100	100	100	100	100	100

* In some cases, the figures in this row are lower than the number of men in the relevant occupational group. These discrepancies are accounted for by replies which were too imprecise to be classified and also by cases in which, owing to an error on the interviewing schedule, the question was not put.

While this is the situation we discover most typically with our affluent workers, it should also be noted that, by contrast, in two special cases our data are highly consistent with the 'human relations' position. The first of these concerns the (quite sizable) minority of craftsmen—14 out of the 56—who reported getting on with their foreman 'not so well' or 'very badly'. Of these 14 men, 11 (79%) explained this negative relationship largely in terms of their foreman's aloofness or sense of superiority and his reluctance

much. In the reports on the studies these 'deviants' are not satisfactorily explained. It is simply suggested that perhaps, in their experience, interaction with foremen was largely job-centred and was disliked for this reason; thus, the importance of supervisors talking to their men about things other than work is held to be re-emphasised. See Turner, 'Interaction and Sentiment in the Foreman-Worker Relationship'.

to talk to them except about their work. The following comments were characteristic.[1]

'I've only spoken to my foreman about two dozen times in two years—and then only about work...He just stands behind you while you're working and says nothing. How would you like it?'

'He's a foreman who's a bit out of touch. He's wrapped up in office work and has lost all contact with the blokes. *When* he speaks it's like he was a higher class than you and you're a lower class.'

'He doesn't bother you and I don't have a lot to do with him, but he thinks he's the little king over the shop. He doesn't have a lot to say to anyone—like a little god.'

The second case is provided by our sample of white-collar workers. The latter, even more than the manual workers, reported favourable relationships with their supervisors: 51 out of 54 (94%) said that they got on 'very well' (59%) or 'pretty well' (35%) with their 'immediate superiors'.[2] But with these workers it was clear that their supervisors' personal attributes and interpersonal skills *were* felt to be of quite considerable importance in creating positive relationships. Of the reasons given in this respect, only a quarter (24%) referred to infrequent contact with immediate superiors, whereas approaching a half (47%) referred to supervisors' 'friendliness', 'willingness to listen' or 'informality', or put the emphasis on 'co-operativeness' and on 'everyone working as a team'.

In both these cases, we would suggest, one is dealing with workers whose expectations from work are not so concentrated, as with the bulk of the manual sample, on economic returns. Work has some meaning other than as simply a means to an end; it is seen as a possible source of satisfaction for expressive and affective needs. Thus, the attitudes and behaviour of supervisors will tend to have a significance which is far greater than where supervisors are regarded merely as the agents of managerial authority. As Dubin has pointed out,[3] individuals whose ego-involvement in their work is relatively high are likely to feel the need for supervisors to confirm, actually and symbolically, their wisdom in choosing this work as a central interest in their lives. Thus, in a situation of this kind, a foreman

---

[1] Reasons given by the men in other occupational groups, who also reported an unfavourable relationship with their foreman, were very mixed—referring *inter alia* to foremen being technically incompetent, ineffective in dealing with complaints, too afraid of breaking rules, and too hard on men who made mistakes.

[2] 'Immediate superior' was substituted for 'foreman' in our interviews with the white-collar workers.

[3] *The World of Work*, pp. 254–7. See also Argyris, 'Understanding Human Behaviour in Organizations: One Viewpoint'.

who shows little personal concern and who restricts interaction to a minimum will very probably arouse resentment and hostility, while on the other hand one who 'takes an interest' and offers recognition and support may well meet with a highly positive response. In other words, such a situation is one in which a 'human relations' approach might be said to have some potential.

By this same argument, though, it is then also implied that for the majority of the workers we studied, or at any rate for the majority of the semi-skilled men, the quality of supervision—in 'human relations' terms —is unlikely to be a highly important consideration. Given that their economic expectations are fairly met, these workers are inclined to look for little further from their present employment. A civil and pleasant supervisor may well be appreciated, but one who 'keeps himself to himself' will cause no great frustration or ill feeling. And certainly there would seem in this case relatively little to be gained, in terms of organisational effectiveness, from attempts at developing supervisors' social skills. As we have seen, the evidence suggests that in the firms we studied supervisor–worker relations in general are relatively smooth in spite of their often formal and 'impersonal' character.

We return, therefore, to what may stand as our major conclusion of this chapter as a whole: that, as men who view their employment in a largely instrumental way, our affluent workers tend for the most part neither to anticipate, nor to experience any strong desire for, a high level of direct 'social' satisfaction from the shared activities and relationships of their workplace. This is the logical consequence, we would argue, of the way in which they typically define their work situation. And this definition of the situation must be regarded, on our evidence, as a factor influencing their attitudes and behaviour on the shop floor that is to some significant degree independent of the in-plant variables which many writers have tended to accept as being of greatest explanatory importance.

4. The worker and his firm

In the previous chapter we have referred to two approaches to the study of social relationships on the shop floor: first, the 'human relations' approach, with its emphasis on the primary work group and on the importance of supervisory 'styles' in patterning worker attitudes and behaviour; and, secondly, a rival approach emphasising the part played by technological constraints in structuring work-roles and role relationships and thus in limiting the extent to which the shop-floor situation can be influenced by the exercise of 'social skills' or 'interpersonal competence'. We have suggested that while both of these approaches, and particularly the latter, are of some relevance in interpreting our findings, both are ultimately inadequate in that they leave out of account the attitudes towards work which workers *bring to* their employment; attitudes, that is, which are formed neither by supervisory practice nor by technological conditions, but which have rather to be regarded as *independent* variables relative to the work situation, and whose origins have to be sought thus in workers' out-plant roles and patterns of association.

In this chapter we are concerned with the attitudes and behaviour of our affluent workers towards their employing organisations. In recent years developments within the 'human relations' tradition and extensions of the 'technological implications' approach have alike led to theoretical formulations regarding the determinants of the effective 'integration' of the worker into the industrial enterprise. Thus, these approaches are again available to us in interpreting our data. However, we would argue that in this case their value is even more limited than before, and again by their inability to go beyond explanations of attitudes and behaviour in terms of the functioning of the enterprise and by their consequent neglect of the worker's definition of the situation. This point we can make most readily by setting our findings against hypotheses, recently advanced by writers such as Woodward and Blauner, concerning the consequences of technology for the quality of industrial relations at plant level. Subsequently, though, we shall argue similarly, if more indirectly, with reference to the organisation theory of writers of the 'neo-human-relations' school such as McGregor and Likert.

The affluent worker: industrial attitudes

If the industrial enterprise is viewed as a social system organised around a particular production technology—the set of means whereby the enterprise achieves its business objectives—then it would seem reasonable to claim that technical organisation will influence not only social experiences and relationships in the immediate work situation but also, through these, the general character of management–worker relations in the plant as a whole. Taking this perspective, Woodward, for example, has argued as follows: 'The climate of industrial relations within a firm [it can be seen] no longer depends entirely upon management's ability to develop sound personnel policies and the kind of procedures for consulting, communicating and negotiating which encourage responsible behaviour on both sides. Employees at both supervisory and operator level are also involved in a system of work organisation and control. This involvement has a more direct and powerful effect upon the pattern of behaviour in the firm than have attitudes to the firm itself. It is his *experience on the shop floor* that is *critical* in determining how hard an operator works, the number and seriousness of the industrial disputes in which he gets involved, and whether he stays with the firm or leaves it.'[1]

On the basis of this kind of argument, therefore, Woodward and others have been prepared to attribute to different types of technology differing propensities for creating harmony or conflict within the industrial enterprise; and, to some large extent, writers of this outlook have shown agreement in the main hypotheses which they have advanced. Assuming a scale of technological complexity running from craft production at one extreme to automated or continuous-flow production at the other, they have tended to locate the technological areas in which industrial relations are most 'difficult' in the *intermediate* ranges of the scale. More specifically, it has been generally held that machine-based, large-batch and mass production, and in particular assembly-line production, are those types of technology which give rise to the most acute problems of 'meaninglessness' in work, of lack of worker autonomy and of impersonal and stringent managerial control; and thus that it is these types of technology which are in turn most frequently associated with expressions of low worker morale and commitment to the enterprise, and with irresponsible and hostile conduct in the industrial relations field.

Blauner, for example, has recently suggested that the degree of worker 'alienation' in modern industry can be seen as following an 'inverted U-curve' in relation to the level of technology in operation.[2] This curve he

---

[1] 'Industrial Behaviour—Is there a Science?', p. 13 (our italics).
[2] *Alienation and Freedom*, pp. 182–3 esp.

sees as rising with technological advance until it reaches its highest point in large-scale assembly industry, as typified by car manufacturing. But then a countertrend occurs as the most advanced levels of technology are attained, so that in the case, say, of a modern chemicals plant, work has become once more a meaningful activity and is carried on in 'a more cohesive, integrated industrial climate'.[1] Woodward's position is one virtually identical to this. Referring to her studies in British industry, she has observed that 'the most intractable problems of organisation and industrial relations seemed to occur in two types of production—batch production and line production based on the assembly of components'; whereas 'organisational and behavioural patterns are much more consistent at...the extremes of the technical scale, in unit production and process industry'.[2] Interestingly enough, Woodward also takes the automobile and chemical industries as paradigmatic cases in putting forward this point of view: 'the motor car industry (including the firms that make components for it) which has been so much criticised for the state of its labour relations, is in the technological area which produces the conditions least conducive to good relationships...On the other hand, process industries like chemicals and oil, which tend to get a lot of commendation for progressive labour policies, are batting on the easiest possible wicket.'[3]

On the basis of the arguments advanced by the writers in question, it would then be expected that we should find within our sample quite marked differences in workers' attitudes and behaviour towards their firms—and in particular one would anticipate contrasts among the semi-skilled men between the assemblers on the one hand and the process workers on the other. It is true that, as was indicated in chapter 1, we selected the three firms from which our sample is drawn not only on account of their differing technologies but also because all were noted for their advanced labour and welfare policies. Thus, it might reasonably be supposed that their similarities in this latter respect would diminish the

[1] *Ibid.*, p. 182.

[2] 'Industrial Behaviour—Is there a Science?', p. 13; see also *Management and Technology*, pp. 18–19, 29–30.

[3] 'Industrial Behaviour—Is there a Science?', p. 14. Woodward refers in this paper to the similarities between her findings, those of the Tavistock Institute team reported in Trist *et al.*, *Organisational Choice*, and also those of Sayles, *Behavior of Industrial Work Groups*. However, on the matter of 'plant climate', Sayles' conclusions appear to diverge somewhat from her own. According to Sayles' results, firms in the intermediate ranges of the technological scale (large-scale assembly production) tended to have *either* very bad industrial relations *or* very good ones. Sayles suggests an interesting explanation for this tendency to extremes in terms of difficulties in communication between union leaders and their rank-and-file. See pp. 113–17.

TABLE 28. *Assessment of present firm as a firm to work for*

Assessment made	Craftsmen (N = 56)	Setters (N = 23)	Process workers (N = 23)	Machinists (N = 41)	Assemblers (N = 86)	All manual (N = 229)	White collar (N = 54)
				Percentage			
'Better than most'	61	78	39	59	73	65	41
'About average'	20	22	44	34	20	25	56
'Worse than most'	13	0	9	5	2	6	4
Other, D.K., D.N.A.	7	0	9	2	5	5	0
TOTALS	101	100	101	100	100	101	101

differentiating effects of technology in the industrial relations field. And certainly, all the firms were alike in that they enjoyed virtually strike-free records. Nevertheless, if technical organisation *is* to be regarded as 'critical' in determining the industrial relations climate, then one might still expect to find some fairly clear indication of its influence underlying this general situation of overt industrial peace. In fact, as will be seen, our data provide no such evidence at all: insofar as differences do emerge within the sample, they are ones which go rather contrary to what would be predicted following the hypothesis we have referred to above.[1]

In discussing their relationship with their firm, one of the first questions we put to our respondents was: 'How would you say [name of firm] compares with other firms you know of as a firm to work for? Would you say it was better than most, about average, or worst than most?' Table 28 shows the pattern of response we obtained across our five occupational groups and also from our white-collar sample. From this table it is apparent that our affluent workers were, in the main, relatively well satisfied with their

[1] As will be seen in what follows, we concentrate on attitudinal data. As we noted above, none of the firms had any analysable strike activity, and furthermore the data available to us made it difficult to establish significant differences between the firms in other behavioural indicators such as labour turnover and absence rates. However, insofar as such differences could be traced, these indicated that, overall, Vauxhall had if anything a *more* stable labour force and certainly no higher level of absenteeism than did the other two establishments. At Vauxhall, over the period 1958–62, the quit rate per annum ranged from 17·5 down to 5·4%, the median figure being 9·7%. The absence rate among hourly paid employees averaged between 4·0 and 4·25% of total hours worked excluding overtime. In both cases, comparative data suggest that these rates are relatively low for a large-scale manufacturing plant. See, for example, the data given in P. Long, *Labour Turnover under Full Employment* (Birmingham, 1951), and J. R. Greystoke, G. F. Thomason and T. S. Murphy, 'Labour Turnover Surveys', *Personnel Management*, vol. XXXIV, no. 321 (September 1952); and H. Behrend, *Absence under Full Employment* (Birmingham, 1951), and British Institute of Management, *Absence from Work* (London, 1963).

TABLE 29. '*Images*' *of management–worker relations*

	Craftsmen (N = 56)	Setters (N = 23)	Process workers (N = 23)	Machinists (N = 41)	Assemblers (N = 86)	All manual (N = 229)	White collar (N = 54)
				Percentage			
'...teamwork means success and is to everyone's advantage'	59	83	52	51	79	67	76
'...teamwork is impossible because employers and men are really on opposite sides'	36	13	44	39	16	28	24
Other, D.K.	5	4	4	10	5	6	0
TOTALS	100	100	100	100	100	101	100

employers;[1] and it is notable that in four out of the five occupational groups, the proportion of men rating their firm 'better than most' is clearly higher than in the white-collar sample. However, the one group which shows significantly *less* than the general level of approval is that of the process workers. Only in this group, in fact, do a majority rate their firm only 'about average' or 'worst than most'. On the other hand, it is interesting to find that the assemblers rank along with the setters—the promoted men—as the groups in which appreciation for the firm as an employer runs highest of all. In the light of these data at least, the emerging stereotypes of 'integrated' chemical workers and 'alienated' car workers are not immediately recognisable.[2]

Doubts in this respect are strengthened by the results we achieved from an attempt to get at the more general conceptions, or 'images', of management–worker relations which the men in our sample held. We put to our respondents the following question: 'Here are two opposing views about industry generally: I'd like you to tell me which you agree with more. Some people say that a firm is like a football side—because good teamwork means success and is to everyone's advantage. Others say that teamwork in industry is impossible—because employers and men are really on

[1] Experience of other employers among the men in our sample was quite extensive. More than half had had from three to five jobs (including their present one) and a third, six or more. Full details are given in table A4.
[2] And it should be remembered here that in terms of their financial rewards the process workers in our sample were a more privileged group within Laporte than were the assemblers within Vauxhall. See n. 1, p. 7 above.

opposite sides. Which view do you agree with more?' From table 29, which shows the response to this question, it would appear that a clear majority of our affluent workers see the enterprise in generally 'harmonistic' terms; or perhaps, to be more precise, have a conception of the enterprise in which recognition of the interdependence of management and labour is generally more powerful than awareness of conflicts between them.[1] The spontaneous comments men made on the question suggested fairly strongly that, in the eyes of the majority, a co-operative attitude towards management was important to the effective operation of the plant and would also, in most cases or 'in the long run', turn out to be in their own best interests:

'Teamwork means success: success means plenty of work and work is what we want.'

'Management and workers can't work without each other. If you get a man out of line—it's like a broken link in the chain...It does no good in the end.'

'At the firm where I started work, they had a motto: "Harmony is necessary to achieve anything." I believe in this.'

'Teamwork is to everybody's advantage. Management gets the work out and we better ourselves financially.'

'We've got teamwork in this firm, anyway. It pays in the end. Management and men are both in the same firm, aren't they?'

The image of the enterprise which is represented here is one which contrasts sharply with the far more 'dichotomous' views, stressing antagonism and exploitation, which have been well documented in the case of miners, dockers and other industrial workers characterised by a more solidaristic orientation and by a relatively highly developed class consciousness.[2] In fact, our affluent workers seem little more likely than the men in the white-collar sample to interpret management–worker relations primarily in 'oppositional' terms.[3] Furthermore, though, in

[1] This is in no way to imply that recognition of such conflicts does not exist—as will be seen below.

[2] On miners see, for example, Dennis *et al.*, *Coal is Our Life*, pp. 32–7, 56–64, and Acton Society Trust, *The Worker's Point of View* (London, 1952), pp. 10–14; on dockers, University of Liverpool, Department of Social Science, *The Dock Worker*, pp. 89–90. The markedly different response to a question similar to ours achieved from a sample of French steel and iron-mine workers is particularly instructive; only 28% of the French workers accepted the teamwork view as against 69% rejecting it. See Alfred Willener, 'L'Ouvrier et l'Organisation', *Sociologie du Travail*, no. 4, 1962, and 'Payment Systems in the French Steel and Iron Mining Industry' in George K. Zollschan and Walter Hirsch (eds.), *Explorations in Social Change* (Boston, 1964).

[3] This finding contrasts sharply with that reported recently by Sykes on the basis of samples of manual and white-collar workers from a Scottish steel firm. In this case it was found that the

turning to the data for the different occupational groups, we find that the assemblers in no way deviate from the general pattern in the direction which Woodward's or Blauner's hypotheses would imply. The reverse, rather, proves to be the case; the assemblers again come close to the setters in the extent of their pro-management sentiments. Four out of five accept the 'teamwork' view. Clearly the idea of the assembly-line man as 'the prototype of the militant worker'[1] is one to which our evidence here can lend little support. At the same time, the data for the process workers give no indication that these men experience any particularly high degree of 'integration' with their firm. On the contrary, this group can be seen to contain a relatively large proportion of workers who doubt the possibility of teamwork and see management and labour as fundamentally divided. Again, therefore, we are forced to conclude that our findings are not what would be expected if the connection between 'technology' and 'industrial relations climate' was always of the nature and importance that have been suggested.

The results from one other question which we put to our interviewees are relevant in this connection. We asked: 'This firm [i.e. the respondent's] has an exceptionally good industrial relations record: why do you think this is?' Table 30 classifies the answers we received.

From this table it can be seen that the kinds of reason by far the most often advanced were ones relating to good industrial relations practice on the part of management or of union leaders. In addition, a further important set of reasons referred to relatively high levels of pay, security and welfare benefits. Generally, one could say, our affluent workers tended to regard their firms' records of industrial peace in a more or less positive light, and explained these in ways which, directly or indirectly, accorded credit to the parties concerned. Only in the case of a minority was a more critical approach taken (at least implicitly) in suggesting that weak unionism or lack of spirit among the rank and file were also factors in the absence of

---

manual workers had overwhelmingly more negative and antagonistic attitudes towards the firm and its management—associated, Sykes argues, with a quite different 'industrial ethos' from that of the white-collar workers. See A. J. M. Sykes, 'Some Differences in the Attitudes of Clerical and of Manual Workers', *Sociological Review*, vol. 13, no. 1 (1965). At the same time, though, we would suggest that, in the case of our respondents, the *meaning* typically given to 'teamwork' differed to some extent between the manual and nonmanual samples: with the former, the major emphasis, as we have implied, was on economic interdependence and reciprocity; with the latter, the idea of co-operativeness in the actual activities and social relationships of work appeared to be more prominent.

[1] Blauner, *Alienation and Freedom*, p. 123. For further discussion of the 'deviant' characteristics of the assemblers in our sample, see John H. Goldthorpe, 'Attitudes and Behaviour of Car Assembly Workers: a deviant case and a theoretical critique', *British Journal of Sociology*, vol. XVII, no. 3 (September 1966).

overt conflict. However, if we examine the distribution of this dissident view, we find that once more it is the process workers who appear to be the most negative in their attitudes towards their firm. As table 30 shows, they alone, among the occupational groups, seem as likely to explain their firm's industrial relations 'success' in terms of labour weakness as in terms of sound policies and procedures:[1] less than half mention management in any approving way. And again, it can be seen that the assemblers stand in marked contrast to the process workers in largely exhibiting attitudes which would most probably be approved of, and shared, by their employer.

On the basis of these findings it is difficult for us to regard technical organisation as influencing the nature of relationships between our affluent workers and their firms in any decisive way. Quite wide variations exist in the types of production system in which these workers are involved; and, as was shown in chapter 2, technology undoubtedly plays a major part in determining the pattern of the immediate rewards and costs experienced by workers in performing their work-tasks and -roles within the enterprise. To this extent, we would reaffirm the importance which writers such as Woodward and Blauner give to technological factors. The point at which our findings must lead us to diverge from their position comes with their assumption that this experience of the individual, in actually carrying out his job on the shop floor, will of necessity be closely associated with his attitudes and behaviour towards the organisation which employs him. In other words, we are unable to accept the idea that the ways in which workers view their firm and act in relation to it will always be primarily determined *within* the enterprise itself, as the result of the in-plant activities and social relations in which workers are engaged.

Rather, our data would indicate that attitudes towards job (in the narrow sense) and firm can, in certain cases, be quite sharply *dis*sociated; that unrewarding and stressful work-roles need *not* lead to a generally negative orientation towards the enterprise as an employer; and, conversely, that more rewarding or less stressful jobs are no guarantee that the organisation which is able to provide them will thereby gain workers' appreciation and attachment. The two groups on which we have so far concentrated in this chapter, the process workers and the assemblers, suggest this point most

[1] One interesting point quite frequently made by process workers in this connection was that as a result of men being split up in twos and threes and scattered around a large area of plant, concerted action and even effective communication between different sections of the labour force were difficult to achieve; thus, plant-based union activity was inhibited. This particular implication of process production technology does not appear to have received the attention it deserves in the current literature.

TABLE 30. *Reasons given for firm's good industrial relations record*

	Craftsmen (N = 56)	Setters (N = 23)	Process workers (N = 23)	Machinists (N = 41)	Assemblers (N = 86)	All (N = 229)
Class of reason			Times mentioned ·			
A. Reasons relating to good management and union practice:						
Effective machinery for consultation and negotiation	9	6	3	6	25	49
Management available and ready to listen to complaints	7	2	3	7	16	35
Responsible and efficient union officials	13	4	1	3	10	31
Effective machinery for quick settlement of disputes	3	2	0	7	18	30
Good supervision	1	2	1	1	5	10
TOTALS	33	16	8	24	74	155
B. Reasons relating to good economic rewards and conditions of employment:						
Good pay and security	18	7	2	11	4	42
Good welfare benefits	1	2	0	0	5	8
TOTALS	19	9	2	11	9	50
C. Reasons relating to weakness of labour:						
Weak union organisation or policy	11	3	8	4	19	45
Workers are unwilling or afraid to strike	12	2	1	9	3	27
TOTALS	23	5	9	13	22	72
D. Other reasons	6	5	9	10	17	47
ALL REASONS	81	35	28	58	122	324
Reasons in class A as percentage of all reasons	41	46	29	41	61	48
Reasons in class B as percentage of all reasons	23	26	7	19	7	15
Reasons in class C as percentage of all reasons	28	14	32	22	18	22
Reasons in class D as percentage of all reasons	7	14	32	17	14	15
TOTALS	99	100	100	99	100	100

clearly.[1] But in *no* group within our sample can we find evidence of 'immediate' job satisfaction being at all closely linked with workers' attitudes towards their firm as an employer. For example, in no case were those men who reported preferring their present job to any other on the shop floor significantly more likely than the remainder to rate their firm 'better than average' as a firm to work for, or to take a 'teamwork' view of management–worker relations; nor were men who reported that their jobs were monotonous or unabsorbing or the pace of work too fast any more likely than others to assess their firms less than favourably, or to see their relations with management in 'oppositional' terms.

We must conclude that in shaping the relationships between our affluent workers and the organisations which employ them, other, and often countervailing, forces are involved in addition to workers' experience 'on the shop floor'. This experience, as we have seen, was frequently associated with deprivation of one kind or another, and was only to a quite limited extent a source of immediate satisfaction. Yet, for the most part, the evidence from our sample confirms outward indications that the plants from which these men came were all ones in which management–worker relations were fairly satisfactory to the parties involved. As we have shown, a majority of those individuals we interviewed, in all occupational groups except that of the process workers, believed that their firm was a relatively good one to work for, accepted a 'teamwork' view of the industrial enterprise, and appeared to regard the absence of overt conflict in their firm as representing a positive achievement. The problem which now arises, therefore, is that of interpreting this state of affairs in a way which can transcend the analytical limitations of the approach that has concerned us so far.[2]

[1] In regard to the assemblers, our findings here once more go contrary to those reported by Turner from the studies he and his associates have made of American car workers. Turner states ('Foreman, Job and Company') that attitudes to job and firm and to foreman and firm were found to be significantly correlated, but not attitudes to job and foreman. He suggests that this last finding may well be peculiar to assembly line production, thus assuming, it seems, that one would normally expect attitudes to job, foreman and firm to be *all* intercorrelated. We see no theoretical basis for such an expectation. For further discussion on this point, see Goldthorpe, 'Attitudes and Behaviour of Car Assembly Workers'.

[2] It should be emphasised here, particularly in regard to Woodward's work, that it is not our purpose to challenge the broad *empirical generalisations* which have been put forward concerning the association between types of technology and patterns of industrial behaviour and relationships. We suspect that these generalisations will prove capable of some refinement (as Sayles' findings imply) but, clearly, statements of probability of this kind cannot be invalidated on the basis of three cases, 'deviant' though these may be; and particularly as the men in our different occupational groups may be atypical precisely because of their affluence. Rather, our argument on pp. 72–6 above and subsequently in this chapter is quite specifically directed against the *theoretical ideas* to which the generalisations in question have given rise,

One possible kind of explanation for the absence of any close link between the nature of work experience and attitudes to the firm among the men we studied would be in terms of these workers' overriding sense of commitment to, and identification with, the enterprise; the argument being that the managements in question had succeeded in creating such an attachment in spite, in some cases, of the 'alienating' character of immediate work-tasks. Such an explanation would, for example, be consistent with the position taken up in recent years by organisation theorists such as McGregor and Likert. These writers would argue that, under the technological conditions of modern large-scale industry, the achievement of organisational effectiveness in fact *requires* this kind of moral involvement of employees, and the integration of their goals, objectively and subjectively, with those of the enterprise as a whole. Only in this way can employees be motivated to high level performance and their capacities fully utilised; so long as traditional theories of organisation are applied and the attempt is made to exercise control through economic means or through formal authority—'carrot and stick' methods—the enterprise will manifestly suffer.[1] Since the firms with which we were concerned were not only successful in the industrial relations field but also had very good business records,[2] it would, then, seem reasonable to examine whether, among their rank and file, a relatively high degree of commitment is shown.

However, an alternative approach is also possible which follows from our concern with workers' orientations towards their employment. It can equally be argued that the lack of association which we have observed between attitudes to job and firm can be explained in terms of the primarily instrumental orientation to work which, we have tried to show, is characteristic of the workers we studied, and in particular of the semi-skilled men. To the extent that workers define their employment as essentially a means of acquiring a certain standard and style of living outside of work, it

and which have been used in attempts to *explain* the regularities observed. And for this we think our data are appropriate.

[1] See Douglas McGregor, *The Human Side of Enterprise* (New York, 1960); Rensis Likert, 'A Motivation Approach to a Modified Theory of Organization and Management', and *New Patterns of Management* (New York, 1961). Argyris has also come close to the position of these writers in his more recent publications; see, for example, *Integrating the Individual and the Organization* (New York, 1964).

[2] Details of Vauxhall's recent record can be found in Aubrey Silberston, 'The Motor Industry 1955–1964', *Bulletin of the Oxford University Institute of Economics and Statistics*, vol. 27, no. 4 (1965). The SKF organisation is the world's largest producer of ball and roller bearings, is the technological leader in this field, and dominates the lucrative replacement market. In the period 1953–62 the firm's sales growth was outstanding, averaging 9·5% per annum. For some details of Laporte's progress, see D. W. F. Hardie and J. Davidson Pratt, *A History of the Modern British Chemical Industry* (Oxford, 1966).

is clearly possible for them to take a negative view of the work-tasks they actually perform while at the same time appreciating a firm which offers pay and conditions that can bring a valued way of life within their grasp. And conversely, in this case, the experience of some direct satisfaction from a job could well co-exist with dissatisfaction with an employing organisation from which the economic returns fell some way short of the level aspired to.[1]

From this point of view, then, the generally positive attitudes towards their firms revealed by the majority of our affluent workers would be seen as deriving not so much from a moral but rather from a largely successful *calculative* involvement with the organisations in question. In other words, the argument would be that the present employment of these workers enables them to come close to achieving their present priorities in wants and expectations relative to work. Thus, an attachment of some strength and functional effectiveness is formed between worker and firm, even though this is of a very limited kind and is, in fact, created primarily through the labour contract itself. And on the other hand, in the case of the dissident minority, the hypothesis would be that what these workers regarded as inadequate pay would prove to be a major source of their discontent.

In evaluating these two possible lines of interpretation, in the light of further data from our interviews, our conclusion must be that it is the latter one which receives by far the greater support. Our evidence points to the fact that the majority of workers in our sample, although they may accept a 'teamwork' view of the industrial enterprise, imply in this way chiefly recognition of certain shared objectives and of a certain interdependence with their employer of a largely *economic* kind. And, moreover, it is also apparent that this area of common interest, while quite widely conceived, is at the same time seen as having fairly definite bounds. There is, in other words, little indication from our findings that our affluent workers have any strong *affective* commitment to their firms of a kind which would be associated with their more or less total integration into the enterprise in the way that is envisaged in 'neo-human-relations' theory.

In the first place, it should be recalled that when asked what it was that kept them in their present employment, the reasons which our affluent

[1] In chapter 2 we argued that 'job satisfaction in terms of workers' experience of their immediate work-tasks and -roles cannot be associated in any direct way with job satisfaction in terms of the worker's attachment to his present employment'. The argument here is simply a development of this. If job satisfaction (in the narrow sense) does not necessarily correlate with attachment to employment, it is unlikely to correlate either with commitment to the firm as an organisation.

TABLE 31. *Assessment of comparable employment advantages in other firms*

Assessment made	Craftsmen (N = 50)	Setters (N = 21)	Process workers (N = 19)	Machinists (N = 34)	Assemblers (N = 83)	All manual (N = 207)	White collar (N = 50)
				Percentage			
Not many firms would give same advantages as present firm	58	72	47	65	69	64	28
Many firms would give same advantages as present firm	38	14	32	26	18	25	68
Other, D.K.	4	14	21	9	13	11	4
TOTALS	100	100	100	100	100	100	100

workers most often gave was that of the level of pay they received.[1] Such an explanation was given by a clear majority of men in all groups other than the process workers; and among the machinists and assemblers more than one man in four stated that the pay was the *only* reason why he remained in his present work. Following on pay, the factor which was next most frequently referred to, by all groups in the sample, was that of job security. Level of pay and security together accounted for over half of all the reasons which were mentioned. Thus, these data in themselves, as was noted in chapter 2, indicate fairly clearly that basic economic considerations are of major importance in attaching these men to the particular organisations in which they work.[2]

In coming to discuss specifically with our respondents their relationship to their firm, we reminded them of the reason or reasons they had earlier given for staying in their present jobs and then asked: 'Do you think there are many firms which would give you these advantages?' The replies we received to this question across our five occupational groups and also for the white-collar sample are shown in table 31—excluding cases where the question proved inappropriate.[3]

As might be expected, the pattern of response here is generally similar to that we obtained when interviewers were asked to compare their present

---

[1] See table 8 above.

[2] And this point is, of course, strongly reinforced by the data on previous jobs and attitudes to these, also reported in chapter 2.

[3] For example, where workers had said that they stayed in their present jobs because they did not want the trouble or risk of changing jobs, or felt too old to move. The replies made by the white-collar workers to the initial question—'What is it then that keeps you here (i.e. in present firm)?'—are given in table A5.

employer with others they knew of (table 28).[1] As can be seen from table 31, a clear majority of our affluent workers, in all occupational groups except that of the process workers, apparently regard their firms as providing particularly attractive employment from their point of view; that is, in relation to the kinds of returns which, for the present at least, they wish primarily to gain from their work. And one point which emerges here still more strongly than in table 28 is the difference in satisfaction with their employers between the manual and white-collar samples. Of the latter group, little more than a quarter felt that they would be unable to find work of comparable attractiveness to them with some other firm; whereas even with the process workers this proportion was almost half, and rose to around 70% with the setters and assemblers. In this way, then, the existence of a relatively powerful instrumental tie between the manual workers and their employers is further suggested.[2]

It might at this point be objected that although a sizable majority of the workers we studied gave the level of pay as a reason for remaining in their present jobs, it does not follow from this that, to a similar extent, pay was a factor which led men to feel that their firms offered them particularly attractive employment. Indeed it might be argued, following McGregor, for example,[3] that while an adequate level of pay may well be an important consideration in holding a man to a job—a minimum requirement, as it were—the aspects of work which are likely to produce a special attachment to an employing organisation are ones which satisfy 'higher level' needs of an expressive and affective kind. Thus, it could prove to be the case that those workers who feel that their present firm offers them particular advantages will tend *not* to be those whose objectives in work are largely restricted to the economic level.

However, by drawing up the appropriate cross-tabulation (table 32) we

[1] A marked association exists within the sample between assessing one's firm as 'better than average' as a firm to work for and believing that comparable advantages to those that attach one to this employment could not be had in many other firms: $\chi^2 = 18.1$; 1 df; $p < 0.001$.

[2] In contrast, one would suggest, to a relatively weak 'bureaucratic' commitment on the part of the white-collar workers. As can be seen by comparing table 28 with table 31, clearly more (though still less than half) of the white-collar workers were prepared to say that their firm was 'better than most' as a firm to work for than felt that not many firms would give them comparable advantages to the ones which they said kept them in their present employment. And unlike the situation with the manual sample, no association exists within the nonmanual sample between these two attitudes. Table A5 indicates that a sizable majority of the white-collar workers (70%) are attached to their present employment primarily by considerations other than the level of pay; but these, it would appear, are less compelling than are the economic attractions which chiefly operate in the case of the manual workers. As noted earlier (table 10), 47% of the latter reported having at some time thought of leaving their present job: with the nonmanual sample, the corresponding figure is 65%.

[3] *The Human Side of Enterprise*, chs. 3 and 4 esp.

TABLE 32. *Assessment of comparable employment advantages in other firms by advantages seen in present employment (i.e. reasons given for staying in present job)*

Occupational group	Reasons for staying in present job	Firms seen as giving same advantages as present one (percentage)				N	Percentage of occupational group
		Not many	Many	Other, D.K.	Total		
Craftsmen and Setters	Level of pay (only)	67	33	0	100	6	8
	Level of pay (+other reasons)	50	43	7	100	44	62
	Level of pay (only or +other reasons)	52	42	6	100	50	70
	Reasons other than pay	86	5	10	101	21	30
ALL		62	31	7	100	71*	100
Process workers, Machinists and Assemblers	Level of pay (only)	73	21	6	100	33	24
	Level of pay (+other reasons)	61	24	15	100	66	49
	Level of pay (only or +other reasons)	65	23	12	100	99	73
	Reasons other than pay	65	19	16	100	37	27
ALL		65	22	13	100	136*	100

* Excludes men to whom the question on comparable employment advantages was not applicable. See note 3, p. 81.

are able to see that such an argument has only limited validity. With the craftsmen and the setters, it is true that men who did not mention the level of pay as something which helped to keep them in their jobs *did* show a greater tendency than the others to say that not many firms could give them employment advantages comparable to their present ones. On the other hand, though, a relatively high proportion of men taking this view of their firm is also to be found among those semi-skilled workers who said that considerations of *pay alone* held them in their present employment. And, moreover, taking the semi-skilled workers as a whole, those who do not mention pay at all prove in this case to be no more likely than the rest to feel that their present firms offer them some special attraction.

Table 32 is thus of value in pointing once more to the fact that the more skilled men in our sample are, on most counts, somewhat less instrumental in their orientation to work than the semi-skilled. As we have remarked earlier, the craftsmen and the setters more frequently have certain wants and expectations from work which go beyond the economic return, important though this may be to them. But, at the same time, we must not lose sight of the further fact, which is also indicated in the table, that, most typically with the workers we studied, the economic aspects of their employment *are* of primary importance; and, as well as binding them to their present jobs, *also* play a quite significant part in creating the relatively widespread feeling of having particularly advantageous employment which we have described. On the basis of table A6, which presents the data of table 32 in a somewhat different form, we can say that of those men who took such a favourable view of their present job, 80% of the craftsmen and setters and 85% of the semi-skilled men saw these advantages, in part at least, in economic terms. In other words, they did not believe that there were many firms which could give them the level of pay, security or fringe benefits which they currently enjoyed.

We would therefore suggest that in the view of the majority of our affluent workers they have made a bargain with their firms, in terms of reward for effort, which provides better than most others available to them for that pattern of rewards which for the time being they wish to pursue; and further, that for all groups in the sample, but most clearly for the semi-skilled men, this pattern is one in which high-level economic returns are given some priority. Thus, these workers are disposed to define their relationship with their firm more as one of reciprocity and mutual accommodation rather than as one of coercion and exploitation. And in this sense at least they are far from being 'alienated'.[1]

At the same time it would follow from our interpretation that this relationship cannot be seen as one which is free from basic oppositions of interest. A situation of fundamental consensus between management and labour might be expected if workers were, in fact, fully integrated into the enterprise socially and psychologically. But the argument that the economic nexus is the major tie between worker and firm—that workers' involvement in the enterprise is not moral but essentially calculative—implies necessarily that co-operation must exist together with some degree of conflict. This is in the very nature of an economically based association. And in fact it can be shown from our data that, in certain specific contexts, most of the men in our sample do have an awareness of at least the potential contrariety of their interests and those of their employers. Notwithstanding the prevalent 'teamwork' image of the enterprise, they recog-

[1] Or at least this is so if 'alienation' is interpreted, as it is by writers such as Blauner, as referring descriptively to a syndrome of 'objective conditions and subjective feeling-states'. If, on the other hand, the term is to be taken as one of *social diagnosis*—as in the classical Marxian tradition—then its applicability is more arguable, although at cost of extending the discussion from the field of sociology into that of social philosophy.

TABLE 33. *Attitudes to work study*

Respondent thinks that	Craftsmen (N = 56)	Setters (N = 23)	Process workers (N = 23)	Machinists (N = 41)	Assemblers (N = 86)	All (N = 229)
	Percentage					
'...work study men are more concerned to make things go smoothly for everyone'	32	35	30	15	33	29
'...work study men are chiefly concerned to make the worker keep up a fast pace all the time'	50	57	52	73	49	55
Other, D.K.	18	9	17	12	19	16
TOTALS	100	101	99	100	101	100

nise that their relationship to their firm may well, on certain issues, become one of opposition and contention.

For example, one matter over which it appeared that some degree of dissensus was always likely to arise was that of work study. Depending on technological conditions and on the way in which wages were paid, the significance of work study varied a good deal from one group to another. Its implications were most immediate in the case of the machinists, since 'standard times' formed the basis for the calculation of their piece rates; while on the other hand it was probably of least consequence for the craftsmen, who were, of course, on time rates and had relatively high autonomy in performing their work-tasks. But, for all groups in the sample, work study was of *some* significance in influencing, directly or indirectly, their intensity of work, and was thus generally of relevance to the 'effort bargain'. We therefore asked all our respondents: 'Do you think work study men are more concerned to make things go smoothly for everyone, or chiefly to make the worker keep up a fast pace all the time?' The replies which were made are classified in table 33. From this, it can be seen that in 4 out of the 5 occupational groups around a third of our affluent workers support the former view as against half adhering to the latter, while among the machinists—the group most directly affected by work study—this negative attitude is yet more clearly marked. In general, the comments which were offered on our question by those taking the majority view made it apparent that work study engineers were seen not as acting in the interests of the enterprise as a whole but rather as being agents of management with specifically managerial interests in mind. Thus, it was necessary that workers should be on their guard against them and should be prepared to counter their efforts.[1] The following extracts from our interview schedules are typical in this respect:

'Work study men are more on management's side. They try to cut times down as much as they can while still getting away with it.'

'Work study men are out for production. That's all they think about. It's their job.'

'The work study men's idea is to get the work done as fast as possible. And if they time a fast man [in establishing a 'standard' time] then it's very hard on a slow one.'

'They are out to get every bit they can from you—but we know that and allow for it. You take it steady when they're timing you. If you gave them a fair crack of the whip you couldn't do the job.'

On the matter of work study the idea of 'teamwork' appears no longer to apply for a sizable proportion of the men in our sample. And this is so, we suggest, because in the context of an instrumental orientation to work, this idea is seen as appropriate only to the extent that the economic interests of employers and labour are felt to coincide. The issues which arise in regard to work study lie beyond the limits of 'teamwork' because, in effect, they concern the very basis upon which such co-operation should rest; and for this reason they are, rather, issues on which a 'two sides' view of the enterprise is most readily taken.

Moreover, on one further question, even more fundamental to the 'effort bargain', an awareness of being in conflict with their firm was still more clearly revealed among the workers we studied. We refer to the question of their remuneration. As we have seen, the level of pay was the most important factor binding the men in our sample to their present jobs; and a majority believed, with economic considerations much in mind, that their present firms offered them particularly attractive employment. Nevertheless, this is not to say that these workers regarded their conditions of service with their firms as being the best they could reasonably expect. We asked our respondents: 'Do you think the firm could pay you more than it does without damaging its prospects for the future?' Table 34

[1] Similar attitudes have, of course, been reported from almost all investigations of employee response to work study. See, for example, Donald F. Roy, 'Quota Restriction and Gold-bricking in a Machine Shop', *American Journal of Sociology*, vol. 57 (March 1952), and 'Efficiency and the "Fix"', *American Journal of Sociology*, vol. 60, 1954–5; also Lisl Klein, *Multiproducts Ltd* (London, 1964).

TABLE 34. *Assessment of firm's ability to pay more without damaging its prospects for the future*

Assessment made	Craftsmen (N = 56)	Setters (N = 23)	Process workers (N = 23)	Machinists (N = 41)	Assemblers (N = 86)	All (N = 229)
	Percentage					
Firm could pay more	79	61	96	49	80	74
Firm could not pay more	20	35	0	44	9	20
Other, D.K.	2	4	4	7	11	7
TOTALS	101	100	100	100	100	101

shows the response to this question, and table 35 classifies the reasons which were given by those men who answered affirmatively.

From these results two things are apparent. First, it is clear that among all groups except the machinists the dominant view is that firms *could* afford to pay their workers higher wages. And, secondly, it is equally clear that by far the most important belief underlying this claim is that firms could give their workers a larger share in the profits they make. The following remarks were characteristic:

'Why do I think the firm could pay more? Well, reading the stocks and shares column in the paper you see their huge profits. They've got a whole lot set aside —and after all, it's the manual worker that earns the profits.'

'Profits are enormous year after year, even when they have to pay for expensive capital works. But they still quibble over a few thousand for the workers.'

'We've just achieved a 15% production increase and it's all profit for the firm. Not enough production increase comes back to the worker as wages.'

'Of course they could pay more! Productivity is increasing and so are sales. They're making an enormous profit and more of it should be passed on.'

The objective validity of comments of this kind does not concern us here: what is relevant is their subjective significance. They show us that the workers in question, although, as we know, generally prepared to see virtue in co-operation with management, are at the same time highly conscious of a divergence of interest over the way in which the product of this co-operation is distributed; and further, that they would for the most part question (at least for the sake of argument) whether they are in fact receiving their proper due.

This again, then, is largely what one would expect on the basis of our contention that these workers take a predominantly instrumental view of

TABLE 35. *Reasons given for thinking that firm could pay more*

Class of reason	Craftsmen (N = 44)	Setters (N = 14)	Process workers (N = 22)	Machinists (N = 20)	Assemblers (N = 69)	All (N = 169)
	Times mentioned					
Workers could be given larger share in profits	27	5	18	11	43	104
Firm could cut waste, become more efficient	18	2	2	3	14	39
Wages should be differently distributed (e.g. between production and non-production grades	7	4	4	1	6	22
Higher wages would lead to improved productivity, quality	3	3	1	5	4	16
Other	8	1	3	2	17	31
ALL REASONS	63	15	28	22	84	212
Reasons relating to larger share in profits as percentage of all reasons given	43	33	64	50	51	49

their work and that their involvement in the enterprise is of a highly calculative kind. For workers with such an orientation to their employment the focus of their industrial relations interest will be on the cash reward they receive for the effort which they expend; and their main concern will be that this economic return should be pushed to the highest possible level. This is not to say that the pressure for ever bigger wage-packets will lead to the general economic position of the firm being totally disregarded. The case of the machinists, with only half believing that Skefko could at present afford to pay more, suggests that the 'long view' may often be taken where circumstances seem to warrant it.[1] As one machinist put it: 'If it's not there, you shouldn't try to get it. Why stretch a firm for a couple of shillings a day and then in twelve months find you're out of work or people are being laid off?'; or more succinctly, in the words of another, 'You don't kill the goose that lays the golden eggs.' On the other hand,

[1] At Skefko at the time the interviews were taking place the firm was facing much greater competition in its field than for some time previously, and this fact was frequently referred to by respondents.

though, it is also interesting to note that the view that wages could be higher was strongest of all among the process workers—the men who showed the most negative attitudes towards their firm as an employer. And comments made by these men throughout their interviews indicate that this is not accidental; that is to say, the relative dissatisfaction with Laporte as an employer appears to stem in some large part from dissatisfaction with the level of pay which was offered. The bargain which the process workers have struck with their firm is, as we saw in chapter 2, enough to attach them fairly firmly to their present employment; and we may also recall that these men had no very marked complaints relating to their immediate work situation.[1] Nevertheless, the feeling that their rightful economic expectations from work were not being adequately met was, it seems, sufficiently powerful to help create among them certainly more anti-employer sentiment than we find in any other group in the sample.[2]

We have here, then, quite consistent evidence that, in the main, our affluent workers do see their relationships with their firms very much in instrumental and contractual terms. This is manifested, one could say, in their fairly general appreciation on the one hand of the economic advantages of their present employment, including the benefits which can derive from 'teamwork', and on the other, of a divergence of interest between employers and labour on issues concerning the actual conditions on which employment rests and 'teamwork' takes place. To the extent, then, that such an orientation is the dominant one among the men in our sample, it is difficult to sustain the hypothesis that these workers are characterised by a high degree of commitment to their firms of an affective and moral kind. Although, by all indications, these firms operate with some considerable amount of success, this they appear able to do without securing the 'integration' of their labour forces in other than a fairly minimal, economic sense.[3]

---

[1] See table 9 above.

[2] In other words, we would suggest that the discrepancy between the level of wages aspired to and that obtained was greater among the process workers than among the rest of the sample. (See below, pp. 138–9.) For the other occupational groups, there is no indication, either statistical or from comments made in the interviews, of any significant association between rating one's firm only 'about average' or 'worse than most' as a firm to work for and feeling that it could afford to pay more.

[3] One further point which it is relevant to note in this connection is that no association exists within our sample between, on the one hand, regarding one's firm as 'better than average' as a firm to work for or taking a 'teamwork' view of the industrial enterprise and, on the other, reporting getting on 'very well' or 'pretty well' with one's foreman. This is consistent with the interpretations we have advanced of the typical character of our workers' relationships with both their immediate supervisors and their employing organisations.

89

Finally, in this chapter we can reinforce this last point through one further set of data from our interview schedules; that is, data on the extent to which our respondents participated in out-of-work activities and associations based on their firms. All three firms had made generous, and indeed sometimes lavish, provision of recreational and 'social' facilities for their employees. Each had a main 'works club' responsible for general social functions and amenities to which employees could belong for a nominal sum;[1] in addition, each supported a wide range of sports clubs and 'special interest' societies which again had very low membership fees. If, then, our affluent workers were at all closely identified with their firms and attached to them in other than an instrumental way, one might expect that a sizable proportion of them would make their firm an important focus of their out-of-work social lives. This, however, we find is not the case: participation in work-based clubs and societies among the workers we studied proves to be generally low. Table 36 brings together the information we collected on this matter from both the 'work' and 'home' interviews.

From these data it emerges that, with the exception of the assemblers, a majority of all occupational groups in our sample did belong to their works' clubs, at least as 'general' members. However, this in itself means only that these men had agreed to a penny or two a week being 'stopped' from their earnings as their subscription; and from this point of view it is perhaps more significant that three-fifths of the semi-skilled men were apparently uninterested in their firms' clubs to the extent of being unwilling even to allow this small deduction. Moreover, it can also be seen from the table that the number of men who had actually joined a special club or society within the larger association was less than half of the number of 'general' members—comprising in fact around a third of the more skilled men and less than a fifth of the semi-skilled. Finally, on the question of attendance, we find that only a minority of those who are club members make use of the amenities provided with any great frequency. Even on a quite modest definition of 'regular attenders', only among the craftsmen does more than 1 man in 4 come into this category; and with the process workers and assemblers, the proportion falls to as low as 1 in 20.

In drawing other than negative conclusions from these findings, a difficulty arises in that we have little comparable data from other samples of workers in British industry which would help us to assess just *how* low is the level of participation we have described. A further complicating factor is that physical and economic constraints, such as distance between

---

[1] The Vauxhall Recreation Club had a basic membership charge of 1*d*. per week, the Laporte Social and Sports Club of 2*d*. per week, and the Skefko Sports and Social Club of 3*d*. per week.

TABLE 36. *Membership and participation in work-based clubs, societies, etc.*

	Craftsmen (N = 56)	Setters (N = 23)	Process workers (N = 23)	Machinists (N = 41)	Assemblers (N = 86)	All manual (N = 229)
Percentage belonging to 'works club' (general membership)	80	65	52	59	29	53
Percentage belonging to a particular club or society	32	35	22	24	14	23
Frequency of attendance of members (at main club and/or special club or society)						
Percentage of members reporting	(N = 45)	(N = 15)	(N = 12)	(N = 24)	(N = 25)	(N = 121)
Never or less than twice a year	36	53	67	39	60	46
More than twice a year, less than twice a month	31	27	25	33	24	29
Twice a month or more	33	20	8	29	16	25
TOTALS	100	100	100	101	100	100
Regular attenders (twice a month or more) as percentage *of total number* in group	27	13	4	17	5	13

home and work and associated travelling costs, must certainly have played some part in limiting the extent to which men went back to their place of work in their leisure time.[1] Nevertheless, we would argue that the data in question do fit fairly convincingly into a pattern of attitudes and behaviour which we have already in part established, that is, a pattern characterised by an instrumental orientation to work and a relatively sharp separation of individuals' working and non-working lives. By any standards, the extent to which the men in our sample were involved in work-based clubs and societies cannot be regarded as high; and it is difficult to believe that this is not *largely* a matter of choice. All our respondents, it should be remembered, were Luton residents,[2] and very few lived more than three miles

[1] The fact that the Skefko employees in our sample tended to live nearer to their place of work than did the Vauxhall or Laporte men is almost certainly reflected in at least the last line of table 36.

[2] With the few exceptions noted on p. 4, n. 2.

4-2

from the site of their firm. The barriers to participation other than psychological ones could, we feel, only rarely have been insuperable.

Furthermore, it may be added that our interpretation here is corroborated in that it is essentially the same as that suggested to us by personnel managers and club officials in all three firms. In each case some disappointment was felt that employees did not respond more positively to the provisions made by their firm for their leisure time; and this was generally recognised as being a problem of 'attitudes to work'. For example, a senior personnel officer at Vauxhall admitted that participation in the firm's club was not nearly so great as had been originally expected, and added that 'even people within easy bus ride don't like coming back to the company. It's their workplace and they don't like it.' Similarly, an official of the Laporte club commented that 'clock people', as compared with staff, 'just weren't interested in recreation within the firm'.[1] And at Skefko a rather disheartened sports club organiser sadly observed that men who were good at games often preferred to join another club rather than the firm's: 'Skefko is identified too closely with the job. Some men even play for other works teams. They say, "I work for Skefko and sleep with it, so I want to get away from it when I can."' In other words, while in brochures and house journals the firms might seek often to present themselves more as communities than as economic organisations, it was widely accepted 'on the inside' that, for the majority of those who make up the manual labour force at any rate, the firm was simply a place where they worked and beyond this had little part or meaning in their lives.

This, we believe, represents a quite realistic assessment of the situation. Moreover, we would question whether, from management's point of view at least, employee attitudes of this kind need be regarded at all unfavourably. As we have tried to show in the course of this chapter, the orientation to work which is in evidence here forms the basis for a generally viable and effective relationship between the worker and his firm; a type of relationship which, in fact, appears to cut across differences in technical organisation and which is largely independent of high-level 'human relations' expertise.

---

[1] In comparison with the manual sample, our white-collar sample (based on Laporte and Skefko) showed a relatively high proportion having general works club membership (72%) and belonging to a particular society (33%). On the other hand, though, the actual participation of these members was quite low: 80% attended less than twice a year, 14% more than twice a year but less than twice a month, and 7% more frequently; that is, only 6% of the total were 'regular attenders'. Discussions with club officials indicated that greater participation occurred among staff with higher status or more technical qualifications.

5. The worker and his union

The data which we have presented in the preceding three chapters reveal a fairly consistent pattern of attitudes and behaviour on the part of the workers we studied in regard to their jobs, their workmates and supervisors and their firms. This pattern can be most readily understood, we have argued, in terms of the largely instrumental view of work which was dominant among the men in our sample. At the same time we have also tried to make clear how, with almost equal consistency, different occupational groups within the sample vary in the degree to which they approximate an 'ideal-type' instrumental orientation. It has been seen, for example, that the craftsmen and setters often have quite important wants and expectations of their work other than purely economic ones, that they do derive some measure of immediate satisfaction from their work-tasks, that they are more likely than the men in other groups to meet their workmates 'socially' outside the factory, and that they are more likely also to participate in work-based clubs and societies. On the other hand, the semi-skilled workers, we have shown, tend to gain little intrinsic reward from their jobs, to be attached to their present employment by more exclusively economic considerations, and to keep their out-plant lives largely separate from their working lives. Furthermore, in almost all these respects we have found that the assemblers represent the extreme case, being most closely matched by the machinists in their concentration on the economic returns from work, but by the process workers in their lack of affective or moral involvement in their employing organisation.

In this chapter, we are concerned with the attitudes and behaviour of our affluent workers towards their trade unions. We shall seek to demonstrate that, once more, an analysis based on the orientation which these workers have towards their employment is an illuminating one and reveals, in fact, much the same themes and variations as we have seen in previous chapters. In other words, our aim here is to show that the relationship of our affluent workers to their unions can be comprehended within the same frame of reference as the other aspects of their industrial lives which we have considered thus far. In this way an advance may be made on both 'human relations' and the rival 'technological implications' approach, the exponents of neither of which have been able to contribute a great deal

93

TABLE 37. *Union membership*

Union belonged to	Craftsmen (N = 56)	Setters (N = 23)	Process workers (N = 23)	Machinists (N = 41)	Assemblers (N = 86)	All (N = 229)
	Percentage					
Amalgamated Engineering Union	79	100	0	100	37	61
National Union of Vehicle Builders	0	0	0	0	41	15
National Union of General and Municipal Workers	9*	0	57	0	0	8
Other	0	0	21	0	1	3
All unions	88	100	78	100	79	87
Non-unionists	13†	0	22	0	21	13
TOTALS	101	100	100	100	100	100

* Five Laporte craftsmen.
† Six Laporte craftsmen and one Skefko craftsman.

to our understanding of the worker as a union member. Indeed, the worker in this role has been largely excluded from their analyses since, in both cases, these start from the idea of the enterprise as a social system and cannot thus incorporate any adequate treatment of the worker's concurrent involvement in a different, and in part opposing, organisation. However, in beginning from the standpoint of the worker himself, we gain the possibility of being able to view his attitudes and behaviour, as employee and unionist alike, in an integrated fashion; and this possibility we have sought to exploit.

In Table 37 we give data which show the extent and pattern of union organisation among the workers in our sample. These data are, however, of little significance in indicating attitudes towards unionism among men in the different occupational groups, since they reflect rather the union situation within each of our three firms. As can be seen, the Skefko workers—craftsmen, setters and machinists—were with one exception all members of the A.E.U., the firm being in principle '100% union'. By contrast, union organisation at Laporte and Vauxhall was less strong; and in fact our assemblers show a level of union membership which is clearly above the estimated figure for all production workers in Vauxhall of around 60%.

TABLE 38. *Trade union experience in relation to present firm by length of service*

Occupational group	Union experience	Length of service (years)			
		0–5	5–15	15+	Total percentage
Craftsmen and Machinists (N = 90)	Became unionists on or after joining present firm	9	12	13	34
	Were unionists on joining present firm and remained unionists*	46	14	6	66
TOTALS		55	26	19	100
Setters (N = 23)	Became unionists on or after joining present firm	4	44	17	65
	Were unionists on joining present firm and remained unionists*	9	22	4	35
TOTALS		13	66	21	100
Process workers and Assemblers (N = 86)	Became unionists on or after joining present firm	22	15	9	46
	Were unionists on joining present firm and remained unionists*	28	20	6	54
TOTALS		50	35	15	100
All manual (N = 199)	Became unionists on or after joining present firm	14	17	12	43
	Were unionists on joining present firm and remained unionists*	34	18	6	58
TOTALS		48	35	18	101

* Though possibly changing unions.

In tables 38 and 39 two other sets of data relating to union membership are presented. These are somewhat more revealing both of the character of unionism among our affluent workers generally and of variations within the sample.

Table 38 gives some indication of how the occupational groups compare in terms of the union experience of their members. In this respect, the craftsmen and the machinists prove to be much alike and can be grouped together,[1] in that more than half are short-service workers and in that a majority too are men with experience of unionism in other firms; that is to say, they were mostly members of trade unions before taking up their present employment: 46 % of the craftsmen and machinists fall into *both* of the above categories. In contrast to this, two-thirds of the setters are intermediate-service workers and a similar proportion have been unionists

[1] The basic data from which table 38 is constructed are given in table A7.

only within their present firm: 44% of the setters are in both of these categories. A different pattern again is then found with the process workers and assemblers. As with the craftsmen and machinists, these men tend to have worked for only fairly short periods in their present firms; but at the same time quite a high proportion only became trade unionists in course of this employment. Thus, something in the region of at least a quarter of the process workers and assemblers could probably be regarded as being relatively 'green' unionists; that is to say, they are men who have become unionists for the first time as a sequel to taking up their present jobs and who have as yet only short experience of union membership. Considering the sample as a whole, it is in fact the sizable proportion of our affluent workers who were employees of their present firm *prior to* being members of their union which appears as the most notable feature. Even including the craftsmen and machinists, this pattern can be said to apply to between a third and two-thirds of those in each occupational group.

Table 39 classifies the results we obtained when we asked our respondents why they had first joined a union. It can be seen that the same lines of differentiation as were evident in table 38 are maintained. The craftsmen and the machinists are again alike in that in both groups we find a relatively high proportion of men who stated that they became union members in part at least on grounds of principle, but also a comparable proportion who gave no other reason for joining than that they were in some way, formally or informally, coerced. One would then suggest, consistently with the evidence of table 38, that workers in these two groups had been mostly employed in firms or shops with strong union traditions and were thus likely either to have internalised these traditions—and to have become 'committed' unionists—or to have experienced them as a constraining force. However, turning to the setters, all of whom had, of course, once been machinists, it would appear that in this case the latter of these two possibilities had been far more often realised than the former. Only one setter in fact claimed to have become a unionist out of principle, while the group had the highest proportion of all of 'reluctant' joiners. The difference is, one would argue, that, unlike the craftsmen and machinists, the setters were, as we know, men who had for the most part been non-unionists before coming to Skefko—a firm in which unionism is virtually compulsory. Thus, in these circumstances, a relatively high degree of involuntary organisation in the case of the setters cannot be regarded as particularly surprising.

Finally, with the process workers and assemblers, we find that there are

TABLE 39. *Reasons given for first becoming a union member*

Class of reason*	Craftsmen (N = 49)	Setters (N = 23)	Process workers (N = 18)	Machinists (N = 41)	Assemblers (N = 68)	All (N = 199)
	Percentage					
Belief in unionism in principle or in worker's duty to join	31	4	17	29	13	20
Advantages of union representation on wages, conditions of service, grievances etc.	4	26	22	10	19	15
Advantages of friendly society benefits, and legal assistance	8	4	33	5	24	15
All workmates were members	8	13	0	10	7	8
Coercion through existence of 'union shop' or pressure from stewards or workmates	29	39	6	32	12	23
Other,† D.K.	20	13	23	14	25	20
TOTALS	100	99	101	100	100	101

* Where more than one reason was given, that coming into the highest of the categories below was counted.

† Mostly too vague or uncertain to classify: e.g. 'I was asked so I joined'; 'it's just what you do'.

clearly fewer men than in the other groups whose entry into unionism was a matter either of principle or of compulsion. Rather, these workers have tended to become unionists, insofar as they had any well-defined reason, because of certain more or less specific advantages which they hoped in this way to gain. This pattern may be seen as deriving from the fact that nearly half of the process workers and assemblers had not been unionists before joining their present firms, and that in these firms unionism was not outstandingly strong. Thus, in their case, union membership was much more a matter of choice than for the other workers in our sample and to some extent, one would suggest, a matter of calculation.[1]

[1] We were informed by an A.E.U. official that in recent years his union had emphasised its friendly society benefits and legal assistance services as a deliberate recruiting tactic. Nonetheless, it is still a notable contrast with our findings that in the case of the members of a branch of the Transport and General Workers Union studied by Goldstein, only 4 respondents out

Taking an overall view, then, in the light of tables 38 and 39 it may be said that not only have a substantial number of our affluent workers been brought into the trade union movement only in the course of their present employment, but also that no more than a small minority appear to have been in any way motivated in this respect through moral conviction. More frequently, these men would seem to have become unionists either with little volition on their own part or because of a belief—often expressed to us—that 'union membership pays'; that is, as a result of a largely instrumental view of unionism which clearly reflects what we would regard as their characteristic orientation towards their working life in general.

However, data on when, and for what reasons, men initially joined a union are not necessarily reliable evidence of what trade unionism implies for these workers at some later point in time. We must turn next, therefore, to the further information which we have on the nature and extent of our affluent workers' present involvement in union affairs.

One set of data which we collected in this connection relates to participation in the union branch. We asked our respondents first of all: 'How often do you go to union branch meetings? Would you say you went regularly, occasionally, rarely or never?' The results produced by this question are given in table 40.[1] From this it can be seen that while the craftsmen have a relatively high proportion of regular and occasional attenders—about half these men having in fact been at some time union officials—the large majority in all the other occupational groups never attend branch meetings or go only rarely. In the case of the setters this is not perhaps surprising in view of what has already been said about the way in which these workers mostly became unionists. But much more striking is the fact that if the three groups of semi-skilled men are taken together, it turns out that only 2% state that they go to meetings regularly and 11% occasionally, as against 16% rarely and 69% never. And it may be noted that the machinists do not in this respect differ very greatly from the process

of 111 mentioned specific union benefits and services as a reason for joining. See Joseph Goldstein, *The Government of British Trade Unions* (London, 1952), pp. 261–2.

It might also at this point be noted that the 30 non-unionists in our sample, all but 7 of whom were process workers or assemblers, were not in the main anti-unionist in principle: 26 (87%) had in fact once been union members. The reasons most often given for not belonging were ones to the effect either that it was 'not necessary' or that there was 'no point in it' *in their present employment*. In other words, these men tended to be as pragmatic in outlook as their unionist workmates.

[1] In the case of those men who answered 'regularly', 'occasionally' or 'rarely', we then also asked: 'And when did you last go to one?' From this it emerged that the very large majority of those saying 'regularly' had attended a branch meeting within the past month, and of those saying 'occasionally', within the past year. Most of those saying 'rarely' had not attended in the past year.

TABLE 40. *Reported frequency of attendance at union branch meetings*

Reported frequency of attendance	Craftsmen (N = 49)	Setters (N = 23)	Process workers (N = 18)	Machinists (N = 41)	Assemblers (N = 68)	All (N = 199)
'Regularly'	22	0	0	0	4	7
'Occasionally'	25	4	0	17	10	14
'Rarely'	25	17	17	24	12	19
'Never'	29*	78	78	59	72	60
Other, D.K.	0	0	6	0	1	1
TOTALS	101	99	101	100	99	101

* Includes all five Laporte craftsmen.

workers and assemblers, in spite of having a higher proportion of men who stated that they became unionists out of principle. Even though it is true that considerable rank-and-file apathy in branch affairs is to be found throughout British trade unionism, these figures for the semi-skilled workers indicate a level of participation which, by any standards, must be regarded as notably low;[1] and particularly so if any allowance is made for possible 'over-reporting' of attendance in the answers we received.[2]

Some idea of the sources of this degree of non-involvement in the branch can be gained from the reasons which we were given when we went on to ask those men who never or only rarely attended meetings why this was. From table 41 it is clear that a general lack of interest and concern in the work of the branch is the most important single factor.

[1] Political and Economic Planning, in its report *British Trade Unionism* (London, 1948), calculated maximum attendance figures at branch meetings for a sample of 16 larger-than-average unions on the basis of voting figures: the range proved to be from 2% to 30% but with a concentration in the range of 15–20%. Subsequently, B. C. Roberts in his book, *Trade Union Government and Administration in Great Britain* (London, 1956), has estimated that in British industry generally the level of attendance among branch memberships is usually between 3% and 15% with a heavy concentration between 4% and 7%. Data on craft-workers and workers in long-established heavy industries suggest relatively high attendance; e.g. average attendance among woodworkers appears to be in the region of 15–20% (Roberts, pp. 95–7) and in the Liverpool study of dockers, 20% of those interviewed stated that they attended at least one branch meeting in four (see *The Dockworker*, p. 122). The previous findings which seem most comparable with the data for our semi-skilled men are those reported by Goldstein for T.G.W.U. members who were largely semi-skilled or unskilled workers and of whom over a third were women: in the branch in question, less than 4% could be regarded as 'active' members and not all of these were necessarily regular attenders at branch meetings (*The Government of British Trade Unions*, pp. 157–8). At A.E.U. branch meetings in the Luton district, at the time when our study was made, average attendance figures ranged from 7 to 25%, according to official figures.

For evidence of a tendency in this direction, see Lois R. Dean, 'Interaction, reported and observed: the case of one local union', *Human Organization*, vol. 17, no. 3 (Fall, 1958).

TABLE 41. *Reasons given for infrequent attendance or non-attendance at union branch meetings*

Class of reason	Craftsmen (N = 26)	Setters (N = 22)	Process workers (N = 18)	Machinists (N = 34)	Assemblers (N = 43)*	All (N = 158)
	Times mentioned					
Not interested in branch affairs, has no knowledge of meetings	11	14	8	23	15	71
Demands of home and family life, leisure activities etc.	8	3	1	8	10	30
Meetings are boring, unintelligible, waste of time	5	3	2	3	1	14
Attendance is not necessary because of link through shop steward	1	2	3	2	6	14
Travelling, shiftwork prevents attendance	2	0	7	3	1	13
Does not believe in unionism, or in need for unions in present firm	4	5	0	2	2	13
Satisfied with union performance, so no need to attend	2	1	3	2	1	9
Other	2	3	0	7	8	20
TOTALS	35	31	24	50	44	184

* This figure excludes A.E.U. members who attended union *shop* meetings regularly or occasionally.

The following comments illustrate the attitude in question:

'I've never known where meetings have been and when. I'm not really interested as long as they look after me in here. I'm prepared to let the other people go.'

'I can't be bothered. The only aspect of the union I'm interested in is what goes on in this factory—what concerns me.'

'I'm just not prepared to find the time. When I go out of that gate work doesn't interest me. The only time I've been to a meeting was when a plant shut down.'

'It's too much trouble—there are other things I'd rather do. I don't find anything of interest in it.'

However, table 41 also indicates that some noteworthy differences do exist within the sample. It can be seen, for instance, that there is a tendency for the reasons given by the setters for not attending meetings to suggest negative as well as indifferent attitudes—unionism is regarded as futile and unnecessary. On the other hand, though, with the semi-skilled men, non-attendance at the branch can less often be assumed to imply total uninterest or disaffection. More frequently with these workers reference is made to the competing demands of home and family or of their work itself; or it is held that branch affairs do not normally require their participation because of the linking role which is played by their shop stewards.[1] The following remarks were characteristic in these respects:

'I can never go [to branch meetings] because of my home commitments. When you've been away at work all day, you can't leave your wife again in the evening.'
'I don't go because of shift work—the meeting falls on my late shift. It's a good excuse, I suppose—I mightn't go often anyway. But I think one should try to take an active part.'
'I used to go but I've dropped off now. I went before I was married. I don't get time now, with the family—and the television. Branch meetings are really for shop stewards.'
'The shop steward tells you all what happened at the branch. I'd go if necessary but no serious issue has ever come up.'

Finally as regards the branch, we asked our respondents how often they voted in branch elections.[2] The answers we received are shown in table 42. Since in general only those men who attended branch meetings were entitled to vote, it is natural that these data should largely follow the pattern of those given in table 40, and thus point again to the extent of non-participation. However, an exception occurs in the case of members of the N.U.V.B., who are allowed to vote for branch officials at their place of work; and it turns out that of the 35 assemblers in our sample who belonged to this union, 26 (74%) said that they voted in these elections regularly. Here again, then, there is perhaps some indication of a readiness to take at least an intermittent interest in branch affairs, provided that this can be done without inroads being made into the individual's non-working life. But at the same time it should be added that the workers in question

[1] Reasons given for not attending at the branch may be re-analysed in terms of the attitude they indicate towards trade unionism on the basis of the following three categories: (i) indifferent ('not interested' etc.); (ii) negative ('meetings are boring' etc., 'does not believe in unionism' etc.); (iii) implicitly positive (all reasons indicating that respondent would attend if it were not for some obstacle or if it were really necessary). Excluding 'other' reasons, it then proves that the percentage of reasons given of types (i) to (iii) respectively was: setters (N = 28) 50, 28, 21; semi-skilled workers (N = 103) 45, 10, 46; craftsmen (N = 33) 33, 27, 39.
[2] The question was analogous in form to that asked about attendance at branch meetings.

TABLE 42. *Reported frequency of voting at union branch elections*

Reported frequency of voting	Craftsmen (N = 49)	Setters (N = 23)	Process workers (N = 18)	Machinists (N = 41)	Assemblers (N = 68)	All (N = 199)
	Percentage					
'Regularly'	35	0	11	7	44*	26
'Occasionally'	20	9	0	7	13	12
'Rarely'	16	13	11	7	3	9
'Never'	29†	78	78	78	38	52
Other, D.K.	0	0	0	0	1	1
TOTALS	100	100	100	99	99	100

* Includes 26 out of 35 N.U.V.B. members who were able to vote in branch elections at their place of work.
† Includes all five Laporte craftsmen.

frequently admitted to voting quite blindly: as one man put it, 'it's really just a case of eeny-meeny-miny-mo'.

So far, then, as the branch is concerned, a fairly clear pattern of attitudes and behaviour among our affluent workers can be discerned. With the exception of the craftsmen, the degree of involvement in the branch is in all groups extremely slight. But while with the setters this would appear to indicate to some extent a lack of enthusiasm for being caught up in a union in any way, with the bulk of the semi-skilled men non-participation may be regarded as having a somewhat different significance. More typically in this case it would seem to result from a feeling that affairs at branch level are of little relevance to what goes on in their particular shops and factories; or, at any rate, from an unwillingness to allow the branch anything more than a very marginal claim on their time and energy outside of work. In other words, the apathy towards the branch which these workers display may be seen as reflecting not so much a general lack of 'union-mindedness' but rather an essentially instrumental and 'self-interested'[1] approach to unionism of the kind to which we have already referred. Moreover, this interpretation is confirmed by the fact that the workers in question prove not to be unresponsive and inactive in union matters in every respect alike. This becomes evident once we turn from the unionism of the branch to what we may call the unionism of the workplace.

As well as asking our respondents how often they voted in branch

[1] On the idea of 'self-interested' unionism, see S. M. Lipset, *The First New Nation*, 'Trade Unions and the American Value System', ch. 5 (London, 1963).

TABLE 43. *Reported frequency of voting at shop steward elections*

Reported frequency of voting	Craftsmen (N = 49)	Setters (N = 23)	Process workers (N = 18)	Machinists (N = 41)	Assemblers (N = 68)	All (N = 199)
'Regularly'	88	61	89	85	84	83
'Occasionally'	2	17	0	5	4	5
'Rarely'	2	4	0	5	1	3
'Never'	6	17	6	5	6	7
Other, D.K.	2	0	6	0	4	3
TOTALS	100	99	101	100	99	101

elections, we also asked them how often they voted in elections for shop stewards. The results given by this question are shown in table 43. From this it is immediately apparent that in all groups in the sample, participation in elections at shop level is considerably greater than at branch level and is, on any reckoning, high. Further, it can be seen that so far as voting for stewards is concerned, differences in participation between the craftsmen and the semi-skilled workers no longer exist; only the setters include an appreciable minority of men who vote other than regularly. To some large extent, of course, this greater involvement in shop elections may be put down to simple convenience: voting is carried out on the spot. However, that this is not the entire explanation is indicated by other of our data. In the case of those men who reported voting 'regularly' or 'occasionally' in shop elections but 'rarely' or 'never' in branch elections, we asked why this was so. The replies we received are classified in table 44. As can be seen, the most immediate explanation—non-attendance at branch meetings—was that most frequently given. But other replies served both to re-emphasise the remoteness of branch affairs from the concerns of our respondents and also to make clear that from their point of view the shop steward was a far more important official than any at branch level. The following comments were typical ones:

'The shop steward affects me more than the branch elections. It don't make a lot of difference which branch you're in so long as you pay your money and support the union. But the steward's the man I deal with if anything goes wrong —I want to know who he is.'

'The shop steward's election is with regard to the man on the shop floor—you like to know who's doing your business. Unions have got so big that they're no longer in touch with the shop floor at all. At the branch they haven't got their finger on the pulse.'

TABLE 44. *Reasons given for frequent voting in shop steward elections but infrequent voting in branch elections*

Class of reason	Craftsmen (N = 17)	Setters (N = 16)	Process workers (N = 14)	Machinists (N = 31)	Assemblers (N = 23)	All (N = 101)
			Times mentioned			
Do not attend branch meetings	9	8	8	15	4	44
Shop stewards are more important than branch officials	3	4	5	9	8	29
Have no knowledge of branch candidates, know shop candidates	2	7	2	10	5	26
Other	4	0	1	3	7	15
TOTALS	18	19	16	37	24	114

'You've always got interest in the things that happen in the shop. You're not all that interested in the affairs of the A.E.U.—except where it concerns yourself.'

'Shop steward elections is to do with the floor. I know the branch has too, but I don't seem to know what goes on there at all. The shop steward is a man on your floor. You know the man and his capabilities. The others you don't know so much about.'

Furthermore, two other items in our interview schedule provide evidence that at least a sizable minority of our affluent workers are quite highly involved in the unionism of the workplace. We asked our respondents, first: 'How often do you talk to your workmates about union affairs? Would you say very often, a good deal, now and then or hardly ever?'; and then (offering the same choices): 'And what about your shop steward—how often do you talk with him about your work and conditions?' Tables 45 and 46 show a pattern of response which suggests that 'informal' participation in union matters in these ways was in fact fairly widespread.[1] It can be seen that with the craftsmen, machinists and assemblers, from a third to a half report talking to their mates about union affairs 'very often' or 'a good deal', while around a third of the workers in these groups also appear to have relatively frequent conversations with

---

[1] In the sample generally there is, as might be expected, a marked relationship between the replies to the two questions. If these are dichotomised—'very often', 'a good deal' as against 'now and then', 'hardly ever'—the positive association is highly significant: $\chi^2 = 24.1$; 1 df; $p < 0.001$.

TABLE 45. *Reported frequency of talking to workmates about union affairs*

Respondent talks to workmates	Craftsmen (N = 49)	Setters (N = 23)	Process workers (N = 18)	Machinists (N = 41)	Assemblers (N = 86)	All (N = 199)
	Percentage					
'Very often'	20	13	11	20	19	18
'A good deal'	31	9	17	22	13	19
'Now and then'	33	61	50	51	47	46
'Hardly ever'	14	17	22	7	21	16
Other, D.K.	2	0	0	0	0	1
TOTALS	100	100	100	100	100	100

their stewards. And, on the other hand, only a quarter or less of the men in these groups would appear to be largely detached from shop unionism. In the case of the process workers and setters, the data point to a clearly lower degree of involvement. However, with the former group this must in part at least be related to the physical barriers which, as we have seen, limit these workers' interaction generally (see table 20) and which are specifically recognised by employees as reducing union strength within the Laporte plant. It is thus only with the setters that there is again some definite indication of a substantial proportion of the group who as a matter of choice have little to do with unionism in any form at all.[1]

The argument that participation in unionism at the level of the workplace is of generally greater significance than more formal participation via the branch is one that has been increasingly emphasised in recent years.[2] We would not, therefore, regard our affluent workers as being very exceptional in showing greater concern with union affairs in the context of their shop and factory than in the context of the union bureaucracy. At the same time, though, we would suggest that, at least with the semi-skilled men in our sample, the disjunction between the unionism of the branch and the unionism of the workplace is carried to an extreme point. While their

[1] One further piece of evidence of a relatively high degree of participation in unionism at workplace level is provided by the case of the *shop* meetings called from time to time by A.E.U. officials in Vauxhall. Of the 32 A.E.U. members among the Vauxhall assemblers in our sample, 22 (69%) reported attending these meetings 'regularly' or 'occasionally' as against 10 (31%) 'rarely' or 'never'.

[2] See, for example, in the American literature Joseph Kovner and Herbert J. Lahne, 'Shop Society and the Union', *Industrial and Labor Relations Review*, vol. 7, no. 1 (October 1953), and Joel Seidman, Jack London, Bernard Karsh and Daisy L. Tagliacozzo, *The Worker Views his Union* (Chicago, 1958), pp. 195–6; and, with reference to Great Britain, Roberts, *Trade Union Government and Administration*, pp. 57–60, 111–12, and George Cyriax and Robert Oakeshott, *The Bargainers* (London, 1960), pp. 68–71.

TABLE 46. *Reported frequency of talking to shop steward about work and conditions*

Respondent talks to shop steward	Craftsmen (N = 49)	Setters (N = 23)	Process workers (N = 18)	Machinists (N = 41)	Assemblers (N = 68)	All (N = 199)
	Percentage					
'Very often'	20	9	6	12	19	16
'A good deal'	16	9	11	17	13	14
'Now and then'	29	35	44	46	44	40
'Hardly ever'	20	44	28	24	22	25
Other, D.K.	14	4	11	0	1	6
TOTALS	99	101	100	99	99	101

participation in the branch is, as we have remarked, notably low, unionism would nonetheless seem to remain an integral part of the working lives of a majority of these men insofar as it is related to the particular conditions and problems of their own employment. Moreover, it is evident that in the eyes of many of our semi-skilled workers, the unionism of the workplace is very largely *dissociated* from what they regard as the official activity of the unions to which they happen to belong. The former is what really matters—'what concerns us'—while the latter they tend often to dismiss as having little at all to do with them. Perhaps the clearest indication of this was given when branch meetings were said to be of no interest or relevance because they dealt with questions which related to 'other firms' or 'all of Luton', or with items which, as one man revealingly put it, 'really only concern the union itself—not the men on the shop floor'.

As we have earlier implied, such an orientation to trade unionism is one which 'makes sense' in terms of what we have already represented as the typical orientation of the workers in question towards their employment generally. That unionism should have little significance for them other than in relation to the immediate 'bread-and-butter' issues of their own work situation is entirely consistent with their definition of work as primarily a means to extrinsic ends: their main interest in the union, as in the firm, is that of the 'pay-off'. Following the suggestion made in an earlier paper,[1] unionism in the style of these workers can be usefully described as 'instrumental collectivism'—collectivism, that is to say, which is directed to the achievement of individuals' private goals, outside the workplace.

[1] Goldthorpe and Lockwood, 'Affluence and the British Class Structure'.

Such an interpretation is supported by the fact that the minority of men in our sample whose attitudes and behaviour are of a clearly different nature are found in greatest concentration among the craftsmen and setters. From our point of view it is not accidental that the craftsmen should provide the highest proportion of branch stalwarts and the setters, so it would seem, of men who are, fairly overtly, unwilling unionists. For in addition to these workers' differing attitudes towards their firms, as indicated in the previous chapter, we would return to the point that the activities and relationships of work have a less narrowly instrumental significance for the men in these two groups than they have for most of the semi-skilled men. And to the extent that the individual's involvement in his work is more than a merely calculative one, the less we would expect him to view his union in an affectively neutral way; for both the 'committed' and the 'alienated' unionist, it is likely that work will have some prominence as a life interest.[1]

If on the basis of the data so far presented, we seek to make comparisons between our affluent workers and workers of a more traditional kind, the main differences, it would then seem, must be looked for not so much in the actual *degree* of participation in union affairs, but rather in the form which this takes and still more perhaps in the *meaning* which union activity appears to have for the majority of the men in question. We have argued that the unionism of these workers is to be understood in terms of the characteristic attitudes which they bring to their employment; that is, as unionism of a markedly instrumental type. We recognise, of course, that all trade unionism, like all work activity, contains a basically instrumental component. Nonetheless, unionism has often represented *more* to workers than simply a means of economic betterment; it has been seen also as a form of collective action in which solidarity was an end as well as a means and as a socio-political movement aiming at radical changes in industrial institutions and in the structure of society generally.[2] In our view, the most distinctive feature of the unionism of the workers we studied is the *extent*

[1] For a similar line of argument and supporting evidence in regard to active unionists, see Lois R. Dean, 'Social Integration, Attitudes and Union Activity', *Industrial and Labor Relations Review*, vol. 8, no. 1 (October 1954); and W. Spinrad, 'Correlates of Trade Union Participation: a summary of the literature', *American Sociological Review*, vol. 25, no. 2 (1960).

[2] On unionism in which solidarity is in part an end in itself, see, for example, the discussion of craft unionism in S. and B. Webb, *The History of British Trade Unionism* (London, 1911), pp. 431–8; and also the account of 'traditional' unionism in F. Zweig, *The British Worker* (London, 1952), pp. 177–9. Further relevant accounts of unionism in particular occupations are to be found in *The Dock Worker*, pp. 115 ff., and, for printers, in A. J. M. Sykes, 'The Cohesion of Trade Union Workshop Organization', *Sociology*, vol. 1, no. 2 (1967).

to which these wider ideals and objectives have ceased to be of significance. In addition to what we have already said about the ways in which these workers became unionists and about the nature of their involvement in union affairs, we can further support this view by evidence of a more direct kind.

Over and above basic economic issues, it may be said that the most important and long-standing concerns of British trade unions have been with questions of authority and power—both within industry and within the wider society. On the one hand, unions have been traditionally engaged with problems of 'the frontier of control'—that is, with problems of establishing workers' rights to some voice in decisions relating to the management of the firms in which they are employed.[1] On the other hand, through their association with the Labour Party, the unions have become deeply involved in national politics. In the course of our interviews, therefore, we sought to discover something of our respondents' attitudes towards both these aspects of the union movement.

In the first place, after discussing with our interviewees the part they played in union affairs, we put to them the following question: 'Some people say unions should just be concerned with getting higher pay and better conditions for their members. Others think they should also try to get workers a say in management. What are your views?' Table 47 shows the general pattern of the replies we received. It can be seen that in four out of the five occupational groups, a majority felt that unions should limit themselves to their specifically economic functions: only among the craftsmen was the idea of greater worker control still largely upheld as a union objective. Moreover, as might be expected from the craftsmen's views on management that have already been recorded, these workers were often prepared to claim not only that a larger share in the running of the firm was the employee's right, but also that this would make for improvements in operating efficiency.[2] By contrast, the comments made by those holding the majority view within the sample revealed both a lack of enthusiasm for any greater involvement in the affairs of the firm and a readiness to accept management's special qualifications and expertise. The following remarks illustrate the attitudes in question.

'The unions shouldn't run the factory—it would be a terrible thing. We have a good deal of say already in conditions and things that concern us—like redundancy. But the men shouldn't have to run the place.'

'I agree with the principle that an employee should be represented to management—and it makes for better relations, like through the [Vauxhall] Advisory

[1] See the remarkable but neglected book by Carter L. Goodrich, *The Frontier of Control: a Study in British Workshop Politics* (London, 1920).　　　[2] See pp. 20–21 above.

TABLE 47. *Attitudes on role of trade unions in industry*

Respondent agrees more with view that	Craftsmen (N = 49)	Setters (N = 23)	Process workers (N = 18)	Machinists (N = 41)	Assemblers (N = 68)	All (N = 199)
			Percentage			
'…unions should just be concerned with getting higher pay and better conditions'	37	61	61	51	59	52
'…unions should also try to get workers a say in management'	61	35	22	46	28	40
Other, D.K.	2	4	17	2	13	8
TOTALS	100	100	100	99	100	100

Council. But workers shouldn't have a say in the management of the firm direct. It's not their business.'

'Workers shouldn't manage the place they're working for. It's not right and they couldn't do it.'

'The average person in a place like this likes to think he could manage, but management is really for educated people who can do it.'

Views of this kind may be taken as reflecting in yet another way the definition of work as essentially a means, which we regard as basic to understanding the general pattern of industrial attitudes and behaviour among the majority of the workers we studied. Given the primarily calculative and contractual way in which they see their relationship with their employing organisations, the position they take up is scarcely a surprising one. Just as they are little interested in being members of a 'plant community' through participation in work-based clubs and societies, so too there is no very widespread desire among these men that their unions should strive to give them a larger role in the actual running of the plant. This is a responsibility in which they are not anxious to share.[1] Their predisposition for what Clark Kerr has called the 'limited-function' firm[2] leads in turn to their favouring also the 'limited-function' trade union— the union, that is, which concentrates its activities almost exclusively on their economic protection and advancement.

In regard, secondly, to the political activities of unions, we began by

[1] Cf. the data presented in chapter 6 on workers' attitudes towards becoming a foreman.
[2] Clark Kerr, 'What became of the Independent Spirit?', *Fortune* (June 1953); see also his *Labor and Management in Industrial Society* (New York, 1964), pp. xvi–xvii.

TABLE 48. *Payment of the political levy*

	Craftsmen (N = 49)	Setters (N = 23)	Process workers (N = 18)	Machinists (N = 41)	Assemblers (N = 68)	All (N = 199)
			Percentage			
Pay levy	61	35	39	46	41	46
Do not pay levy, have contracted out	31	30	28	29	15	25
Say do not pay levy but have not contracted out / Do not know anything about levy	8	35	33	24	44	29
TOTALS	100	100	100	99	100	100

asking our respondents, once we had established that they were union members, whether or not they paid the 'political levy'—that is, whether or not they contributed to their union's political fund and thus, in effect, to the Labour Party. In the case of those men who said that they did not, we then asked further if they had 'contracted out'. The results which these two questions produced are given in table 48.

Since in the unions with which we were chiefly concerned the political levy and union dues were 'compounded' into a single payment, it may be assumed that men who had not contracted out were in general paying the levy, regardless of the way in which they replied to our question. Thus, table 48 can be taken to indicate that in four out of the five occupational groups in the sample, the proportion contributing to the political fund was around 70%. The exception is provided by the assemblers, who show an appreciably larger percentage. However, even allowing for this, it would seem that, overall, the incidence of contracting out among our affluent workers is relatively high. According to estimates made by Harrison,[1] the proportion of all trade unionists paying the political levy in the late 1950s was around 80%; and this figure takes into account exemptions from the levy, non-payment without contracting out, and other causes of non-payment which do not arise with the men in our sample. Thus, the proportion of unionists generally who actually do contract out must be well under 20%—a level which, among the workers we studied, is clearly exceeded in all groups apart from the assemblers.

[1] Martin Harrison, *Trade Unions and the Labour Party since 1945* (London, 1960), p. 33.

As an extreme contrast to the situation found in our investigation, we may note the data which have been recorded for the membership of the National Union of Mineworkers. In this latter case, less than 4% of the total membership had contracted out (1958)—and over 95% of these men were colliery officials and staff.[1] Clearly then, we may say that our affluent workers are very far indeed from having the degree of solidarity which these figures reflect, and which makes contracting out an act of 'disloyalty' that only the determined outsider will be likely to undertake.

Moreover, one other point emerging from table 48 calls for comment. If we consider those men who may be regarded as paying the political levy, it would appear that in all groups except the craftsmen from a third to a half are making their contribution without realising this; that is to say, either they do not think that they pay the levy but have not contracted out or they admit to having no knowledge of the levy at all. This means, then, that, in addition to the relatively high proportion of those who do contract out, we must recognise also a further sizable category of men who have no awareness of the main way in which, as union members, they are implicated in political affairs. As the table shows, it is in fact only among the craftsmen that a majority of the unionists pay the political levy and know that they do; in the other groups this proportion averages out, with no very great variations, in the region of only two-fifths.

On the basis of this evidence, therefore, it would appear, first, that in the consciousness of many of our affluent workers the political involvement of their union is not a matter of any great saliency; and, secondly, that of those who are more politically aware, a sizable number are not prepared to support their union in its affiliation to the Labour Party. In sum, it is fairly clearly indicated that these workers are not to any large degree committed to the traditional idea of the trade unions and the Labour Party as forming the industrial and political 'wings' of an integrated labour movement.

In order to confirm this interpretation, we may turn to the findings from a further question which we put to our respondents in course of the 'home' interviews, in which we discussed their political views at some length. We asked: 'As you know, most trade unions support the Labour Party; do you approve of this, or do you think they ought to keep themselves separate?' The pattern of replies we received is shown in table 49. This reveals that, once more with the exception of the craftsmen, a majority of our affluent workers do not believe that the unions and the Labour Party should continue in their present relationship; the skilled workers alone largely

[1] *Ibid.* p. 43.

TABLE 49. *Attitudes towards trade union support for Labour Party*

	Craftsmen (N = 49)	Setters (N = 23)	Process workers (N = 18)	Machinists (N = 41)	Assemblers (N = 68)	All (N = 199)
	Percentage					
Approve of trade union support for Labour Party	61	26	49	44	37	45
Think trade unions and Labour Party should keep themselves separate	39	74	51	50	59	53
Other, D.K.	0	0	0	6	4	2
TOTALS	100	100	100	100	100	100

approve of the historic alliance. Moreover, this result is all the more significant when the further information is added that of the union members in our sample over two-thirds have never voted other than for the Labour Party, and that, when interviewed, 69% had the intention of voting Labour at the forthcoming General Election (1964). Even if we consider only these Labour supporters, we find that among the setters and semi-skilled men still only 51% favour the unions' close association with their Party as against 49% taking the opposing view.[1]

Finally, the results of one further question, which we asked immediately after the one discussed above, are also relevant to an understanding of our respondents' views on the position of the unions in the wider society. The question was: 'Some people say that the trade unions have too much power in the country: would you agree or disagree, on the whole?' The answers that were given are recorded in table 50. In the case of the craftsmen and setters, the pattern of replies is very much what would be expected on the basis of previously presented data. With the semi-skilled workers, however, the situation is somewhat less straightforward. To begin with, it may be noted that while, as we have seen, a majority of these men do not support the unions' alliance with the Labour Party, there is also a majority—albeit a small one—against the view that union power is too great. In other words, some proportion of those who would like to see the

[1] With the craftsmen, the corresponding figures were 68% and 32%. In the Liverpool study of dockers, only 17% of those interviewed said they disapproved of the close connection between trade unionism and the Labour Party, and this attitude appeared to be chiefly associated with disapproval of the wage-freeze policy which was felt to have been accepted by the union at the request of the Labour government. See University of Liverpool, *The Dock Worker*, p. 132.

TABLE 50. *Attitudes towards trade-union power*

	Craftsmen (N = 49)	Setters (N = 23)	Process workers (N = 18)	Machinists (N = 41)	Assemblers (N = 68)	All (N = 199)
			Percentage			
Agree that trade unions have too much power	27	70	39	44	43	41
Disagree that trade unions have too much power	69	30	59	56	56	56
Other, D.K.	4	0	2	0	1	4
TOTALS	100	100	100	100	100	101

unions cut their official political ties would nonetheless not wish to see the unions' position in the country made weaker—an outlook which is, of course, entirely consistent with the idea of 'instrumental collectivism'.[1] At the same time, perhaps the most significant point remains that as many as two-fifths of the men in question were prepared to agree that the organisations by which as wage workers they are represented *are* too powerful on a national level. Here, we would suggest, is further evidence of the extent to which these workers fail to identify at all closely with their unions above the level of the workplace, and in effect see little connection between the unionism which they themselves practice and the national organisations to which they formally belong.

In several different ways, thus, the evidence that we have brought forward demonstrates the fact that, leaving aside the craftsmen, the majority of our affluent workers take a view of the functions of trade unionism which is of an obviously restricted kind. Neither as a way to greater worker participation in the affairs of the enterprise nor as a political force is unionism greatly valued. Rather, one could say, the significance which unionism has for these workers is very largely confined to issues arising in their employment which are *economic* in nature and which are *local* in their origins and scope. One must be careful not to exaggerate the extent to which among more traditional industrial workers the wider aims and aspirations of the union movement are, or were, adhered to; undoubtedly, immediate questions of wages and conditions of service have

[1] The proportion is in fact almost exactly a half. Within the sample as a whole there is no significant association between disapproving of the unions' support for the Labour Party and agreeing that the unions have too much power.

always been of primary concern to union members. Nevertheless, insofar as we have been able to make use of comparative data, it is, we suggest, fairly clear that the unionism of the workers we studied is distinctive in its instrumental and 'self-interested' emphases.

In the light of the discussion of this chapter, it might well appear that among our affluent workers trade unionism is in some sense in decline—that it has lost its emotional appeal, its moral force, and its ability to extend men's social and political horizons. And certainly, on the evidence we have presented, it would not be easy to gainsay such a view. However, the point to which we wish to return in conclusion is the following: that given the way in which the work situation was most typically defined among the workers we studied, it is difficult to conceive of their style of unionism being markedly different from that we have described. The orientation of workers towards trade unionism reflects their orientation towards their employment generally; and where the latter is predominantly instru-mental, it is not to be expected that unionism, any more than work itself, will be seen as a way of satisfying other than economic needs. In other words, the situation with our affluent workers must not be viewed as one in which trade unionism is, as it were, 'losing its hold' upon these men, but rather as one in which they themselves are changing the character of unionism and are creating, in effect, a new type of unionism consistent with the wants and expectations which they bring to their work. The validity of such an analysis is clearly indicated by the 'deviant' case of the craftsmen. As we have seen, with these workers, whose orientation towards their employment is significantly less instrumental than that of the semi-skilled men, a far more traditional and 'solidaristic' pattern of attitudes and behaviour towards their union is still prevalent: just as they seek more from their work than economic returns alone, so too do they seek more from their trade unionism.

Thus, while the argument of 'trade unionism in decline' remains a tenable one, it is so only on the basis of certain fixed assumptions about what must be regarded as the 'essential' characteristics of the union move-ment. On the basis of a less static and more flexible conception of the nature of trade unionism, what is seen as decline might be alternatively viewed as the beginning of yet a further stage in an already lengthy and complex process of institutional development.

At all events, it should be recognised that even at its most instrumental and 'particularistic' the unionism of our affluent workers is still an important form of collective action; and that these workers' reliance upon such action remains closely associated with their position and role as men who sell their labour power to an employer in return for wages. Within modern industry, participation in action of this kind, via union membership, still typically differentiates manual from non-manual employees,[1] and in this way reflects certain continuing differences between these two groups, both in their objective work situation and in their orientations towards work. For instance, of the 54 men in our sample of white-collar workers, only 1 proved to be a union member. Although a majority (63%) said they had no serious objections to unionism and nearly half (42%) had in fact once belonged to a union, unionism appeared to have little appeal for these men in their present circumstances;[2] and these findings are very much in line with those of other studies of white-collar employees in industrial concerns.[3] Thus, in seeing the unionism of our affluent workers in a proper perspective, the white-collar employee must also be taken as a point of reference as well as the more traditional manual worker. The relevance and importance of the former comparison will, we hope, be more fully brought out in course of the succeeding chapter.

[1] J. R. Dale, *The Clerk in Industry* (Liverpool, 1962), p. 37, estimates that only *c.* 5% of clerks in industrial or commercial concerns are union members. For manufacturing industry at the beginning of 1964 Bain makes the somewhat higher estimate of 10·5%. See G. S. Bain, 'The Growth of White-Collar Unionism in Great Britain', *British Journal of Industrial Relations*, vol. IV, no. 3 (1966).

[2] The 31 men who had not been union members were asked: 'Have you ever seriously thought of joining a union?'; 27 (87%) said that they had not. The 23 men who had belonged to a union were asked: 'Why did you leave?'; 18 (78%) explained that they left as a result of changing their employment or on being promoted to a 'staff' position.

[3] See, for example, Dale, *The Clerk in Industry*, ch. 4, and Sykes, 'Some Differences in the Attitudes of Clerical and Manual Workers'.

6. The worker and his economic future

So far in this monograph our main aim has been to describe and analyse the current realities of the industrial lives of our affluent workers. In this chapter, however, the focus of our interest changes somewhat: we turn our attention to the hopes and expectations which these workers have for the years ahead. In particular, we try to understand to what extent the instrumental orientation to work, which we have shown to be dominant among our respondents, patterns not only their present attitudes and behaviour but also their view of what is desirable and possible so far as their economic future is concerned.

Once again, thus, we consider our affluent workers not primarily as members of a given industrial organisation but rather, in this case, as men who, in some more or less conscious way, have 'projects'[1] for themselves and their families which they seek to realise through work in one form or another. Already in adopting an instrumental approach to their employment—in aiming to maximise the extrinsic, at the expense of the intrinsic, rewards from their work—the majority of the men we studied would appear to have committed themselves to a fairly distinctive course of action. We must now consider the implications of this for the way in which they evaluate further possible means of advancing their projects and of achieving their objectives.

In the course of this chapter, we examine in some detail the attitudes of the workers we studied to several different 'ways ahead' which, in principle at least, are open to them. But, prior to doing this, it is necessary that something should be said concerning the social and psychological context of their response. Most importantly, it should be noted that, in comparison with many workers in older age-groups, or with workers in less prosperous regions of the country, the men in our sample have had relatively little direct experience of economic insecurity thus far in their working lives; and further, that they appear to feel no great anxiety about their basic security for the future. In restricting our sample to workers between the ages of 21 and 46, one of our main concerns was in fact to eliminate men

---

[1] By 'project' is meant some *chosen course of action* through which the individual seeks to create for himself a new life situation. See A. Touraine and O. Ragazzi, *Ouvriers d'Origine Agricole* (Paris, 1961).

TABLE 51. *Experience of unemployment*

Longest period of unemployment*	Craftsmen (N = 56)	Setters (N = 23)	Process workers (N = 23)	Machinists (N = 41)	Assemblers (N = 86)	All (N = 229)
	Percentage					
Never unemployed (other than transitionally)	98	96	91	78	83	88
Up to 3 months	2	4	4	12	13	8
3–12 months	0	0	4	5	5	3
Over 12 months	0	0	0	5	0	1
TOTALS	100	100	99	100	101	100

* Only two men had had more than three periods of unemployment.

whose entire range of industrial attitudes and behaviour might have been shaped by prolonged unemployment in the inter-war period. With the wider aims of our research in mind, we wished rather to concentrate on workers who were likely to have spent their adult lives under generally more favourable economic conditions. Table 51 shows the extent to which we were successful in this respect. It proves to be the case that only 3% of the craftsmen and setters and 17% of the semi-skilled workers had ever been out of a job for any appreciable length of time.

Moreover, since our sample was taken from relatively successful firms, sited in an area of rapid industrial expansion, it is not particularly surprising that the majority of the men in question should also be reasonably confident about the stability of their present employment. We asked our respondents: 'How secure do you think your job is in [name of firm]? Would you say it was dead safe, fairly safe, rather insecure or very insecure?' As is shown in table 52, only among the process workers did a sizable minority take a somewhat pessimistic view,[1] and, overall, this was the case with less than 10% of the sample. We also asked our respondents what considerations led them to feel the way they did; table 53 classifies the answers we received from the large majority who regarded their present jobs as being either 'dead safe' or 'fairly safe'. From this it can be seen that workers in different occupational groups and different firms tend to emphasise different sources of security. For example, while the crafts-

[1] A short while before our interviews took place, a plant producing titanium had been closed at the Laporte factory. The shutdown had been planned six months ahead and to a considerable extent the redundancy problem had been handled by letting the labour force run down through natural wastage. Nevertheless, a small number of men with less than three years' service were laid off.

TABLE 52. *Assessment of security of present job*

Assessment made	Craftsmen (N = 56)	Setters (N = 23)	Process workers (N = 23)	Machinists (N = 41)	Assemblers (N = 86)	All (N = 229)
	Percentage					
'Dead safe'	32	39	9	2	14	18
'Fairly safe'	64	57	65	85	77	72*
'Rather insecure'	4	4	26	5	6	7
'Very insecure'	0	0	0	5	1	1
Other, D.K.	0	0	0	2	2	1
TOTALS	100	100	100	99	100	99

* Of the 165 men saying 'fairly safe', it is interesting to note that 42 (25%) remarked that '*no job is dead safe*'. It was our impression that a good number of these men felt that their job was really a *very* secure one, but that it would be almost tempting providence to assert this too strongly.

men set particular store on their possession of scarce skills and on the competitive strength of Skefko, the setters and machinists are reassured more by the firm's past record in avoiding major lay-offs;[1] and the assemblers, having no special skills and being in an industry in which redundancies are endemic, see the safety of their jobs as lying chiefly in their seniority.[2] However, the main point is that, on one basis or another, the bulk of the workers we studied were able to feel that they could reasonably expect to retain their present jobs. And, to this extent at least, they could thus look to the future without the doubts and fears which were inescapable in the case of most industrial workers in the past and which still remain very real for many today. Furthermore, as will emerge more clearly later in the chapter, the degree of security which our affluent workers enjoyed encouraged them to abandon the 'fatalism' about the future which was the traditional worker's characteristic defence against the constant uncertainties of his economic life.[3] Having already some assurance of security, it was possible for them to look ahead to achieving still better economic conditions, and in a generally optimistic way. At the same time,

[1] The last time men were laid off at Skefko was in 1926.
[2] All our assemblers were 'Grade I' men; i.e., had been employed at Vauxhall for at least six months and, other than in exceptional cases, for more than two years. Their average length of service was just over eight years. Between the end of the war and the time when our interviews were carried out, there had been only one occasion on which men with more than one year's service had been made redundant at Vauxhall. So far as hourly paid workers were concerned, the firm invariably followed a strict policy of 'last in — first out'.
[3] See, for example, the perceptive account given in Richard Hoggart, *The Uses of Literacy* (London, 1958), pp. 60–72.

TABLE 53. *Reasons given for assessing present job as 'dead safe' or 'fairly safe'*

Class of reason	Craftsmen (N = 54)	Setters (N = 22)	Process workers (N = 17)	Machinists (N = 36)	Assemblers (N = 78)	All (N = 207)
			Times mentioned			
Have high seniority, grading	4	5	1	7	56	73
High, stable demand for firm's product	15	5	5	9	19	53
Firm has good record in avoiding redundancy	13	9	2	19	0	43
Have skills that are in demand, are good workmen	20	5	3	4	8	40
Firm is strong competitively	19	0	2	5	6	32
Other reasons	0	0	0	1	3	4
ALL REASONS	71	24	13	45	92	245

though, as we shall now try to show, the specific nature of their aspirations reflects the fact that these men are still wage-workers: men who have achieved their present affluent condition primarily through selling their labour power to the highest bidder, and whose future life chances are fairly clearly delimited by the nature of the position and role which they occupy within the total economic system.

One possible and perhaps the most obvious, 'way ahead' for rank-and-file industrial workers is that of promotion within their firm—first, in most cases, to some supervisory grade and thence, conceivably, to a managerial position. A progression of this kind would lead, eventually at any rate, to greater economic rewards, to more responsibility and authority within the enterprise, and to higher social status in the outside world. Thus, it might well be thought that the idea of advancement in this fashion would be an attractive one to workers who have to some extent broken free from traditional patterns of working-class life and who are prepared to seek out new styles of living for themselves in a relatively individualistic way.

However, so far at least as the men in our sample are concerned, such an expectation is not in fact well supported. Attitudes towards promotion proved to be negative as often as positive, and it was evident that for the large majority of workers we studied promotion did not figure at all significantly in their future plans.

TABLE 54. *Attitude towards idea of becoming a foreman*

Would like idea of becoming a foreman	Craftsmen (N = 56)	Setters (N = 23)	Process workers (N = 23)	Machinists (N = 41)	Assemblers (N = 86)	All manual (N = 229)	White collar (N = 54)
	Percentage						
'Very much'	20	39	17	22	29	25	46
'Quite a lot'	43	22	17	12	20	24	41
'Not much'	18	9	9	22	28	21	11
'Not at all'	13	30	57	42	22	28	2
Other, D.K.	7	0	0	2	0	3	0
TOTALS	101	100	100	100	99	101	100

We asked our respondents first of all, 'How about the idea of becoming a foreman? Would you like this very much, quite a lot, not much or not at all?' We then also asked: 'Have you ever thought seriously of becoming a foreman?'; and to those men who said that they had, we put the further question: 'What have you done about it?' The answers we received to these questions are given in tables 54 and 55. From the former table, it can be seen that among the more skilled workers around 60% said that they liked the idea of becoming a foreman 'very much' or 'quite a lot', but that this was the case with only between a third and a half of the semi-skilled men. A marked contrast is apparent here with our sample of white-collar workers, 87% of whom regarded the idea of promotion in a positive way. Furthermore, table 55 makes it clear that in all groups alike only a small minority had ever regarded promotion as at all a serious prospect, and that fewer still had taken any steps towards realising such an ambition. Differences between the groups are in these respects of obviously less importance than the overall pattern. Considering the sample as a whole, we find, in fact, that only 17% of our affluent workers were both positive in their attitudes towards the idea of becoming a foreman and had thought seriously about this, and that only 8% were both positive and had taken some action to this end.[1]

On the basis of these data it is, then, apparent that far from being a particularly marked aspiration among the workers we studied, promotion is not a matter which has any very great significance for them. Indeed, comparisons with the findings of other studies made in British industry would suggest that the workers in our sample are certainly no more likely than others to be actually seeking to 'get ahead' in this way and that, if anything, they are somewhat *less* likely to express an interest. For example,

[1] See table A8.

TABLE 55. *Action taken in regard to becoming a foreman*

	Craftsmen (N = 56)	Setters (N = 23)	Process workers (N = 23)	Machinists (N = 41)	Assemblers (N = 86)	All (N = 229)
	Percentage					
Have never thought seriously of becoming a foreman	71	74	70	93	67	74
Have thought seriously of becoming a foreman but have taken no action	18	22	17	5	17	16
Have applied for, enquired about a foreman's job	9	0	13	2	9	7
Have taken other action —e.g. attended training courses	2	4	0	0	6	3
TOTALS	100	100	100	100	99	100

in the investigations made by the Acton Society Trust in five large-scale manufacturing plants, 21% of the skilled men interviewed and 9% of the semi-skilled and unskilled had put in applications for supervisory jobs, and 50% of the former group and 41% of the latter reported that they were 'very interested' in being promoted.[1] Again, among the workers covered by Banks in his case-study of 'industrial participation' 13% of the skilled maintenance men had actually applied for promotion and a further 35% had this in mind, while among semi-skilled production workers the corresponding figures were 10 and 23%.[2] The only cases in which men have been shown to be clearly more averse to the idea of promotion than are our affluent workers are in fact ones in which promotion tends to be more or less directly *rejected* as a result of strong feelings of class solidarity and of antagonism towards management. For instance, several writers on traditional mining communities have noted that promotion is not widely sought, since for a man to take up a supervisory post means in effect 'going over to the other side' and is thus tantamount to an act of class disloyalty.[3] Similarly, Sykes has reported that among a sample of highly class-conscious workers from a Scottish steel manufacturing plant, only 10%

[1] See Acton Society Trust, *Management Succession* (London, 1956), pp. 64-5.
[2] J. A. Banks, *Industrial Participation* (Liverpool, 1963), p. 34.
[3] See, for example, the sources cited in Goldthorpe, 'Technical Organisation as a factor in Supervisor–Worker Conflict', notes 24 and 27; also Dennis *et al.*, *Coal is our Life*, pp. 31-2.

TABLE 56. *Anticipated reaction of workmates if respondent became a foreman*

Anticipated reaction of workmates	Craftsmen (N = 56)	Setters (N = 23)	Process workers (N = 23)	Machinists (N = 41)	Assemblers (N = 86)	All (N = 229)
	Percentage					
Generally unfavourable	23	30	13	49	23	28
Mixed; i.e., some unfavourable, some favourable	46	26	13	29	19	28
Generally neutral	16	35	30	10	24	21
Generally favourable	9	9	26	5	23	15
Other, D.K.	5	0	17	7	11	8
TOTALS	99	100	99	100	100	100

wanted promotion and over 80% believed that to accept promotion would give rise to 'problems' with their workmates.[1]

With these comparisons in mind, then, it is of interest to investigate the sources of our respondents' apparent lack of enthusiasm to move off the shop floor. To begin with, we can examine directly the extent to which, in our case, the anticipated reactions of fellow workers were an inhibiting factor. We asked our respondents: 'Just supposing you did become a foreman, what do you think your mates would feel about it?' Table 56 gives a classification of the replies we received in terms of the favourability or otherwise of the feelings which were thought likely. It can be seen that although relatively few men would expect their promotion to be received positively, in no group would a majority anticipate a generally *un*favourable reaction; and that only among the machinists was the proportion in this category greater than a third. In all groups, between a third and two-thirds would expect mixed or generally neutral feelings. Moreover, further analysis reveals that in those cases where a hostile reaction was anticipated, this was far more frequently thought of in terms of accusations of 'favouritism' and 'brown-nosing' rather than of 'going over to the other side' and 'disloyalty'. Less than a third of the men in question would expect their mates' reaction to be of this latter kind.

From this evidence it would seem unlikely that work-group pressures deriving from a solidaristic orientation to work are of any major importance in shaping our respondents' attitudes and behaviour in regard to promotion. And this conclusion is, of course, one entirely consistent with

[1] 'Some Differences in the Attitudes of Clerical and Manual Workers', pp. 299–301.

our previous findings that very few of our affluent workers reveal an orientation to work of this kind, or are in fact implicated in work groups which possess a high degree of cohesiveness.

To corroborate this line of argument further, and also to arrive at some more positive conclusions, we may turn next to the data we obtained when we asked our respondents in an open-ended manner actually to explain why they regarded the idea of promotion in the way they did. Table 57 classifies the reasons which were given by those workers who had expressed negative attitudes.

From this table, it may be noted in the first place that men who did not much, or who did not at all, like the idea of becoming a foreman only rarely referred to problems of relationships with other workers when explaining their lack of enthusiasm. In fact, less than 1 in 10 of the men in question gave a reason of this nature. This, then, confirms our view that group constraints are of relatively little significance.

Secondly, it is apparent that the factor which was by far the most important in creating negative attitudes towards promotion was one which involved economic rather than social considerations; namely, the extent to which supervisory posts were seen by our affluent workers as being *disadvantageous* in comparison, implicitly or explicitly, with the rank-and-file jobs which they currently occupied. In terms of its demands, its content or its financial rewards, the foreman's job was frequently viewed by our respondents in a decidedly unfavourable light. The following comments are illustrative in this respect:

'The foreman has too much responsibility. I don't mind a bit of responsibility but when we do things wrong we only get told off. When things go wrong for the foreman—he's really in trouble. It wouldn't be worth it.'

'I was a foreman in a previous firm and I didn't like it. The reward isn't sufficient. Look at the worry—a foreman's a whipping boy for management *and* workers. A foreman's money is no more than a skilled man's and he takes his worries to bed.'

'I think I could have been a foreman—but I probably get more money anyway. I like to know when I'm coming in and out; I like to be an ordinary worker.'

'Why don't I like the idea of becoming a foreman? The money! Drop a third of your wages just to be known as a foreman? Not likely!'

'I wouldn't become a foreman—not in this firm anyway. All the foreman here is, is a dishrag—pushed around by people who don't know what they are talking about. And financially he's no better off, despite his sick pay and days off.'

On the basis of table 57, we would then suggest that our respondents' tendency to approach their employment in a largely instrumental way is

TABLE 57. *Reasons given for negative attitudes towards idea of becoming a foreman*

Class of reason	Craftsmen (N = 17)	Setters (N = 9)	Process workers (N = 15)	Machinists (N = 26)	Assemblers (N = 43)	All (N = 110)*
	Times mentioned					
A. Reasons relating to undesirability of foreman's job:						
Foreman's job involves too much responsibility, stress, pressure	11	5	7	11	14	48
Prefers content of present job to that of foreman's job	4	3	5	6	4	22
Is better off financially as ordinary workman	2	3	7	0	1	13
TOTALS	17	11	19	17	19	83
B. Reasons relating to respondent's unsuitability:						
Does not have right kind of personality, attitudes for foreman's job	3	3	1	8	9	24
Is too old	0	0	0	0	5	5
Lacks required education, training	0	0	0	1	2	3
TOTALS	3	3	1	9	16	32
C. Reasons relating to social pressures						
Does not want to leave workmates, move into another class	2	0	0	4	4	10
D. Other reasons	1	1	1	3	8	14
ALL REASONS	23	15	21	33	47	139
Reasons in class A as percentage of all reasons	74	73	90	52	40	60
Reasons in class B as percentage of all reasons	13	20	5	27	34	23
Reasons in class C as percentage of all reasons	9	0	0	12	9	7
Reasons in class D as percentage of all reasons	4	7	5	9	17	10
TOTALS	100	100	100	100	100	100

* I.e. men who replied 'Not much' or 'Not at all' to the question on how they would like the idea of becoming a foreman.

yet again in evidence. Where the idea of promotion is not found a particularly attractive one, the main reason for this proves to be that the 'pay-off' from the foreman's job is not felt to match up to the degree of involvement in, and commitment to, the enterprise which such a post requires. In other words, in terms of a 'money for effort' calculation, the foreman's job is not regarded as being worth while.

Moreover, such an interpretation also helps to account for the differences between occupational groups which table 57 reveals. It can be seen that among the assemblers, and to a lesser extent the machinists, the emphasis on the undesirability of a foreman's job is not so pronounced as in other groups, and that a sizable number of men explain their lack of interest in promotion on the grounds, rather, of their personal unsuitability for a supervisory position. These data may be set alongside the further facts that in Vauxhall it was the fixed policy of the firm to pay foremen at a clearly higher level than could be regularly achieved by their subordinates,[1] and that in Skefko some earnings differential usually existed between foremen and the rank-and-file machinists. On the other hand, the range of earnings of Skefko craftsmen and setters appeared to overlap to some appreciable extent with that of foremen, and so too did that of craftsmen and of the higher-paid process workers in Laporte.[2] Thus, in the case of the assemblers and machinists, it may be said that a greater likelihood existed that a supervisory job would be accepted as a 'paying' proposition, even if, for other reasons, it was still not desired.

We may note, incidentally, that the argument here is further supported when we turn to the explanations which were given by those respondents who held positive attitudes towards promotion. Table 58 reveals that the assemblers and machinists among this number, in comparison with those from other groups, tended to place greater stress on the extrinsic rather than on the intrinsic rewards of a foreman's job. More than the other workers in our sample, these men would stand to gain something from promotion in economic terms.

At the same time it must also be recognised that, in all groups apart from the assemblers, at least half of those men who favoured the idea of promotion referred to the *non*-economic attractions of a supervisory position. These respondents, we would suggest, often saw in promotion a way out of

[1] A foreman's basic salary was actually calculated through a formula taking into account the pay of the workers he supervised. At the time of our study, salaries of foremen and general foremen in Vauxhall ranged from around £900 to £1,400 per annum. Moreover, foremen were paid for overtime in the same way as hourly paid workers.

[2] In Skefko foremen were not paid for overtime. In Laporte only overtime amounting to more than eight hours per month was counted, and this could be compensated for, if management wished, by additional holidays rather than by overtime payment.

their present dilemma of having to forfeit direct satisfaction from work in order to obtain a level of earnings appropriate to their out-plant objectives. A foreman's job in their view offered more inherently rewarding work while, at the worst, entailing only a relatively slight loss on the financial side. The following comments were characteristic in this respect:

'I like the idea of becoming a foreman because of the bigger variety of work. I had a couple of stripes in the army. I like responsibility—it swells my head a bit but I like it. The more active my mind and body is, the better I like it.'

'As a foreman, you're a bit further up the industrial ladder. The job has more interest; it's more responsible and secure. I get the feeling I have a lot of latent abilities never called on.'

'I wouldn't be frightened of the job; I'd like to try it. There would be satisfaction in getting a job done—a whole sequence of jobs being put together, not just the one job I do myself which is really only part of a job.'

However, in regard to those men who favoured the idea of promotion, the main question which arises here is, of course, why so few had taken any action towards this end, or had even given the matter their serious consideration. Why, in other words, were such aspirations as existed in this direction so lacking in conviction? In large part, we would suggest, the explanation of this must be given in terms of the assessments which our workers made of their actual promotion opportunities. Our data indicate that although some workers might see a foreman's job as an attractive one, they were for the most part fairly well aware of the barriers they faced in seeking to achieve this position; and that a sizable proportion recognised that, whatever action they pursued, their chances in this respect were somewhat less than hopeful. Thus, to become a foreman was an aspiration which often did not appear to merit thinking about in any serious way.

For example, we asked our respondents: 'If you decided to have a go at this (i.e. promotion), how would you rate your chances of getting to be a foreman? Would you say they were very good, fairly good, not too good, or hopeless?' Table 59 shows for both our affluent workers and our white-collar sample the replies of those men who had previously expressed positive attitudes towards the idea of promotion. It can be seen that not one of the manual workers in question would regard his chances of becoming a foreman as 'very good', and that about as many men rate their chances 'not too good' or 'hopeless' as rate them 'fairly good'. In comparison, of those white-collar workers who were keen on promotion, 13% appear highly optimistic about achieving this promotion and a further 53% moderately so. What this means, then, as can be seen from the last

TABLE 58. *Reasons given for positive attitudes towards idea of becoming a foreman*

Class of reason	Craftsmen (N = 35)	Setters (N = 14)	Process workers (N = 8)	Machinists (N = 14)	Assemblers (N = 42)	All (N = 113)*
	Times mentioned					
A. Reasons relating to extrinsic rewards of foreman's job:						
Foreman's job is a means of 'getting on', 'bettering oneself'†	16	7	1	8	16	48
Foreman's job is better paid	8	0	2	3	12	25
Foreman's job has greater security	8	1	2	3	7	21
TOTALS	32	8	5	14	35	94
B. Reasons relating to intrinsic rewards of foreman's job:						
Would like authority, responsibility	14	5	4	3	8	34
More variety in work	4	1	0	1	4	10
More opportunity for learning new skills	3	1	1	1	1	7
Other	4	3	1	2	6	16
TOTALS	25	10	6	7	19	67
C. Other reasons	1	1	1	2	9	14
All reasons	58	19	12	23	63	175
Reasons in class A as percentage of all reasons	55	42	42	61	56	54
Reasons in class B as percentage of all reasons	43	53	50	30	30	38
Reasons in class C as percentage of all reasons	2	5	8	9	14	8
TOTALS	100	100	100	100	100	100

* i.e. men who replied 'Very much' or 'Quite a lot' to the question on how they would like the idea of becoming a foreman.

† It is possible that in some cases 'intrinsic' considerations were also implicit; e.g. gaining more authority or responsibility in work. But the explicit elaboration of reasons counted here was always in terms of material success.

line of table 59, is that while a clear majority of the white-collar sample both favour the idea of promotion *and* rate their chances as at least 'fairly good', the same is true of only a rather small minority of the men in our manual sample—in fact of something less than a quarter overall.

In the case of those manual workers who rated their chances of promotion

TABLE 59. *Assessment of chances of becoming a foreman by men with positive attitudes towards promotion*

Chances rated as	Craftsmen (N = 35)	Setters (N = 14)*	Process workers (N = 8)	Machinists (N = 14)*	Assemblers (N = 42)	All manual (N = 113)	White-collar (N = 47)
				Percentage			
'Very good'	0	0	0	0	0	0	13
'Fairly good'	43	57	63	7	52	45	53
'Not too good'	29	43	13	21	38	32	30
'Hopeless'	20	0	25	71	7	19	4
Other, D.K.	9	0	0	0	2	4	0
TOTALS	101	100	101	99	99	100	100
Percentage of *all* in group who are positive towards promotion *and* rate chances as 'very good' or 'fairly good'	27	35	22	2	26	22	57

* Since in Skefko the grade of setter is normally intermediate between that of machinist and foreman, the marked differences between these two groups are not surprising. If the two groups are taken together, as might seem reasonable in the case of this table, a pattern of response much closer to that of the other occupational groups is produced: namely, 'fairly good', 32%; 'not too good', 32%; 'hopeless', 36%. The corresponding figure in the last line of the table would be 14%.

as 'not too good' or 'hopeless', we also asked: 'What, then, do you think would stop you becoming a foreman?' Table 60 classifies the reasons that were given both by those of our respondents who were positive towards the idea of promotion and by those who were not. As might be expected, the reasons are quite varied: some imply that the perceived barriers to promotion might not be permanent; others that the respondent is perhaps unfairly discriminated against. But, as can be seen, three types of reason were advanced a good deal more frequently than any other: those relating to the respondent's lack of education etc., to the fact that the respondent was 'not known' in his firm, and to the fact that openings for promotion did not exist. Among all groups except the setters, who had of course already experienced some promotion, such reasons accounted for around 60% of all reasons given. The following comments are illustrative of the views in question:

'What would stop me becoming a foreman? Lack of education. You need knowledge and schooling these days—for example, in subjects like maths. There's more opportunity for this now than there was in my time.'

TABLE 60. *Reasons given for negative assessment of chances of becoming a foreman*

Class of reason	Craftsmen (N = 33)	Setters (N = 13)	Process workers (N = 10)	Machinists (N = 39)	Assemblers (N = 50)	All (N = 145)
			Times mentioned			
Lack of education, training, opportunity to learn new skills	5	2	4	23	16	50
Is not known in firm, does not know any managers	11	2	0	2	15	30
No openings for promotion exist	7	4	3	8	3	25
Is too young	3	5	0	7	1	16
Is too old	1	1	0	3	10	15
Does not have right kind of personality	1	3	1	6	4	15
Is too good a worker to be taken off present job	3	0	1	0	4	8
Has poor record, reputation with management	4	0	0	1	2	7
Other reasons	5	1	2	3	4	15
ALL REASONS	40	18	11	53	59	181

'The trend today—and rightly so—is to use trained engineers as foremen. They know the theoretical as well as the practical side.'

'I look around me and I see blokes who've been doing the same job for twenty or thirty years, and who are still in the same place. Why should they pick me? Unless you are known, you don't stand a chance.'

'Opportunities for promotion don't arise very often—perhaps not for ten years at a time in this shop. And in any case the trend now is to get someone from outside—someone with technical knowledge.'

What is chiefly significant about such reasons for pessimism over promotion chances is that, for the most part, they are highly realistic ones. For example, very many of our affluent workers *were* lacking in qualifications for promotion. The large majority had left school at the minimum age and relatively few, apart from the craftsmen, had subsequently received any appreciable amount of industrial training.[1] Then again, although all three

[1] The proportion having left full-time education at 14 or under, or at 15 since this became the minimum age, was 85%. 15% of the sample had some experience of further part-time education of a vocational character.

firms from which our sample came operated schemes of 'promotion from within', for a worker to be taken up as a candidate for promotion still involved 'catching the eye' of a superior;[1] and in a large-scale enterprise this is almost inevitably a fortuitous matter to some extent. Finally, there can be no doubt at all about the limited opportunities for promotion. In Laporte, the ratio of rank-and-file production workers to foremen ranged from 1:20 to 1:60; in the Vauxhall assembly departments the range was from 1:30 to 1:55; and in the Skefko machine shops the ratio was in no case lower than 1:120.[2]

In general, then, we may conclude that the attitudes of our affluent workers towards promotion must be understood in relation both to their characteristic orientation towards their employment and to their objective chances of advancement. A foreman's job might be regarded as offering insufficient compensation for the demands that it makes in the form of involvement and commitment; alternatively, it might be seen as providing an opportunity for work which affords a relatively high level of both intrinsic and extrinsic rewards. But the point to be stressed is that, in either case, the way in which the possibility of promotion is viewed derives from an orientation to work in which a calculative element is highly developed. Promotion is not almost automatically accepted as desirable, as with white-collar employees for whom a career is a moral expectation; nor is it widely rejected out of group or class solidarity, as with some more traditional industrial workers. It is, rather, critically assessed in terms of its costs and rewards in relation to the individual's present work situation. And thus, as our data show, some degree of diversity exists in the detailed positions which are taken up as the outcome of this highly circumspect approach. At the same time, though, even in those cases where promotion is regarded as desirable, it is likely that it will not be treated as a very serious prospect; and primarily so, it would seem, because, for the

[1] In Vauxhall, any worker could apply to be considered for a supervisory position and need not be sponsored by a foreman or manager; but in the case of candidates who were actually called before the selection panel, performance reports were obtained from both their foremen and their area managers. In Skefko, men could not apply to become foremen. Supervisory vacancies were filled by senior managers for whom the main sources of information and advice were existing foremen. Moreover, men chosen to become foremen were, in most cases, already chargehands, and chargehands were nominated directly by their foremen. In Laporte, vacant supervisory posts were normally advertised and the selection was then made by a three-man interviewing board. This always included the departmental head or manager under whom the supervisor would work.

[2] In Vauxhall, there also existed the position of 'group leader' and in Skefko that of 'chargehand' between the rank-and-file and the foremen. But neither group leaders nor chargehands were expected to fulfil supervisory functions and this was clearly reflected in their conditions of service. Moreover, group leaders, unlike chargehands, were not necessarily regarded as being supervisory 'material'.

majority of the men in question, it cannot be reckoned as an ambition which carries any reasonable possibility of being eventually achieved.[1]

As an alternative to promotion within the firm, one other conceivable 'way ahead' for the industrial worker is to abandon his role as a wage-earner and seek to establish himself in business on his own account. This, of course, was the mode of economic and social ascent classically pre-scribed for ambitious members of the industrial labour force by the ideologues of capitalist society in its 'heroic', nineteenth-century phase. However, in the context of modern, 'post-capitalist' society it has appeared generally more appropriate to emphasise the opportunities offered by other channels of upward mobility. Consequently, the doctrine of self-help in the form of independent business enterprise is today clearly neither preached nor accepted with the conviction of earlier times. Rather, the idea has grown up that this doctrine survives, in any significant form, only in the 'American Dream', which in some way manages to retain its power in spite of the realities of contemporary economic and social structure.[2] At the same time, the fact remains that attempts by individuals to 'set up on their own' are still being made in all advanced societies in relatively large numbers, and the extent to which such a possibility appears as an attractive one to our affluent workers is thus a matter of some interest.

After raising the issue of promotion with our respondents, we then went on to put the following question: 'Another way a man might improve his position (i.e. other than by promotion) is by starting up in business on his own. Have you ever thought of doing this?' In the case of those men who said that they had, we also asked if they had taken the matter any further and, if so, how. Table 61 presents the results we achieved.

On the basis of these data, it could in fact be argued that, among the workers we studied, interest in having their own business ran at a relaitvely high level. As can be seen, only among the setters had more than a third of our respondents never thought about the idea at all; while on the other hand, in all groups other than the setters, between a third and a half had either considered the matter seriously or had actually made the attempt.[3]

---

[1] This may, of course, have been also a factor in inducing some men to say that promotion was not desirable; i.e. to 'rationalise' in this way their probable inability to achieve promotion. But it is important to make clear—as we have tried to do—that for many of our affluent workers quite 'rational' grounds *did* exist for not regarding a foreman's job as being a particularly attractive proposition.

[2] See Ely Chinoy, *Automobile Workers and the American Dream* (New York, 1955).

[3] The main types of business which had been either considered or attempted were the follow-ing: small shop (most often grocery and general, or newsagent and tobacconist); public house; boarding-house; cafe; motor repairs; small farm. The variety was, however, considerable.

TABLE 61. *Attitudes and action taken on possibility of starting own business*

	Craftsmen (N = 56)	Setters (N = 23)	Process workers (N = 23)	Machinists (N = 41)	Assemblers (N = 86)	All manual (N = 229)	White-collar (N = 54)
				Percentage			
Have never thought of this	21	48	26	17	29	27	44
Have thought of this but not seriously	45	30	26	39	35	37	37
Have thought seriously of this*	27	13	22	24	27	25	15
Have tried to run own business in past, or are trying now part-time†	7	9	26	19	9	12	4
TOTALS	100	100	100	99	100	101	100

* I.e. have made definite plans, have started saving, have investigated specific possibilities, have
tried to assess chances of success etc.
† In total, there were 21 men in the former category and 7 in the latter.

Thus, it could at all events be said that starting up their own businesses was an idea with somewhat more appeal for our affluent workers than that of gaining promotion: as will be remembered, only 17% of the sample proved both to favour the idea of promotion and to have treated this as a serious possibility. Moreover, it is also worth noting that among the men in our sample the level of interest in going into business on their own account appeared to be at least as high as that reported by Chinoy in his study of American workers—despite the greater normative pressures to hold such an ambition to which the latter are supposedly subjected.[1] Finally, it may be further observed that while in the matter of promotion the men in our white-collar sample were clearly more ambitious than our manual workers, the reverse is true as regards the prospect of becoming self-employed. The venture of starting one's own business, one may suggest, is, in principle at least, generally more attractive to men who either do not want promotion or who believe they have little chance of this than to men who see in promotion their 'natural' way of 'getting on'.

From the point of view of our affluent workers, the specific appeals of

[1] Chinoy reports that of his 62 respondents 37 (60%) said that they were interested in having
their own businesses, but that, of these men, 25 did not really expect to leave their present
employment. Thus, in all, only 12 men (19%) could be regarded as pursuing the idea of self-
employment in a serious way. Moreover, none of Chinoy's respondents was currently running
a business in his spare time (*Automobile Workers and the American Dream*, ch. VII).

becoming self-employed are not difficult to appreciate. We did not ask a question directly on this matter but most of the men concerned made some spontaneous comment. From these remarks, it was fairly clear that, as with those men who favoured the idea of promotion, what was most frequently sought was a form of work which would offer a relatively high level of *both* economic *and* inherent rewards; and in the latter respect the main attraction in having one's own business was, of course, that of being independent and autonomous—of 'working for yourself' and of 'being your own boss'. Once more, then, the particular nature of our workers' aspirations is most clearly perceived against the background of their current work experience and of the orientation towards work which has led the majority into their present employment. The following comments captured the spirit of many others:

'If you have your own business, you work for yourself; you get the profits and you're your own boss. It's all a matter of money. Anyone with money and sense would work for themselves.'

'I should like to engage in some business where I wouldn't be limited. I don't know what that would be—catering or a boarding-house perhaps, or I fancy myself as a publican. But I'd like something where I could make my own way.'

'I've been thinking about it for over a year. There's an opening for me making sports trophies for my father's firm, but I need the capital to buy machinery. If I could get this, I'd be alright. There's a lot of money in it and it's interesting work—craftsmanship you could say.'

However, while the degree of interest shown by our respondents in having their own business is of some significance, the crucial question for present purposes still remains open: that of the extent to which their aspirations and hopes in this respect were strong enough to lead them to the decisive step of actually trying to establish themselves as 'independents'. We know that a few men had already attempted this (and had given up) and that a still smaller number were making a start on a part-time basis. But what of the remainder—how likely were these men to throw up their jobs and seek to turn their 'dream' into reality? In general, the evidence we have would suggest that, for the majority, the probability of this happening was not high; that, in other words, most aspirations for self-employment—as for promotion—were held with no great expectation that they would one day be fulfilled.

In the first place, we may reaffirm the point made in chapter 2 that, for the most part, the men in our sample appeared to be fairly firmly attached to their present jobs. As was noted, only in one occupational group—the craftsmen—had more than half ever thought of leaving, and, again with the exception of the craftsmen, only 20–30% had ever gone as far as to investigate alternative employment opportunities. Moreover, of the 108 men who said that they had at some time considered leaving, only seven (6%) gave as a reason for this the possibility of starting up in business on their own (table 11). And conversely, we also find that those men who later in the interview said that they had seriously thought of becoming self-employed were not significantly more likely to have considered leaving than were the remainder of the sample.

Secondly, we had some further check on the degree of realism in aspirations for self-employment through a question included in our 'home' interviews. We asked husband and wife if they had ever discussed together the possibility of trying to set up their own business. Comparing the replies we received with those given by the husbands in the 'work' interviews, it turned out that of the men who said they had thought about having their own business, though not seriously, two thirds (66%) had apparently never bothered to talk this over with their wives, and that the same was also true of over one third (37%) of the men who claimed to have gone into the possibilities in a serious way.[1] What then is implied here is that, taking the sample as a whole, less than 1 man in 6 claimed both to have considered self-employment seriously and to have raised the matter within his family.

Finally, our data also indicate that just as our affluent workers were fairly clear-sighted about the barriers to gaining promotion, so too were they well aware of the difficulties which confronted the aspiring entrepreneur. In the case of those men who said that they had thought about trying to start their own business but had not taken any further steps, we asked why this was and what was holding them back. Table 62 classifies the replies that were made. From this it is evident that there was widespread appreciation among the men in question of the objective economic problems which they faced—most notably, that of raising the required capital. As can be seen, this difficulty was referred to far more frequently than any other. Moreover, though, it may be noted that table 62 also suggests that, for a number of men, yet further hesitancy about self-employment resulted from the doubts which they had (or which had been brought home to them) on the wisdom of putting in hazard their present, not unfavourable, economic position; the position that in most cases they had built up through having secured employment which afforded them higher

[1] I.e. 50 men out of 76, and 21 out of 57 respectively. Data were not available for nine men in the former category and six in the latter. In both categories, a further eight men (11% and 14% respectively) stated that they had *deliberately* not discussed the idea of self-employment with their wives because this was nothing to do with them.

TABLE 62. *Reasons given for not going ahead with idea of own business*

Class of reason	Craftsmen (N = 28)	Setters (N = 9)	Process workers (N = 12)	Machinists (N = 22)	Assemblers (N = 36)	All (N = 107)*
Lack of capital	16	3	5	16	26	66
Risk involved for family, present standard of living	9	3	2	10	2	26
Lack of openings, too much competition	6	1	1	1	2	11
Opposition from family	1	0	1	0	4	6
Other reasons	4	2	1	2	7	16
TOTALS	36	9	10	29	41	125

* Includes men who had previously had their own business; these men were asked why they had given up.

earnings than would most other kinds of work available to them. In other words, it was far from being the case that our affluent workers had 'nothing to lose' through a venture into self-employment. Thus, the question arose for them not simply of whether it was possible to get a business started off, but also of whether the resources they could command were sufficient to make the risks of eventual failure ones worth taking. And given the fact that many of these men had already made considerable sacrifices in attaining their existing standard of living—particularly through enduring inherently unrewarding and stressful jobs—a reluctance to jeopardise their achievements is all the more readily understood.[1]

Although, then, the idea of having their own businesses was attractive to a large proportion of the workers we studied—clearly more than were attracted by the idea of promotion—there would appear in the end to be no great difference in the numbers who actually pursued these two goals with any real sense of purpose. In both cases, it turns out that only a quite small minority of our respondents could be said to have aspirations of a serious kind. With the remainder, promotion and self-employment alike had apparently been little considered beyond the level of mere reflection; or, at all events, aspirations in these directions had not given rise to positive action—had not been transformed into 'projects'. Basically, we would suggest, these 'ways ahead' were seen by our respondents as being ones

[1] It is also worth noting that since the domestic standard of living of most of our respondents was to some extent based upon credit, in the form of mortgage or hire-purchase arrangements, an incursion into self-employment would probably have had immediate negative consequences through lowering their 'credit rating'.

primarily for *other* people: for those with education and 'qualifications' who could look forward to a genuine career within their employing organisations, or for those with the financial backing to give a business venture a fair chance of success. They were not regarded as offering generally realistic opportunities for rank-and-file wage-workers. And from their own position as *affluent* workers, our respondents had often less motivation than others to struggle in such ways against the odds which would have faced them.

If, then, the workers we studied did not for the most part have serious aspirations either for promotion or for self-employment, in what form did the forward-looking attitudes to which we earlier referred actually appear? How *was* the possibility of material advancement envisaged?

At the very end of our 'home' interviews, we asked our respondents the following, deliberately general question: 'Looking ten years ahead, what improvement in your way of life would you most hope for?' The answers we received are given in table 63, and show a quite similar pattern in all occupational groups. From group to group it can be seen that clearly the most widespread kinds of aspiration held by our affluent workers were those which related to increased consumer capacity and to higher standards of domestic living. And most important of all, it would appear, was the simple aspiration to have more money to spend and more goods and possessions. In all groups, around 3 men out of 5 saw this as their major objective for the years ahead. By comparison, aspirations relating to individuals' working lives were far less prominent, and the conclusions of earlier sections of this chapter were strongly confirmed by the fact that in no group did more than a very small minority place their hopes for the future in job advancement[1] or in starting their own business. Next in importance to aspirations for higher levels of consumption were aspirations for children and aspirations which, in one way or another, reflected a desire for a less taxing, more pleasurable existence; that is to say, aspirations which suggested the respondent's own abandonment of striving for 'success' in any individualistic sense.

In the light of these data, it would then appear that with the majority of the workers we studied the pattern of their hopes for the future implied a process of advancement in the sphere of consumption, but one unaccompanied by any change in their present status in the sphere of production.

[1] Moreover, what was hoped for in this respect was not always promotion but in some cases a move to another shop-floor job which would give greater intrinsic rewards without entailing any reduction in level of pay.

TABLE 63. *Improvement in way of life most hoped for in next ten years*

Class of aspiration	Craftsmen (N = 56)	Setters (N = 23)	Process workers (N = 23)	Machinists (N = 41)	Assemblers (N = 86)	All (N = 229)
			Times mentioned			
A. Aspirations relating to consumer power, domestic standard of living:						
To have more money to spend, more goods and possessions	36	14	13	24	50	137
To buy own house	16	4	5	11	17	53
To have better, larger house	7	2	4	1	12	26
TOTALS	59	20	22	36	79	216
B. Aspirations relating to work:						
To have more secure employment	7	1	2	3	5	18
To have better job (other than one simply providing more money)	7	1	0	0	6	14
To have own business	3	2	0	3	5	13
TOTALS	17	4	2	6	16	45
C. Other aspirations:						
To see children getting good job, education	4	6	3	10	9	32
To have easier, more relaxed, comfortable or happier life	5	6	3	6	12	32
To have more leisure time, activities	10	0	3	6	11	30
Miscellaneous	8	6	5	9	21	49
TOTALS	27	18	14	31	53	143
ALL ASPIRATIONS	103	42	38	73	148	404
Aspirations in class A as percentage of all aspirations	57	48	58	49	53	54
Aspirations in class B as percentage of all aspirations	17	10	5	8	11	11
Aspirations in class C as percentage of all aspirations	26	43	37	42	36	35
TOTALS	100	101	100	99	100	100

The advancement they looked to, it must thus be supposed, was one of a primarily *collective* kind; one which would result from general increases in the level of economic rewards accruing to all who occupied a similar position and role to their own within the social division of labour. In other words, the hopes of our respondents for the future were ones which were not related to their chances of individual ascent but, rather, ones that they would realise along with their fellow workers or not at all.[1]

However, in further contrast to aspirations for promotion or self-employment, aspirations for a rising level of consumption did appear to be quite widely regarded as realistic ones. Indeed, in this respect, aspiration tended in many cases to merge into expectation. Moreover, one important source of this optimism was not difficult to appreciate. For the most part, the workers in question were conscious of having achieved improvements in their living standards in the recent past, and were thus inclined to believe that such improvements could, in some degree or other, be maintained in the future. Further of our data enable us to indicate the prevalence of this frame of mind.

For example, in the course of the 'work' interviews, we asked our respondents: 'How much would you say your standard of living had risen over the last ten years? Would you say it had risen a great deal, quite a lot, not very much, or not at all?' We then followed this up by asking further: 'How about the next five years? Would you expect things to be better, about the same, or worse?' Results produced by these two questions are given in tables 64 and 65. From the former table it can be seen that in all occupational groups a clear majority of our respondents believed that in course of the past decade their standard of living had risen substantially; and that, overall, only around one in ten felt that they had not gained in any way.[2] From the latter table, in which data from the two questions are cross-classified, the relationship between appreciation of past gains and

---

[1] Cf. Chinoy, *Automobile Workers and the American Dream*, ch. x. It should be made clear that by 'fellow workers' we do not imply the whole of the manual labour force. As our respondents generally recognised, through holding the jobs they did they were in a relatively advantageous position compared with the majority of other industrial workers. They had, in effect, benefited from individual initiative insofar as this had resulted in their securing such employment.

When a similar question about hopes for the future was put to our white-collar sample, the pattern of response produced was not greatly different from that of the manual sample. The form of the question may possibly have encouraged answers in terms of consumption rather than of work, and it followed on a number of questions dealing with respondents' earnings and possessions. However, from other data we do, of course, know that most white-collar workers did hold serious aspirations for promotion, while most manual workers did not.

[2] The fact that the process workers had the highest proportion of men in this category—and the lowest proportion feeling that their living standards had risen 'a great deal'—corroborates the argument advanced in chapter 4 (pp. 88–9) to account for the relatively high degree of anti-employer sentiment within this group.

TABLE 64. *Assessment of rise in standard of living over last ten years*

Standard of living rose	Craftsmen (N = 56)	Setters (N = 23)	Process workers (N = 23)	Machinists (N = 41)	Assemblers (N = 86)	All (N = 229)
	Percentage					
'A great deal'	21	26	13	24	17	20
'Quite a lot'	34	44	44	39	47	42
'Not very much'	30	26	22	24	23	25
'Not at all'	14	0	22	10	11	11
Other, D.K.	0	4	0	2	2	2
TOTALS	99	100	101	99	100	100

optimism about the future becomes evident. Of those who reported that their standard of living had gone up 'a good deal' or 'quite a lot' in the past ten years, in the region of 80% or more in each occupational group expected things to be 'about the same' in the next five years—that is, that the rise in their living standards would continue; or that things would become even better—that is, that living standards would rise still more rapidly.[1] On the other hand, of those who believed that their standard of living had risen 'not very much' or 'not at all', on average only around a third expected some improvement in the future as against some 60% who expected no change or took a yet more pessimistic view.

In other words, a marked propensity existed among our respondents to extrapolate their experience of the relatively recent past into the years ahead. And since, in the majority of cases, this experience was favourable, it is not surprising that the view taken of the economic future—in terms, at least, of living standards—should for the most part be favourable too.

At the same time it should also be noted from table 65 that it was more likely that men who felt they had gained little or nothing in the past ten

[1] It must be admitted that some possibility of ambiguity arose in the answers men gave on their expectations for the future in that these might not always have been intended to be understood in relation to the answer given on the experience of the past; e.g., men who reported that their standard of living had risen substantially in the past and who then said they expected things to be 'about the same' in the next five years might have wished to imply that they did not expect that living standards would rise at all in this period, rather than that the previous upward trend would be maintained. However, interviewers quickly became aware of this difficulty and endeavoured to ensure that respondents did give an answer to the second question which was to be understood in conjunction with their answer to the first. A useful check that this had been achieved was provided through the answers to the next question, on why the respondent saw the future in the way he did (see below, pp. 141–2).

TABLE 65. *Assessment of rise in standard of living over last ten years and expectations for next five years*

Rise in last ten years	Expectations for next five years	Craftsmen (N = 56)	Setters (N = 22)	Process workers (N = 23)	Machinists (N = 40)	Assemblers (N = 84)	All (N = 225)*
Number saying 'a great deal' or 'quite a lot'		31	16	13	26	55	141
	Percentage saying 'better'	42	25	54	50	46	44
	Percentage saying 'about the same'	42	69	46	38	32	41
	Percentage saying 'worse'	16	6	0	0	9	8
	Percentage uncertain	0	0	0	12	13	7
	TOTALS	100	100	100	100	100	100
Number saying 'not very much' or 'not at all'		25	6	10	14	29	84
	Percentage saying 'better'	32	67	40	29	31	35
	Percentage saying 'about the same'	52	33	20	64	48	48
	Percentage saying 'worse'	8	0	30	7	10	11
	Percentage uncertain	8	0	10	0	11	7
	TOTALS	100	100	100	100	100	101
Percentage of 'optimists'† in each group		61	83	74	66	61	65

* The four men who were classed as 'Other, D.K.' in table 64 are omitted from this table.
† I.e. men reporting that their standard of living rose 'a great deal', or 'quite a lot' in the last ten years and expecting things to be 'better' or 'about the same'; or men reporting that their standard of living rose 'not very much' or 'not at all' but who were expecting things to be 'better'.

years would, even so, be optimistic about the future than it was that men who felt their living standards had risen substantially would be pessimistic. This suggests, therefore, that the 'optimists' were not influenced by their past experience alone, and that some other grounds existed for their expectation of 'good times' ahead. After our respondents had answered the two questions on which tables 64 and 65 are based, we asked each man why he viewed the future in the way he did. Table 66 classifies the

TABLE 66. *Reasons given by 'optimists' for their views of the economic future*

	Craftsmen (N = 34)	Setters (N = 19)	Process workers (N = 17)	Machinists (N = 27)	Assemblers (N = 52)	All (N = 149)
			Times mentioned			
General economic progress will continue, is inevitable	13	7	4	9	18	51
Own industry or firm will continue to advance because of competitive position, technical innovation, efficient management etc.	5	4	2	2	7	20
Some present types of expenditure will end; e.g. mortgage will be paid off, children will leave school etc.	5	1	2	6	5	19
Beneficial effects likely from joining Common Market	1	1	0	2	8	12
Beneficial effects likely from a change of Government, from having Labour in power	3	0	2	3	1	9
Expects to better own position through upgrading, promotion or starting own business	2	1	0	1	5	9
Other reasons	5	3	2	1	6	17
ALL REASONS	34	17	12	24	50	137
No clear reason given, D.K.	1	2	5	3	2	13

replies which were offered by the 'optimists'; that is, by those men—some two-thirds of the total sample—who had reported that their standard of living had risen 'a good deal' or 'quite a lot' in the past and who expected things to be 'better' or 'about the same'; or who had reported that their standards of living had risen 'not very much' or 'not at all' but who expected things to be 'better' nonetheless. These data help one to gain a somewhat fuller understanding of the basis on which our respondents' hopes for the future were founded.

From table 66, it is in fact evident that quite a wide variety of considerations influenced the way in which our respondents assessed their prospects for the years ahead, including, it may be noted, political as well as directly economic ones. The relevance of different phases of consumption associated with the life-cycle is also indicated, and for some of the workers in the sample the expectation of declining commitments was apparently of greater weight than that of increased income. However, it is equally clear from the data of table 66 that still the most important factor giving cause for optimism was that simply of a belief in the continuing nature of economic progress—either of a general kind or, at any rate, in the case of those industries or firms in which our respondents were themselves engaged. In all groups, as can be seen, reasons reflecting such a belief were offered much more frequently than were any others. The outlook in question is well illustrated by the following extracts from our interview schedules:

'Why do I think things will be better? Well, I'm considering the last ten years. Things have steadily progressed and there's no reason to say that they won't still. Things have been getting steadily better—and surely this won't stop. It would be strange if it did.'

'Things will keep on improving. We're moving with the times—not moving back. It will affect everybody in every walk of life. In a few years there will be no slum areas; unemployment in the North will improve. We've *got* to move with the times: if we don't, somebody will move us.'

'We're improving all the time. This must continue. We can't think of going back. People wouldn't stand for it.'

'Luton was once a small town: now they improve everywhere, always. There was a little college—now that's big. There's a new library to help everyone and improve facilities. In a few years we will have new roads and other things for the people. This is a boom town.'

'Things must get better. We seem to be on an upward trend. The prospects look brighter all round—even the world situation looks brighter. Things will *have* to improve—that's evolution!'

Our conclusion must then be that the attainment of progressively higher standards of domestic living represents the typical 'project' among the workers we studied. For these men and their families, we would suggest, there are no longer well-established patterns of consumption with which they are content to conform, but rather they are aware of a wide range of possibilities out of which many different life-styles may be created. The recognition of such possibilities generates the desire for ever-increasing consumer power. At the same time, though, it is not typically part of their designs for the future that they should secure this rising consumer power through individual advancement in their occupational lives: as we have seen, the aspirations which existed among our affluent workers for promotion or for self-employment were not in most cases being actively pursued. To a large extent, this may be regarded as the result of a realistic assessment of the very limited chances of success. For certainly, both promotion and self-employment did have some strong attraction for a number of men, notably as a possible means of escaping from a situation in which they were able to gain high level economic rewards from their work only at the cost of sacrificing more direct satisfactions. But in some part also, it would seem, this lack of commitment to occupational ambition arose from the fact that, *given* the present economic position of our affluent workers, neither promotion nor self-employment appeared as an objective which it was now worth while for them to aim at. Looked at in the highly calculative way which is characteristic of our respondents' orientation to economic life in general, it was sometimes the case that these 'ways ahead' could not in fact be accepted as offering any clear or certain advantage.

However, whether through the operation of constraint or of choice, the outcome remains that only a small minority of our affluent workers seriously envisaged any change in their present role as rank-and-file employees. For the large majority, their hopes for the future were pinned rather on gaining an increasing amount of income, as rank-and-file workers, in consequence of more or less general improvements in wages and conditions of service. As individuals, the most they could do to further their interests was thus to seek to retain their present jobs, or to obtain still better-paying ones if opportunity occurred. But for the most part, as it seems our respondents well recognised, the shaping of their economic future was not in their own hands. It would be determined basically by the economic fortunes of the country in general and of their own industries and firms in particular; and in some measure also—though this point was not much stressed—by the success of their unions at the different levels of collective bargaining. The general optimism about their future which our respondents revealed reflects, therefore, as was shown, not so much a belief in their own individual capacities to 'make good' as, rather, a belief in the probability or inevitability of uninterrupted economic advance along a broad front.

In their view of the future, then, as in the present, work remains for most of the men in our sample an area of their lives in which they expect little opportunity for self-realisation in any form. It remains, rather, primarily a means to the achievement of ends which lie outside of itself. It is essentially through work that these men seek to realise their projects: yet their working lives do not figure significantly in these projects. Their existence outside of work represents for our affluent workers the realm of at least relative freedom; as consumers, as home-makers, they can exercise some autonomy and creativity in shaping the pattern of their lives. But the price of this is that work itself must be accepted as the realm of necessity.

7. Orientation to work and its social correlates

In the foregoing chapters our major aim has been to indicate a certain homogeneity in our sample of affluent workers in terms of their orientation to work and associated attitudes and behaviour in the work situation. Variations in these respects have been observed from one occupational group to another. But, we have argued, these can best be understood as variations on, or sometimes as deviations from, a central tendency: that of regarding work in a predominantly instrumental way. This instrumental orientation, we have tried to show, is one which, to some significant degree, extends across occupational divisions reflecting differences in skill and status and which would appear to override perhaps yet more decisively the possible effects upon industrial attitudes and behaviour of differing production technologies. Most notably, among the semi-skilled men in our sample—the process workers, the machinists and the assemblers—no attitudinal or behavioural patterns are in evidence that can be systematically related to the contrasting technological environments in which these men perform their daily work.

In this penultimate chapter, our main purpose will be to consider the *sources* of the instrumental view of their employment which our affluent workers most typically adopt. But, first, it will be useful if we set out in summary form some of the findings presented earlier which are of greatest relevance in characterising the orientation in question. The following may be regarded as an adequate list.

(i)   There is no evidence that within our sample any association exists between job satisfaction (or deprivation) in terms of workers' immediate shop-floor experience and their attachment to their present employment. This attachment appears rather to be based upon predominantly extrinsic —that is to say, economic—considerations. The level of pay was the reason by far most frequently given by respondents for staying in their present work, being referred to by 65% of the more skilled men and 67% of the semi-skilled. Moreover, 87% of the former group and 82% of the latter explained their attachment in part at least by reference to economic considerations of one kind or another—level of pay, degree of security, or extent of 'fringe' benefits. In contrast to this, liking the nature of the work they performed was given as a reason by only 29% of the craftsmen and setters and by only 14% of the process workers, machinists and assemblers. At the same time, there is no evidence to indicate that the entry of the workers we studied into their present employment was the result of constraint rather than of choice. Of the men in semi-skilled jobs, for example, only 27% had never previously had a job at a higher skill or status level.

(ii) Only a small number of the workers in our sample appeared to be members of solidary work groups. In some cases, though not in all, this could be related to technological conditions; but, quite apart from this, there was no indication that the majority of our respondents were greatly concerned to maintain close relationships with their workmates, either within or outside the workplace: 76% of the more skilled men and 66% of the semi-skilled said that they would be 'not much bothered' or 'not bothered at all' if moved to another job away from their present mates; and while 40% of the former reported having a workmate friend or friends with whom they would arrange to meet for social activities outside of work, this was true of only 20% of the latter group.

(iii) For the most part, the workers we studied were reasonably satisfied with their firms as employers. Overall, only 6% rated their firm as being 'worse than most' as a firm to work for. Associated with this, a majority of the men in all occupational groups except one, and overall 64% of the sample, believed that few firms could give them comparable employment advantages to the ones—largely economic—which kept them in their present jobs. At the same time, though, it was also evident that, in the main, these workers saw their relationship with their firms as an almost exclusively contractual one, founded upon a bargain of money for effort. And again in all groups except one, a clear majority believed that their firm could afford to pay them more without damaging its prospects for the future. Moreover, consistently with their conception of the enterprise as an essentially economic association, relatively few men participated actively in work-based clubs and societies: only 23% of the craftsmen and setters and only 8% of the semi-skilled workers attended as often as twice a month.

(iv) The large majority of our affluent workers (87%) were union members, but between a third and two-thirds in each occupational group had become unionists only in the course of their present employment. Overall, only 20% gave any indication that they had first joined a union, in part at least, as a matter of principle or duty. Participation in union affairs at shop level was apparently quite extensive but the unionism of the workplace was seen as something largely separate from the 'official' union activity of the branch, and participation at branch level was, in the main, extremely low. While 22% of the craftsmen reported attending branch meetings regularly' and 25% 'occasionally', for the men in the other occupational groups the figures were 2% and 10% respectively. Furthermore, the functions of trade unionism tended to be conceived of in a generally restricted way; that is, as being limited to issues arising directly out of the employment contract: 61% of the craftsmen but only 33% of the rest of the sample thought that it should be one of the objectives of unions to get workers a say in management. And so far as political action was concerned, only among the craftsmen did a majority support the alliance with the Labour Party and knowingly pay the political levy.

(v) Finally, in regard to their economic future, the majority of the workers in our sample appeared to concentrate their aspirations on securing a continuing improvement in their standard of domestic living rather than on advancement of any kind in their occupational lives. In other words, their hopes were pinned on the likelihood of rising consumer power resulting from general increases in wage levels rather than from changes in their individual roles within the sphere of production. Only 29% of the craftsmen and setters and 19% of the semi-skilled men were both attracted to the idea of promotion and believed that their chances of this were relatively favourable; and taking the sample as a whole, only 8% liked the idea of promotion *and* had taken some positive action to this end. Similarly, so far as the possibility of self-employment was concerned, while 25% of the sample said that they had considered this seriously (apart from the further 12% who had at some time made the venture) only 3% reported that they were thinking, or had thought, of leaving their present employment specifically in order to start up in business on their own. Predominantly for these men, work remained for the future, as well as for the present, a necessary means to extrinsic ends rather than an area of social life which offered possibilities of achievement in itself.

In what ways, then, is this orientation to work and its associated syndrome of attitudes and behaviour socially generated and sustained? What accounts for the fact that in the light of the comparative data we have been able to assemble, our affluent workers reveal such a markedly instrumental approach to their work-tasks, their work associates and their work organisations? Answers to questions of this kind are, in any circumstances, hard to establish; and, moreover, it is at this juncture that the difficulties which stem from our study being a more or less unforeseen by-product of a larger investigation become particularly acute. In a number of respects we lack what would be the most useful and relevant material. Thus, our treatment of the problem we have posed will of necessity be a tentative and in no way conclusive one. Nevertheless, it remains possible for us to advance some hypotheses which, in our view, make theoretical sense, and also in some cases to produce a certain amount of supporting evidence.

At an earlier point in this monograph, we advanced the view that regardless of their affluent condition, the men in our sample were still wage-workers, engaged in selling their labour power in a market situation, and that consequently they were to some significant degree constrained to regard their work in an instrumental way—more so, say, than bureaucratic employees in whose relationship with their employing organisations important moral as well as economic elements are recognised. At the same time, though, we also suggested that the workers we studied were particularly motivated to increase their economic returns from work—and thus their power as consumers—even if this entailed the sacrifice or devaluing of more immediate satisfactions of an expressive and affective kind. We have now shown at some length that such a pattern of motivation is in fact in evidence; that in a variety of ways the attitudes and behaviour of our affluent workers contrast clearly enough with those of workers with a more solidaristic orientation. Thus, put in more specific terms, our problem is that of characterising the social context within which the motivation in question is created.

The first factor which must be taken into account here is one which was 'built in' to the initial design of our study; that is, the position of our respondents in the life-cycle. As we have described, our sample was limited to men who were between the ages of 21 and 46 and who were married. Not surprisingly, thus, as can be seen from table 2, the large majority (83%) had one or more dependent children. Men who are in this position, we would suggest, are, *ceteris paribus*, more likely than men at either an earlier or a later stage in the life-cycle to take up an instrumental orientation towards their work.

To begin with, the financial demands and responsibilities falling upon the worker will generally increase, if not with marriage, then certainly with the coming of children. Apart from children causing additional expense, the entry of the wife into the period of active motherhood will limit her opportunities for contributing to the family income. Studies of teenage workers have indicated that in their case a concern with relatively high wages tends not to be an overriding one in determining job choice or, more realistically, job attachment: considerations relating to the nature of work-tasks, working conditions, workmates and superiors are generally of at least comparable importance.[1] But once the economic obligations associated with the roles of husband and father are assumed, then the motivation to give higher priority to extrinsic, economic returns is likely to increase, and a different pattern of wants and expectations in regard to work may be expected to develop.[2] As is indicated by comments previously recorded, some incidental evidence did emerge from our interviews of men having taken their present jobs, in place of lower-paying but intrinsically more rewarding ones, chiefly as a result of feelings of family responsibility or of wifely pressure.[3] And while no exact statistical treatment is possible, a rough estimate from our data suggests that most of the workers in the sample who expressly preferred some previous job to their present one (55% overall) left the former work only after they became 'family' men. On the other hand, it would also seem likely that as workers move into older age-groups than those covered by our sample, and their children become employed themselves, the motivation to maximise the economic 'pay-off' from work will weaken and allow more weight to be given to other considerations. For example, as we have noted (table 63), when we asked our respondents what improvements in their way of life they most hoped for over the ten years ahead, some were already looking forward to having a less stressful life or to enjoying greater leisure; and these things prove to be more frequently mentioned in succeeding age-groups.[4]

Furthermore, as well as imposing pressure upon him to increase his income, the role obligations of the worker with a young family may also come into conflict with his extensive association with workmates outside the factory or with any high degree of participation in union affairs or work-based clubs and societies. The demands made upon him as husband and father are at this stage likely to be given relatively high priority on his time and energy outside of work in comparison with demands which pertain to his roles as a member of a work group, trade union or social

[1] See, for example, the studies discussed in Michael Carter, *Into Work* (London, 1966), pp. 138–9, 162–6.

[2] See, for example, the studies discussed by Sylvia Shimmin, 'Extra-Mural Factors influencing Behaviour at Work', *Occupational Psychology*, vol. 36 (July 1962).

[3] See pp. 34–6 above.

[4] Ranging from 6% of all aspirations mentioned in the 21–25 age group to 18% in the 41–46 group. The 'cycle' we are suggesting here may perhaps be regarded as the analogue in the 'affluent society' of today to Rowntree's famous 'poverty cycle' of half a century ago. See B. S. Rowntree, *Poverty: a study of town life* (London, 1901), ch. v.

club.[1] Alternatively put, the most 'significant others' in his life will tend to be his wife and children rather than his 'mates', fellow unionists or leisure companions. As we have seen, in explaining their non-participation in union affairs in particular, our respondents referred relatively frequently to their overriding commitment to their families (table 41); and a number added, as if in mitigation of their present 'apathy', that they 'went fairly regular' until the time they married. In this way the consequences of his familial obligations reinforce the consequences which are in any case likely from the worker's own definition of his job in essentially instrumental terms: the sharp dichotomy between work and non-work is established. Family life is looked to as a major source of expressive and affective satisfactions, while little is expected or sought from working life other than the wherewithal for the pursuit of extrinsic ends.

There are, then, good grounds for believing that in restricting our sample to married men in the younger age-groups we increased the probability of encountering instrumental orientations to work. To this extent, our findings reflect decisions taken in the design of our research. However, it is fairly obvious that the position of our respondents in the life-cycle cannot be the whole, or even the major part, of the explanation of their instrumental outlook on work. For one thing, the great majority of workers do of course pass through the financially difficult stage of having young families; yet clearly it is not the case that all are equally motivated at this time to increase their economic returns from work at the cost, if necessary, of more immediate satisfactions. The alternative possibility exists of accepting some fall or 'plateau' in living standards, and undoubtedly this is a choice which many make. Then again, it by no means *always* occurs, even in the early years of marriage, that familial role obligations are interpreted so as to give them general priority over commitments felt towards workmates or work organisations. This is made most evident by studies of the family life of such 'traditional' workers as miners, steelworkers and trawlermen.[2] In this way, therefore, the question of the extent to which the economic and social implications of having a young family will lead to an instrumental view of work must become ultimately one of values; specifically, that is, one of the value which is set on a steadily rising standard of domestic living and on devoting one's non-working life to one's wife and children.

[1] See the perceptive analysis of this situation in Bernard Barber, 'Participation and Mass Apathy in Associations', in A. W. Gouldner (ed.), *Studies in Leadership* (New York, 1950); also H. Wilensky, 'Life Cycle, Work Situation and Participation in Formal Associations', in R. W. Kleemeier (ed.), *Aging and Leisure* (New York, 1961).

[2] See the references given above, p. 54, n. 2 and n. 3, p. 60, n. 2 and n. 3; also the useful synthesis attempted in Josephine Klein, *Samples from English Cultures* (London, 1965), vol. I, ch. 4.

TABLE 67. *Region of upbringing* and of location of immediately previous job*

Region†	Upbringing		Immediately previous job	
	N	Percentage	N	Percentage
Luton area	68	30	114	50
London and South-Eastern	55	24	52	23
Eastern	12	5	8	4
Midlands and North Midlands	10	4	5	2
Southern and South-Western	10	4	5	2
East and West Ridings and North-Western	7	3	4	2
Northern	9	4	0	0
Wales	6	3	1	(1)
Scotland	5	2	4	2
Northern Ireland and Eire	32	14	6	3
Other overseas	11	5	4	2
Not classifiable,‡ no information	4	2	26	11
TOTALS	229	100	229	101

* I.e. region in which the respondent spent the majority of his years prior to entering employment.

† Apart from 'Luton area' (which covers all territory within 10 miles of the town boundaries) these are Standard Administrative Regions or groupings of these, plus Eire and 'other overseas'.

‡ Because of variety of regions lived in or because job was not related to any one geographical base (e.g. as with some men in the Armed Forces).

With the workers we studied, it is clear that these were both matters of considerable value-emphasis. This is indicated by the very fact that an instrumental orientation to work was prevalent, and it is amply confirmed by evidence of a more direct kind.[1] As well, then, as explaining our respondents' approach to their employment in terms of their position in the life-cycle, we must also account for their concern to *maintain* their relatively prosperous and rising standard of living and for their *inclination* towards a family-centred style of living. In both these respects, we believe that attention can be most usefully directed towards the experience of our respondents in terms of *geographical* and of *social mobility*.

In the light of the comparative material available, our sample of affluent workers must be regarded as being geographically highly mobile. For example, from Thomas's survey of labour mobility in Great Britain over the period 1945–9, it emerged that more than three-quarters of the

[1] See, for example, the data on aspirations presented in the previous chapter, pp. 136–8, and also, for a full account, our final report, *The Affluent Worker in the Class Structure*, ch. 4.

working men and women in the sample had never been employed outside the region in which they lived at the time they were interviewed, and that almost half had worked throughout their lives in one town only.[1] In contrast to this, table 67 reveals that of the workers we studied only 30% had lived chiefly in the Luton area up to the time they were first employed, and that nearly half had grown up outside the entire London and South-Eastern region. Furthermore, only half of the sample had been working in the Luton area in the job they had held immediately before their present one.[2] This preponderance of migrants is found in all the occupational groups which our sample comprises, and it is also worth noting that, overall, a majority of respondents' wives had been likewise brought up outside the Luton area.[3]

That this degree of geographical mobility is evident within our sample could again be regarded as the consequence of a decision on our part: that of choosing Luton as the *locale* for our investigation. For, over the decade which preceded our study, net migration contributed appreciably more than natural increase to the steady growth in Luton's population.[4] However, a situation of this kind might well be found in any town in which high-paying jobs exist in any number. What is chiefly important to note here is that this demographic characteristic of Luton *as a community* is also very relevant to our present interest. Because Luton is, as it were, a town of migrants, even those inhabitants who have not themselves been geographically mobile are nonetheless significantly affected by the mobility of others. For example, as a result of the continuous growth in population, post-war housing development in Luton has been at a very high level,[5] and this has been associated with considerable residential mobility among 'natives' and migrants alike.[6] Then again, in any given neighbourhood,

---

[1] G. Thomas, *Labour Mobility in Great Britain, 1945–1949*, Ministry of Labour and National Service (London, 1951), pp. 39–40.

[2] These findings may also be contrasted with those reported by Jefferys in her study of labour mobility in Battersea and Dagenham: less than 10% of those interviewed (1951) had worked outside London and the Home Counties during the post-war years, even including Service experience. See Margot Jefferys, *Mobility in the Labour Market* (London, 1954), pp. 110–11.

[3] This was the case with 51% of the wives of the skilled men and with 58% of the wives of the semi-skilled men.

[4] Over the period 1951–61, the population of Luton grew from 110,400 to 131,600; i.e. at an average rate of around 1·8% per annum. The average annual rate of natural increase over the same period was 0·7%.

[5] This is true in particular of private building. See the comparative data given in C. A. Moser and Wolf Scott, *British Towns* (Edinburgh and London, 1961), appendix B.

[6] Only 30% of the couples in our sample had not changed their place of residence since marriage or since coming to Luton as a couple. Of the remainder, 30% (21% of the total sample) had been in their present accommodation for not more than two years and 64% (44% of the total) for not more than five years.

TABLE 68. *Reasons for moving to Luton (men who moved after marriage)*

Class of reason	Craftsmen (N = 25)	Setters (N = 10)	Process workers (N = 9)	Machinists (N = 25)	Assemblers (N = 35)	All (N = 104)
			Times mentioned			
House available there, or better quality or value in housing than in area previously lived in	18	6	7	19	13	63
More secure work, higher wages than in area previously lived in	13	3	3	9	20	48
Other reasons	1	1	0	1	5	8
ALL REASONS	32	10	10	29	38	119

native Lutonians live alongside, and are perhaps outnumbered by, the families of newcomers, often with sufficient subcultural differences to give them a certain distinctiveness. And from our interviews and from a reading of the local press, it was apparent that in Luton consciousness of such differences was a quite definite influence on individuals' attitudes and behaviour towards each other.[1]

How, then, are these facts of geographical mobility related to the orientation to work which our respondents typically display? There are two main connections which we would suggest.

In the first place, we have data to indicate that to a large extent the migrants in our sample came to Luton specifically in search of material improvement, notably in regard to housing and jobs. In the case of those couples in our sample who had come to the town together, we asked: 'Why did you move to Luton?'; and then further: 'What sort of changes did this involve?'—encouraging here discussion of relative advantages and disadvantages in comparison with the area they had previously lived in. The results produced by these questions are shown in tables 68 and 69.

From these data, it is clear that it was overwhelmingly the attraction of better living conditions and higher incomes which brought these couples

[1] Londoners, Irish, Scottish and 'northerners', together with 'Lutonians' themselves, were the groups most frequently singled out for comment. Articles and exchanges of letters on the 'natives'-versus-'immigrants' issue occurred frequently in *The Luton News*. See, for example, the numbers of 28 March and 6 June 1963 and numbers immediately following.

TABLE 69. *Advantages and disadvantages involved in moving to Luton (men who moved after marriage)*

	Craftsmen (N = 25)	Setters (N = 10)	Process workers (N = 9)	Machinists (N = 25)	Assemblers (N = 35)	All (N = 104)
Advantages			Times mentioned			
Availability, quality or value of housing	18	4	7	19	16	64
Higher income, better-paying work	11	3	3	12	25	54
More amenities, more pleasant physical environment	4	0	1	5	3	13
Better social life, people are more friendly, likable	2	0	0	4	4	10
Nearer to kin	1	1	1	1	1	5
Other advantages	1	2	0	0	3	6
ALL ADVANTAGES	37	10	12	41	52	152
No advantage mentioned	1	1	0	0	0	2
Disadvantages						
Separation from kin and friends	13	4	3	1	16	37
Poorer social life, people are less friendly, likable	9	0	5	5	6	25
Fewer amenities, less pleasant physical environment	3	1	1	6	9	20
Higher cost of living	0	1	1	1	3	6
Other disadvantages	4	0	2	1	8	15
ALL DISADVANTAGES	29	6	12	14	42	103
No disadvantage mentioned	7	5	2	15	6	35

to Luton,[1] and, further, that almost invariably they felt that they had achieved advantages in these respects. At the same time it also appears that, once more in a majority of cases, some kind of disadvantage, usually non-economic in nature, had been experienced along with the material gain. Over a third of the couples complained of being separated from kin and friends, a quarter of a less rewarding social life, and a fifth of the amenities and physical environment of Luton.

[1] Couples mentioning the attractions of housing were concentrated among those coming to Luton from London and the South-East. The low proportion of assemblers referring to housing reflects in part the fact that within this group the proportion of 'Londoners' was relatively small.

The significance of these findings in the present context is therefore twofold. Most importantly, it is indicated that our sample was one which was in some degree 'self-selected' for a high level of motivation towards material advancement; that is to say, it was one which comprised a high proportion of men who were found together in Luton *because of* a decision on their part to leave a former area of residence in quest of improvement, in one way or another, in their living standards. In addition, it is also revealed that taking such action more often than not entailed social costs. Thus, it may be supposed that in view of this, our respondents would be all the more concerned that their decision to move should produce the 'pay-offs' which were the main objective. In other words, the migrants in our sample had often something at stake in their attempt to achieve and to maintain a materially satisfying existence; and it might then be expected that their motivation in this respect would be correspondingly reinforced.

Secondly, our respondents' orientations to work were also importantly shaped, in our view, by the *generalised* effects of there being in Luton a particularly large number of geographically mobile persons. As we have already seen, relatively few of our affluent workers had close relationships with workmates either within or outside the workplace. But, furthermore, the findings of our 'home' interviews reveal that neither were our respondents typically involved in tightly knit social networks based on kinship or locality.[1] The migrants, as might be expected, were for the most part physically separated from the main body of their kin; and very few of the sample, whether migrants or natives, appeared to live in neighbourhoods which displayed the communal solidarity of 'established' working-class districts. Both the degree of residential mobility and the social heterogeneity of neighbourhoods which are characteristic of Luton militated against this pattern of community living.

Thus, in the absence of many of their kin and of solidary local communities, the majority of our respondents were led to adopt a style of life which was decisively centred on the home and the conjugal family. Their major emotional investments, we would suggest, were made in their relationships with their wives and children, and these relationships were in turn their major source of social and psychological support.[2] Consequently,

---

[1] For a full account of respondent's patterns of sociability, see *The Affluent Worker in the Class Structure*, ch. 4.

[2] Essentially similar findings have, of course, been produced by a number of recent studies of physically (chiefly residentially) mobile workers and their families. For a useful survey, see Klein, *Samples from English Cultures*, vol. 1, ch. 5; also, Lockwood and Goldthorpe, 'The Manual Worker: Affluence, Aspirations and Assimilation'.

their familial role obligations were in general given clear priority over those arising from their membership in other, to them less significant, groups and associations—such as those based on their place of work. Work, that is to say, tended to be devalued in other than its economic aspects; the family rather than work was for these men their central life interest. Moreover, it should be recognised that while this pattern must in part be seen as the result of constraints—notably those deriving from geographical mobility[1] —once established, it becomes, like all patterns of social affiliation, in some degree self-maintaining.[2] To the extent that his non-working life is committed to his immediate family, the individual is the less able, and the less motivated, to enter into involvements which might interfere with his family life through placing seriously competing claims upon his time and energy. And, further still, it is also the case that a home- and family-centred mode of existence is one clearly more compatible with a concern for maximising the economic returns from work than with an orientation to work which embodies important wants and expectations of a non-economic kind.

In sum, then, our argument is that geographical mobility is associated with our affluent workers' instrumental view of their employment in both a direct and an indirect way. On the one hand, there is an immediate connection, in that many of our sample had come to Luton specifically in order to raise their material standards of living. On the other hand, there is evidence that in Luton, as a town of migrants, a common style of social life is a largely 'privatised' one, which is conducive to and supportive of a definition of work as essentially a means to extrinsic—that is to say, largely familial—ends.

Turning now to social mobility, it cannot be argued that in this respect our sample of affluent workers is so obviously distinctive as it is in terms of geographical mobility. Nevertheless, there is evidence that among the workers we studied a relatively high proportion had experienced *downward* mobility in one form or another.

As is shown in table 70, in the region of three-quarters of the more skilled men in our sample had fathers who were themselves manual workers. However, among the semi-skilled men some considerable variation in the pattern of social origins can be seen to occur. Over 80 % of the process workers are from manual workers' families but this is the case with clearly less than half of the machinists. Moreover, a third of the machinists

[1] But also, in some cases, from overtime and shiftwork and from wives working.
[2] cf. the discussion in R. K. Merton, *Social Theory and Social Structures* (Glencoe, 1957), pp. 268–71.

The affluent worker: industrial attitudes

TABLE 70. *Experience of social mobility—occupational status of father*

Occupational status of father*	Craftsmen (N = 56)	Setters (N = 23)	Process workers (N = 23)	Machinists (N = 41)	Assemblers (N = 86)	All (N = 229)
	Percentage					
'White-collar'	18	17	9	32	19	20
'Intermediate'	2	13	9	27	11	11
'Manual'	80	70	83	42	70	69
No information	0	0	0	0	1	(1)
TOTALS	100	100	101	101	101	100

* For further details of the occupational classification used see appendix C. The occupational status accorded to a father is based on his son's account of the kind of work he did for the greater part of his life.

(and a fifth of the assemblers) have unambiguously 'white-collar'[1] origins. These figures may be compared with what is known about rates of intergenerational social mobility in British society at large. From the results of the investigation directed by Glass it can be calculated that of the skilled and semi-skilled workers in the national sample which was taken, 71% of the former group and 78% of the latter were the sons of manual workers, whereas probably not more than 15% and 10% respectively could be reckoned as being of white-collar parentage in terms of our classification.[2] Thus, it may be said that both the machinists and the assemblers in our sample, though notably the former, show more downward mobility intergenerationally than would be expected on a national basis.

Further data relevant to our respondents' experience of social mobility are given in table 71—in this case, data on intragenerational or 'career' mobility. It can be seen that from a sixth to a quarter in all occupational groups have at some time held a white-collar job, but that the machinists and assemblers were much more likely than men in other groups to have had jobs of 'intermediate' status. Consequently, only around half of the machinists and assemblers had spent the whole of their 'careers' in manual employment. We have no exactly comparable data of a national character,

[1] Where 'white-collar' is used to refer to social origins or occupational status, it is to be taken in a broader sense—i.e. as indicative of a certain status level—than where it is used to refer to a certain type of work. As can be seen from appendix C, the 'white-collar' occupational status categories cover some types of work which would not be described as white-collar in the stricter usage of the term—e.g. some forms of self-employment.

[2] These figures are based on the reworking of the results of the Glass study by R. K. Kelsall which is contained in S. M. Miller, 'Comparative Social Mobility', *Current Sociology*, vol. IX, no. 1, 1960. The original results are given in D. V. Glass (ed.), *Social Mobility in Britain* (London, 1954).

TABLE 71. *Experience of social mobility—highest occupational status achieved**

Highest occupational status achieved	Craftsmen (N = 56)	Setters (N = 23)	Process workers (N = 23)	Machinists (N = 41)	Assemblers (N = 86)	All (N = 229)
			Percentage			
'White-collar'	16	26	17	24	16	19
'Intermediate'	5	13	4	29	31	20
'Manual'	79	61	78	46	52	61
TOTALS	100	100	99	99	99	100

* The slight differences between the results given in this table and those given in table 16 are explained by the fact that in the latter table jobs lasting less than a year were not counted.

but on the basis of material presented by Thomas, it is clear that in the two groups in question the proportion of men with experience of nonmanual work is high, and this would seem most probably true for the sample as a whole.[1]

Finally, it is worth noting that what is perhaps a relatively large proportion of our affluent workers have *siblings* who are of white-collar status;[2] that is, brothers who hold white-collar jobs or sisters married to such men: 63% of the sample have at least one such sibling and 27% have two or more. These respondents, and particularly the latter group, may also be thought of as being downwardly mobile, if in no other way, at least in a *relative* sense; that is to say, they have stayed at the same status level as their family of origin or they have moved downwards while others of their generation have succeeded in establishing themselves in white-collar positions. Although the form of social mobility in question here is not a generally recognised one, it is nonetheless one which we believe may be of some relevance in the present context.

Given that at least within some groups in our sample the experience of downward mobility is more extensive than might generally be expected, what connection is to be made between this fact and our respondents' characteristically instrumental view of their employment? The relationship which we would hypothesise is a double one.

[1] See Thomas, *Labour Mobility in Great Britain, 1945–49*, p. 30. It should be noted, however, that in many cases the downward mobility which is in question here is of a somewhat special kind in that it follows upon previous upward mobility; that is, where men of manual origin held a nonmanual job before reverting to manual status. Moreover, it would, of course, be generally the case that the moves made to this lower occupational status were of a voluntary nature. No association exists within the sample between having held a white-collar job and being of white-collar origin.

[2] No comparable data collected on a national basis are available.

On the one hand, we would suggest that, in view of the data we have set out, it is probable that feelings of 'relative deprivation' have been comparatively frequent among the workers we studied. A sizable proportion of the men in the sample are, it would seem, in situations in which it is likely that they will have had white-collar persons, with 'middle-class' living standards, among their reference groups or reference individuals; often these persons would be members of their own families. Yet, as we have indicated earlier, very few of our respondents have the qualifications required to give them any real chance of achieving white-collar jobs themselves, other than ones of a low-paying type. A situation of the kind in question may equally well occur in the case of men who have not done well enough educationally to maintain their white-collar origins; or of men who have held nonmanual jobs but who were not equipped to reach the higher income levels of the white-collar hierarchy; or of men who have always been in manual work but who have seen their siblings move into white-collar positions which they are not themselves qualified to obtain.[1]

In all these cases, we would argue, strong motivation is likely to be generated to acquire a relatively high standard of living—one comparable to that enjoyed by the persons by reference to whom the individual assesses his own achievement.[2] But this motivation must be accommodated to the constraints which result from inadequate education and training. A logical and perhaps the most readily available solution is then to adopt an orientation to work of a predominantly instrumental kind: to seek work and to follow a pattern of work behaviour in which clear priority is given to the level of economic return over all other considerations. The resort to such a solution is most clearly revealed in our sample in the attachment of the semi-skilled men to jobs which offer a high level of pay not in return for the knowledge or skill they demand but rather as compensation for the stress and strain they impose.[3]

On the other hand, we would suggest that once they have become the occupants of high-paying manual jobs, our affluent workers have not

[1] On the importance of siblings as a reference group in occupational life, see William H. Form and James A. Geschwender, 'The Social Reference Basis of Job Satisfaction: the Case of Manual Workers', *American Sociological Review*, vol. 27, no. 2 (1962).

[2] It should be emphasised that this does not *necessarily* imply seeking also to emulate specifically white-collar *life-styles*, still less to gain acceptance into 'middle class' society (although it would appear that the minority of workers in our sample who do reveal these further aspirations *are* likely to be men with multiple 'white-collar' affiliations). For a further example of how relative deprivation may affect work behaviour, see H. L. Wilensky, 'The Moonlighter: a Product of Relative Deprivation', *Industrial Relations*, vol. 3, no. 1 (1963).

[3] In addition, though, it should be recalled that the craftsmen too revealed some propensity to give priority to economic returns from work in that a number had taken jobs at Skefko and

infrequently found themselves in a further social situation of a kind likely to reinforce their instrumental outlook on their work: that is, a situation of 'status incongruency'.[1] This would derive from the fact that while in many cases they had affiliations of some kind or other with white-collar society,[2] and certainly had the level of income required to sustain a white-collar standard of living, they were nonetheless still of generally lower status in occupational terms. They remained manual wage-workers, in fact —and often in jobs of an inherently unattractive kind—as a *condition of* their relatively prosperous existence.

In such circumstances it is not to be expected that these men would wish to live out any more of their lives than was strictly necessary on the basis of work relationships or within the scope of their work organisations. Conversely, the domestic *milieu* would be that in which the advantageous aspects of their situation would be most manifest and the disadvantageous ones least intrusive. From this point of view our respondents' tendency to establish a dichotomy between their working and non-working lives, both psychologically and socially, becomes readily intelligible. And so too does the emphasis which they gave to their familial roles over against those associated with their workmates and workplace.

In the foregoing paragraphs, we have argued that in two ways—in their experience of geographical and of social mobility—the workers we studied prove to be in some degree distinctive; and, further, that in both respects their experience and the situations in which they currently find themselves are probable sources of the values and motivations which characterise their approach to their employment. In the remainder of this chapter, our aim will be to provide some empirical support for the hypotheses we have advanced.

Ideally, the way to test our arguments on the social sources of instrumental orientations to work would be through the comparative analysis of samples

---

Laporte in succession to jobs in smaller, lower-paying firms in which their work had apparently been of a less specialised and routine character. See p. 37, n. 1, above.

[1] We take this term from Stuart Adams, 'Status Congruency as a variable in Small Group Performance', *Social Forces*, vol. 32 (1953). It has been subsequently applied in a more specifically sociological context by Homans and, under the name of 'status crystallization', by Lenski. See G. C. Homans, 'Status Congruence' in *Sentiments and Activities* (Glencoe, 1962); and Gerhard Lenski, 'Status Crystallization: a non-vertical dimension of social status', *American Sociological Review*, vol. 19 (1954).

[2] In addition to the familial and occupational affiliations already referred to, it should also be noted that 19% of the skilled men and 26% of the semi-skilled workers had married the daughters of 'white-collar' fathers, and that 53% of the former group and 41% of the latter had wives who had at some time held a white-collar job. Moreover, these different white-collar connections show no significant tendency to be associated with each other within our sample.

	'Instrumentalism' Scores		
Item	o	I	2
Nature of attachment to present employment: Reasons given for staying at present firm	Level of pay not mentioned	Level of pay together with other reasons	Level of pay only
Involvement with workmates: Feelings about being moved away from present mates and level of out-plant association with workmate friends	Would feel 'very upset' or 'fairly upset' if moved *and* visits with or has arranged outings with workmate friend(s)	Would feel 'very upset' or 'fairly upset' if moved *or* visits with or has arranged outings with workmate friend(s)	Would not feel upset if moved and does not visit or have arranged outings with workmate friend(s)
Organisational participation: Participation in work-based clubs and societies and attendance at union branch meetings	Participates in at least one club or society* *and* attends 'regularly' or 'occasionally' at branch†	Participates in at least one club or society *or* attends 'regularly' or 'occasionally' at branch	Does not participate in any club or society and does not attend branch 'regularly' or 'occasionally'

* I.e. attends at least twice a year.
† I.e. approximately once a month or once a year respectively—see p. 98, n 1.

such as ours along with others comprising workers with markedly different orientations. However, this is not a possibility open to us within the context of the present study. Rather, we must limit ourselves to comparisons that can be made *within* our sample; that is, to comparisons between workers who approximate to a greater or lesser degree the instrumental orientation which we have shown to be dominant. To do this means, therefore, devising some measure of 'instrumentalism'[1] which will differentiate among our respondents and which will do so in such a way as to give us divisions of the sample of reasonable size for comparative purposes. Such a measure—albeit of a very crude kind—can be obtained if we categorise the replies made to a number of questions on our interview schedule and then score these in terms of the degree of 'instrumentalism' which they may be taken to indicate. The choice of questions must of course be to some extent arbitrary, and equally the method of scoring. Nonetheless,

[1] By this term we refer to the entire attitudinal and behavioural pattern which is revealed by the data summarised at the beginning of this chapter.

TABLE 72. *'Instrumentalism' scores*

Score	Craftsmen (N = 56)	Setters (N = 23)	Process workers (N = 23)	Machinists (N = 41)	Assemblers (N = 86)	All (N = 229)	
			Percentage				
6	0	0	9	5	9	5 ⎫	Highly
5	16	26	35	34	40	31 ⎭	instrumental
4	30	26	30	22	29	28	Intermediate
3	41	39	17	20	16	25 ⎫	
2	13	4	9	12	6	9 ⎬	Less
1	0	4	0	7	0	2 ⎪	instrumental
0	0	0	0	0	0	0 ⎭	
TOTALS	100	99	100	100	100	100	

it seems to us that a measure of some utility can be arrived at in this relatively simple way. The diagram opposite shows the particular scheme we have adopted, which incorporates items indicative of the nature of respondents' attachment to their present employment, the extent of their involvement with workmates, and the extent of their organisational participation.

On this basis, as can be seen, the most instrumentally oriented individuals of all would score 6. These are men who report staying in their present job simply because of the level of pay, who do not think they would be upset if moved away from their present workmates, who have no workmate friends whom they see outside the workplace other than more or less casually, who do not participate in any work-based club or society, and who only rarely, if ever, attend their union branch. On the other hand, the least instrumentally oriented men would score 0. These would be men who do not mention the level of pay as a reason for staying in their present job, who do feel they would be upset if moved away from their workmates, who have at least one workmate friend whom they see outside work in an organised way, who participate in at least one work-based club or society, and who report attending their union branch 'regularly' or 'occasionally'.

The way in which our sample is distributed in terms of the scoring in question is shown in table 72. This clearly reflects the prevalence of an instrumental pattern since there is in fact no zero score, only 2 % of the sample score 1, and only 9 % score 2. At the same time, the semi-skilled men, as would be expected, reveal generally higher scores than the more skilled. The modal score for the former is 5—that is, in what we have termed the 'highly instrumental' range—while the modal score for the latter is 3—that is, in the 'less instrumental' range.[1] The division of the sample into these ranges, together with the 'intermediate' one (score 4), gives us three roughly equal groups on which our subsequent analyses can be based.[2]

In regard to our hypotheses linking an instrumental orientation to work with geographical mobility, the possibilities of empirical testing on the basis of the present research are extremely limited. We have argued above that the implications of Luton containing a high proportion of migrants go beyond those who are migrants themselves and affect life-styles and social values in a quite general way. If this is so, it would not necessarily follow that the native Lutonians in our sample should be markedly less instrumentally oriented than those men who had actually experienced geographical mobility.[3] In the event, the relevant cross-tabulation of our data

[1] If 'highly instrumental' scores are set against 'intermediate' and 'less instrumental' scores, the tendency for semi-skilled men to come into the former range is highly significant: $\chi^2 = 15 \cdot 5$; 1 df; $p < 0 \cdot 001$. The term 'less instrumental' is used advisedly to emphasise the fact that most of the men in this range could, on a general view, be still regarded as quite instrumentally oriented in their industrial attitudes and behaviour. For example, a man would achieve a score of as low as 3 simply by reporting that some other consideration as well as the level of pay kept him in his present job, by having just one workmate friend whom he occasionally visited or accompanied on outings, and by attending his union branch once a year. Given the overall character of our sample, we were, of course, forced to allow such relatively weak criteria for entry into the range in question in order that this would comprise a reasonably large proportion of the sample.

[2] It should be noted here that the items we included in our measure of 'instrumentalism' did not 'scale' nor were scores on these items very closely related. While the former attribute was not expected, we have, of course, tended to think of 'instrumentalism' as constituting a syndrome of attitudes and behaviour on the lines indicated in the ideal type set out in chapter 2; and the items we chose as the basis for our measure were intended to reflect this. What we in fact discover is that while scores on different items do show a general tendency to be associated, the associations are not, taken individually, of a statistically significant kind. This might be taken to imply that 'instrumentalism' should not be thought of as a single syndrome which individuals display to a greater or lesser degree, but rather that the various elements in what we have regarded as the instrumental pattern have no particular tendency to co-exist. However, it should be remembered that, as noted above, our method of scoring was devised specifically in order to differentiate within a sample in which, collectively, 'instrumental' attitudes and behaviour were found to predominate. The distinctions made so as to split the sample up into sizable sub-divisions had to be relatively fine ones. It might still be the case that the application of more basic distinctions to a less homogeneous sample would in fact confirm the assumption of an 'instrumental' syndrome. On our reading of the literature of industrial sociology, we would think this result more likely than not. At all events, we do not believe that the weak association between the scores on our items is in itself enough to require that such an assumption be abandoned. Finally, it may also be noted that scores on the different items included in our measure regularly co-vary in relation to the independent variables we introduce. For example, semi-skilled workers not only have higher total scores than the more skilled men, as we have seen, but also come out higher on each of the three component scores.

[3] There is also, of course, the point that native Lutonians who wished to give priority to high-level economic returns from work would not need to be geographically mobile to find suitable employment opportunities.

shows that while some tendency in this direction is present, this is only very weak and, moreover, disappears altogether once skill level is held constant.

However, we did previously suggest that among the workers we studied there would be special reasons for expecting a strongly instrumental view of work on the part of men who had moved to the Luton area from some other region. In an attempt to arrive at some test of this particular argument, despite the difficulties posed by the generalised effects of mobility, a further hypothesis might be developed on the following lines: that those men in the sample who have in some sense experienced the 'greatest' geographical mobility, and thus presumably, the sharpest break with their former lives, will show a correspondingly greater degree of 'instrumentalism'—and one which will in fact distinguish them from the rest of the sample, even though all our respondents are inhabitants of a town in which migrants predominate.

In order to examine this possibility, we can divide the geographical regions introduced in table 67 into two categories: one comprising the regions which make up the whole central and south-eastern part of the British Isles, the other comprising all those regions to the north and west— largely those of the 'Celtic fringe'—which are not only physically, but also subculturally, the further removed from Luton.[1] We can then investigate whether those of our respondents who originated in these latter regions reveal a more pronounced instrumental pattern than do the remainder. Taking the sample as a whole, there is a statistically significant tendency in this direction.[2] However, on making the necessary division of the sample by skill level, it becomes evident that this effect results to some major extent from the more skilled men being less likely than the semi-skilled to have experienced migration of a 'long-range' kind. As table 73 shows, some association between such migration and 'instrumentalism' does still appear *within* the two skill categories: but, while this is perhaps enough to prevent our hypothesis from being rejected forthwith, the pattern revealed is clearly not one of sufficient strength to be accepted as effective validation.

Thus, so far as geographical mobility is concerned, our views on the social sources of an instrumental approach to work must be left only a little above the level of conjecture—to be corroborated or otherwise by the

---

[1] The regions falling in the first category are: London and South-Eastern, Eastern, Southern, Midlands and North Midlands, East and West Ridings and North-Western; and in the second: South-Western, Wales, Northern, Scotland, Northern Ireland and Eire.

[2] Comparing 'highly instrumental' scores against 'intermediate' and 'less instrumental' scores and counting the 11 men brought up overseas as also having experienced 'long-range' mobility: $\chi^2 = 4.7$; 1 df; $p < 0.05$.

TABLE 73. *Degree of 'instrumentalism' by skill level and experience of geographical mobility*

Skill level	Geographical mobility	Highly instrumental	Intermediate	Less instrumental		N
			Percentage			
Semi-skilled	Long-range	50	22	28	100	58
	Other	43	29	28	100	89
Skilled*	Long-range	27	36	36	99	11
	Other	18	28	54	100	67
All		36†	28	36	100	225†

* Craftsmen and setters.
† The four men not classified in table 67 are excluded.

findings of further research. All that may be added is that such indications as can be gained from existing studies encourage us to believe that it is the former outcome which is the more probable.[1]

In comparison with hypotheses relating to geographical mobility, the arguments we have advanced concerning social mobility and 'instrumentalism' are, in principle at least, far more readily testable within the limits of our present study.

To begin with, we can divide our respondents into two groups on the basis of their fathers' occupational status: those whose fathers were unambiguously 'white-collar' and the remainder whose fathers' occupational status was either 'intermediate' or 'manual'. The former group we can regard as being downwardly mobile intergenerationally and the latter we can treat as being in this respect more or less 'stable'. Following the hypotheses we have put forward, we would then expect our downwardly mobile respondents to show a more emphatic instrumental orientation than the remainder.

If the sample is considered as a whole, such an association does prove to exist and is of a statistically significant kind.[2] Moreover, in this case, holding constant the level of skill has only a limited effect and the association

[1] Most notably, recent French studies of workers who have migrated to industrial centres from outlying rural areas indicate that these workers have a predominant interest in the economic return from their employment ('*l'économisme*'), are relatively unconcerned with 'social' satisfactions from work, and remain largely uninvolved in union affairs even though they are likely to adopt militant attitudes on economic issues. See Touraine & Ragazzi, *Ouvriers d'Origine Agricole*, ch. III esp.; and also the more general discussion by Touraine and B. Mottez, 'Classe Ouvrière et Société Globale' in Friedmann & Naville (eds.), *Traité de Sociologie du Travail*, vol. 2, pp. 236–40.

[2] Comparing 'highly instrumental' scores against 'intermediate' and 'less instrumental' scores: $\chi^2 = 5.2$; 1 df; $p < 0.025$.

TABLE 74. *Degree of 'instrumentalism' by skill level and experience of social mobility (intergenerational)*

Skill level	Social mobility by reference to occupational status of father	Highly instrumental	Intermediate	Less instrumental		N
			Percentage			
Semi-skilled	Downward	58	19	23	100	31
	Stable	42	30	28	100	118
Skilled*	Downward	36	28	36	100	14
	Stable	15	30	55	100	65
All		36	28	35	99	228†

* Craftsmen and setters.
† The one man for whom there was no information in table 70 is excluded.

remains fairly marked among both the skilled and semi-skilled groups. This can be seen from table 74.[1] Of particular interest here are the two 'extreme' situations. Of the 65 skilled men whose fathers had also been manual workers, it can be seen that only 15% are 'highly instrumental', while a majority—55%—fall into the 'less instrumental' range. In contrast are the 31 semi-skilled men whose fathers are, or were, of white-collar status—in other words, the men who may be regarded as downwardly mobile to the greatest degree. In this case, we find that only 23% are in the 'less instrumental' range, while by far the largest proportion— 58%—are scored as 'highly instrumental'. It can therefore be claimed that these results are in general highly consistent with the hypothesis which we have put forward.

Furthermore, going back to our arguments concerning possible relative deprivation and status incongruency among our respondents, other testable propositions suggest themselves: most obviously that a pronounced instrumental orientation to work should be prevalent not only among those men who were downwardly mobile intergenerationally but also among those who were downwardly mobile in 'career' terms or in a relative sense *vis-à-vis* their siblings.

In regard to the first of these possibilities, our findings are negative; that is to say, men who at some point in their work histories had held a white-collar or other nonmanual job do not turn out to be more instrumentally

[1] A similar, though somewhat weaker, pattern is also obtained if we take as downwardly mobile those men whose fathers' occupations were classed as 'white-collar' *or* 'intermediate' in status.

oriented than others—if anything they are somewhat less so. To this extent, then, our expectations are not upheld. Moreover, in regard to the second possibility, only a limited tendency in the anticipated direction is found. Men who had two or more white-collar siblings were more markedly instrumental in their attitudes and behaviour than were the remainder; but this effect was not a strong one and was in fact confined to the semi-skilled workers[1]—to those groups in which the status gap between our respondents and their white-collar siblings would tend to be widest.

Such results do not appear particularly encouraging from the point of view of the conjectures we have made. However, on elaborating our analysis, one further interesting—and reassuring—point emerges. It would seem to be the case that being downwardly mobile in 'career' terms or in relation to siblings is far more clearly associated with pronounced 'instrumentalism' where this experience *co-exists* with downward mobility intergenerationally. In other words, those men whose downward movement from the occupational status of their parents is 'compounded' by either of the two other types of downward mobility are particularly likely to have adopted a highly instrumental approach to work. For example, there are 11 men in the sample who are of white-collar parentage and who have also at some stage had a white-collar job themselves: of the 11, 8 (73%) fall into the 'highly instrumental' range as against 2 (18%) who are 'less instrumental'.[2] Again, among the semi-skilled men, there are 16 who are of white-collar origin and who have two or more siblings of white-collar status: 10 of these (63%) prove to be 'highly instrumental' and only 2 (13%) 'less instrumental'.[3] The difficulty here is, of course, that one is dealing with unfortunately small numbers, and percentage figures may well be misleading. But a somewhat more reliable basis for our argument can be provided, in the way shown in table 75, where downward 'career' mobility and mobility relative to siblings are considered together.

[1] For men with two or more white-collar siblings (N = 43) the percentages in the 'highly instrumental', 'intermediate' and 'less instrumental' categories respectively were: 54, 26, 21; and the corresponding figures for the remainder (N = 106) were 42, 28, 29.

[2] An explanation of the absence of any association between downward 'career' mobility and pronounced 'instrumentalism', except where downward mobility intergenerationally had also occurred, could be suggested on the following lines. Inspection of our data shows that men of white-collar origins who had themselves held white-collar jobs had tended to do so at the *beginning* of their work careers, whereas this was not the case with men of manual origins who had held such jobs. In moving down to manual work, the former group were in fact *at the same time* failing in an attempt to maintain their familial status; but in the case of the latter group, their downward mobility, as already noted (p. 157, n. 1, above) was often of a rather special kind, signifying perhaps no more than the end of a brief white-collar 'interlude'. For this reason, then, it would be far less likely to generate feelings of relative deprivation.

[3] Five out of the 10 and 1 out of the 2 were also downwardly mobile in 'career' terms.

TABLE 75. *Degree of 'instrumentalism' by experience of social mobility* (*intergenerational and other*)

Mobility experience	Highly instrumental	Intermediate	Less instrumental		N
		Percentage			
Downwardly mobile inter-generationally—compounded*	59	23	18	100	22
Downwardly mobile inter-generationally—not compounded	44	22	35	101	23
Not downwardly mobile inter-generationally	32	30	38	100	182
All	36	28	36	100	227†

* I.e. by downward mobility in 'career' terms or relative to siblings or both.

† The one man for whom there was no information in table 70 is excluded and also one man for whom there was no information on siblings.

From the table, it can be seen that there is a fairly clear difference in degrees of 'instrumentalism' between those men who had experienced 'compounded' downward mobility and those who had experienced downward intergenerational mobility only; in fact, this difference is somewhat greater than that between the latter group and the remainder of the sample who were not of white-collar origin. With the benefit of hindsight this is not perhaps very surprising. The psychological impact of downward mobility, relative to parental status, may be expected to be greater where this movement occurs as part of the individual's own occupational history (rather than being in effect determined before, or at the point of, his entry into the labour market) or where his lower status is underlined by the continuing higher status of a number of his siblings.

In sum, a fair amount of evidence can be produced from our study to lend support to the idea that downward mobility, in some forms at least, may be a source of a markedly instrumental view of work. This is so whether or not the particular causal connections which we have hypothesised are in fact the effective ones. Conversely, it does not automatically follow from the evidence in question that these connections are established. This last issue, we recognise, must remain a very open one, and it is one which calls for further, more specific, investigation.[1]

[1] This need is also pointed to by the fact that previous studies of the implications of downward mobility for the attitudes and behaviour of industrial workers have led to somewhat different conclusions in different societies. Lipset and Gordon, for example, have produced evidence to suggest that in the American case downwardly mobile workers remain oriented to 'middle

However, as a conclusion to this chapter, we present three 'case studies' which are taken from among those men in our sample who fell into the 'highly instrumental' category. These serve to show that the links which we have suggested between 'instrumentalism' and both geographical and social mobility are not at any rate entirely fanciful but can rather be seen at work in the lives of particular individuals. In the first case the effects of geographical mobility appear to have been of greatest importance; in the second, the effects of social mobility; while in the third the effects of both are in evidence.[1]

Case one: Mr Doyle

Mr Doyle is a machine operator at Skefko. He is in his early thirties and has four children all under the age of five. He and his wife are devout Catholics. Both were born and bred in rural districts in Eire. Mr Doyle's father, who is now retired, worked throughout his life in the family business—a small butcher's shop. Mr Doyle describes the living his family made as being 'a very poor one' and he now regularly sends money back to his parents to 'help out'.

After leaving 'ordinary' school at sixteen, Mr Doyle became an apprentice cinema projectionist. He liked the work but soon became dissatisfied with his pay and prospects. He was once out of work for several weeks after a cinema closed down. For a time he considered trying to start his own mobile cinema but was eventually forced to abandon the idea; he had no capital of his own and did not wish to borrow from his family in case the venture failed and he brought them into debt. Instead, Mr Doyle decided to come to England where projectionists' wages were much higher. He found a job in a large cinema in Manchester and remained there, very happy in his work, for several years. In his mid twenties,

class' values—this being reflected in their low level of participation in trade unionism and in a relatively high level of involvement in, and commitment to, their work. See S. M. Lipset and Joan Gordon, 'Mobility and Trade Union Membership' in Lipset and R. Bendix (eds.), *Class, Status and Power*, 1st ed. (London, 1954). In contrast, Touraine and Mottez ('Classe Ouvrière et Société Globale') have argued on the basis of French data that downwardly mobile workers, while not identifying with the labour movement, are nonetheless likely to reveal a relatively high degree of resistance to change and to support restrictive practices. Our results point to a third possibility: that workers of the kind in question will tend to remain little involved—other than in a calculative way—in either unions or their employing organisations and will define their work as an area of essentially instrumental activity to be 'insulated' as much as possible from other areas of their social lives. If more extensive research were to confirm these differing patterns, it would be interesting to consider their explanation in terms of differences in the nature of social stratification in the three societies—leading to varying social consequences and subjective meanings of downward mobility from case to case.

[1] In order to prevent identification of the actual individuals concerned, we have in each case altered a large number of facts of a non-essential kind.

however, Mr Doyle again began to feel doubtful about his level of income and security, and particularly since he was now planning to marry. Through Irish friends he heard about the 'big money' available in Luton and eventually he decided to move there and take a factory job. Shortly afterwards his marriage took place and within a year his first child was born. About the same time he left the firm he had originally joined: 'There was obviously a strike coming up and I couldn't afford to lose several weeks' pay.' He then went straight into his present job at Skefko.

Mr Doyle finds his work irksome because of its lack of variety—'Though I suppose this is a good thing on piece rates since you lose less time on new set-ups.' The pace of work is often 'a bit of a strain' and he misses using the mechanical skills he learnt as a projectionist. However, he has no thought of leaving Skefko: 'The pay's very good here; there aren't many places where you could do better.' He readily admits that where work is concerned he gives pay priority, and he stresses in this respect the responsibility he has to his wife and children. Although he would not like to move away from the men he now works with, he rarely sees them outside the factory other than by chance. He belongs to the Sports and Social Club but has only played very occasional games of snooker there. During his time at Skefko, he has attended only one union branch meeting: 'The family comes first; I like to spend all the time I can with them. Shift work makes it difficult enough as it is.'

This emphasis on the family is in fact the dominant feature of Mr Doyle's social life in general. He and his wife have two or three 'good friends' in Luton—all but one of whom are also Irish; but apart from these ties and the more limited acquaintances they make at monthly meetings of Catholic societies, they are more or less isolated. Mr Doyle regards many of his compatriots in Luton as being 'rowdy' and 'cheap', and both he and his wife find native Lutonians hard to get on with. Both have experienced difficulties in trying to become more integrated into the local community. Mr Doyle, for example, planned to join a working-men's club to which several of his workmates belonged but then withdrew because he believed it was being run by a Communist clique. He would also like to join an angling club but has not done so since this would mean being away from his family at week-ends.

The Doyles write to their relatives in Ireland every week and they visit Ireland almost every holiday. But they have no plans for returning there permanently. They look forward to building on the prosperity they have achieved in Luton—to buying their own house, to giving their children a good education and, eventually, to having more time to themselves to enjoy their domesticity.

Case two: Mr Taylor

Mr Taylor is an assembler at Vauxhall. He is in his late twenties and has two small children. He was brought up in a suburban district to the east of London. His father was employed for some time in an insurance broker's office in the city and then became manager of a small commercial concern. He is presently helping to manage a trading firm in which he has an ownership interest.

Mr Taylor was the eldest of four children, having two brothers and a sister. All the boys were privately educated, at least in part. Mr Taylor attended a private 'college' until he was fourteen and then went on to a municipal art school. He hoped to become a commercial artist but decided after a year that he would not make the grade: 'I'm a bit slow really.' He then looked around for clerical work and eventually found a job in a large City bank. He remained there up to the time of his National Service and returned afterwards. A year or so later he moved to a job as a wages clerk in an industrial firm. Meanwhile, both of Mr Taylor's brothers had become launched on successful careers, one as a shipping executive, the other as a chartered accountant.

Mr Taylor found his new job very attractive: 'some responsibility and plenty of freedom' but promotion prospects were slight. Moreover, by this time he was envisaging marriage and felt that he should try to find work of a better-paying kind. After several short-lived jobs he decided to 'go the whole hog' and got work as an assembler at a big car-manufacturing plant sufficiently close to his home town to enable him to go on living there after his marriage took place. However, he and his wife had great difficulty in finding suitable accommodation and it was this which chiefly led them to think of moving to Luton. In addition, Mr Taylor was 'fed up with the bickering and stoppages' at his existing firm and liked the idea of working at Vauxhall. The next time vacancies occurred there he got himself taken on, and shortly afterwards the Taylors made a down payment on a house in a new private estate on the outskirts of Luton.

While appreciating Vauxhall's good industrial relations, Mr Taylor makes no secret of the fact that it is first and foremost 'the money' that keeps him in the firm's employment. He finds that he can 'tolerate' assembly-line work but is often bored and irritated by the restrictions it imposes. He misses the variety of work and of social contacts which he had in his clerical jobs. Nevertheless, he would only think of leaving Vauxhall if he could accumulate enough capital to start up a business of his own. Mr Taylor is very conscious of the fact that, as he puts it, 'I've done worse than the rest of the family'; and he would like one day to 'make good' himself. But at least until he is in a position to make his bid, his main concern remains that of getting the best-paying work which is available to him.

Apart from the cash nexus, Mr Taylor's ties with his work and workplace are virtually non-existent. He 'gets on alright' with his workmates but 'they are not friends'. He never sees them outside work other than casually—'even though some of them live almost next door'. He does not belong to the Vauxhall Recreation Club and, although a union member, he has never been to a union meeting of any kind: 'I joined for the friendly benefits, that's all.'

The Taylors' social life in Luton is in general very restricted. There is only one couple—met through their children—whom they visit or go out with. Although before coming to Luton they had belonged to a number of clubs and societies, Mrs Taylor now belongs to none and Mr Taylor to only one—the local cricket club where he plays once a week in summer. Both of the Taylors still regard their 'real friends' as being back in their home district and they still see them frequently when visiting their parents. They also telephone friends and kin quite regularly.

Mr Taylor's 'dream' for the future is to go back 'home' to start his own business: to reassume, one would feel, his position in middle-class society. However, his more realistic aspirations are those of 'doing well at Vauxhall—getting promotion perhaps', buying a larger house in a more 'select' area, and sending his children to a private school.

Case three: Mr Grant

Mr Grant is also a Vauxhall assembler. He is forty years old and has four children aged between three and twelve. He was born in Ireland but before coming to Luton had lived for the greater part of his life in Scotland. His father, who has remained in Ireland, has a grocery business and is also a publican. Mr Grant has four brothers and two sisters. All have come to England in search of employment and have mostly been successful. Mr Grant's elder sister started her own small business in London and subsequently married a university lecturer; a younger brother has become a director of a publishing firm: 'They've done well—we don't see much of them now.'

Mr Grant intended to make his own career in the Merchant Navy. After leaving school at fifteen he was at sea for ten years. During this time he worked his way up to the position of second mate, and then started taking courses at a technical college for his first mate's certificate. However, after some months he abandoned this because of bad eyesight and financial difficulties. Shortly afterwards he left the Merchant Navy and for the next two to three years had a variety of jobs in different parts of Scotland, working chiefly as a barman, bar manager, or clerk. This unsettled period ended with Mr Grant's marriage, when he decided he should take a 'steady job'. He found work as a machinist in an engineering firm on Clydebank and was there for nine years. During the late 1950s, the firm ran into difficulties and Mr Grant had doubts about his security; he was also dissatisfied with the level and uncertainty of his earnings on piece rates. After some hesitation, he and his wife finally decided to move to Luton when they heard that jobs were available at Vauxhall and that they would be able to buy their own house—'which didn't seem to be the done thing in Scotland, at least in the working element'.

Mr Grant dislikes most aspects of the work he does at Vauxhall; he finds it 'very boring', yet stressful both physically and psychologically: 'It gets on your nerves the way it ties you down.' He has tried several times to get himself moved off the assembly line but without success. However, he has never seriously thought of leaving Vauxhall: 'I brought my family down here and the money's very good; I've got to make a go of it.' He has no close ties with any of his workmates and although he joined the Recreation Club when he first came to Vauxhall, he has never participated in any way. He has been to 'one or two' union meetings—the last eighteen months ago: 'I've had too much time to put in on the house since then.' He sees Vauxhall as 'the place where I work—that's all'.

Mr Grant is similarly limited in his appreciation of Luton. He stresses that he came there 'for the job and the house'—'I didn't come because of any personal liking for Luton. It's a big place commercially but the people have a market-town mentality.' On the estate to which the Grants have recently moved (to a newer and larger house than their first) they find the people 'more respectable than most' but they have so far made little contact with their neighbours and do not seem anxious to do so: 'I like people to mind their own business...I spend ninety-five per cent of my time with my wife and children.' The only people the Grants see at all regularly in Luton are also migrants—Mrs Grant's parents and younger sister who have moved down from Scotland and an old school friend of Mr Grant. Their other main social contacts are with three of Mrs Grant's brothers and their families who are now living in the London area. One is a B.B.C. engineer, another a production manager and the third a science teacher. Visits take place 'fairly often', the brothers mostly coming to Luton 'because they have cars'.

Mr Grant admires these men, it seems, even more than his own success-ful kin: 'They have all got on even though they didn't have the benefit of a very good education to begin with. They did it all on their own—part-time in the evenings.'[1] He often thinks now that he should have persevered more himself in the Merchant Navy and that it was a mistake to leave: 'I should have kept on and tried to get further.' In his present position he no longer has any real hopes for promotion. He believes that the best he can look forward to is to have 'still a bit more money coming in—a win on the pools perhaps or a rise so that I could put something in the bank'. But, one way or another, he thinks that 'things will go on improving.'

[1] In this case, then, it was his *wife's* siblings, more perhaps than his own, who formed an important reference group for the respondent. In any research specifically concerned with the consequences of 'relative' downward mobility, it would be necessary to take this possibility systematically into account.

8. Conclusion

In the introductory chapter to this monograph, two aims were set out: first, that of describing the industrial attitudes and behaviour of our sample of affluent manual workers; second, that of using this descriptive material as a basis for raising and discussing a number of theoretical problems in industrial sociology. We hope that by now these two aims have, in some manner, been achieved. It may, however, be of some further value if in this brief concluding chapter we develop or restate certain points to which we attach major importance.

So far as the descriptive purpose of our study is concerned, our salient findings, reflecting our respondents' predominantly instrumental orientation to their employment, have already been summarised at the beginning of the previous chapter. Here, therefore, we may concentrate on the question of what wider significance these findings may be said to have. As we stated at the outset, our sample is not one on the basis of which any far-ranging generalisations of a direct kind can safely be made: on the contrary, it was expressly devised so as to represent a special, critical case. And, as we have repeatedly tried to show in course of the monograph, the attitudes and behaviour of our respondents appear often divergent from those of most other industrial workers who have been studied in different, more 'traditional' contexts. Nevertheless, while these contrasts are, of course, central to the argument of the monograph, we have at certain points found reason to speculate that our affluent workers may perhaps be revealing a pattern of industrial life which will in the fairly near future become far more widespread. The main respects in which we believe this may prove to be the case, and our grounds for thinking so, are as follows.

(i) It is in our view probable that, in the conditions of modern British society, the tendency will increase for industrial workers, *particularly unskilled or semi-skilled men*, to define their work in a largely instrumental manner; that is, as essentially a means to ends which are extrinsic to their work situation. The more traditional modes of working-class life are now steadily being eroded both by such factors as urban redevelopment and greater geographical mobility and also, one may suppose, by the 'demonstration effect' of those workers and their families who have already become 'affluent'. One may then expect that as this process continues, the pressure on the mass of manual workers to increase their consumer power will intensify. Models of new standards and styles of living will become both more evident and more compelling. In the case of those men at least who do not possess skills which are in high demand, there will be mounting inducements to relegate work to the level of merely instrumental activity and to seek employment which offers a high economic return if only as compensation for its inherent 'disutility'. Moreover, such a tendency is likely to be encouraged by the reorientation of working-class family and community life which would now seem to be taking place on a fairly large scale. One major outcome of this is to bring the conjugal family into a more central position than previously in the life of the manual worker, and thus to widen and strengthen the expectations which are held of him as husband, father and family provider. And to the extent, then, that his out-of-work life becomes dominated by home and family concerns, the link between this and the worker's occupational life is likely to be narrowed down to one of a largely economic kind.[1] In other words, a privatised social life and an instrumental orientation to work may in this way be seen as mutually supportive aspects of a particular life-style.

(ii) Following on from the above, we would also expect our affluent workers to be to some extent 'prototypical' in the limited, affectively neutral, nature of their involvement in their work organisations. We are not inclined, on existing evidence, to share in the view of Blauner and others who see the more advanced forms of production technology as being generally conducive to more normatively integrated industrial enterprises.[2] We would not give the same weight as these writers to the effects of technology in determining attitudes to work and the structure of work relationships. As a factor of greater potential importance, we would again refer to ongoing changes in working-class life outside work, and most notably in this respect to changes *within* the family. In consequence of the conjugal family assuming a more 'companionate' or partnership-like form, relations both between husband and wife and between parents and children would seem likely to become closer and more inherently rewarding; certainly more so than could generally have been the case under the economic and social conditions of the traditional working-class community.[3] If workers are better able to satisfy their expressive and affective

---

[1] cf. Klein, *Samples from English Cultures*, pp. 283–99.   [2] See above, pp. 70–1.

[3] See, for example, Klein, *Samples from English Cultures*, pp. 288–302; and J. and E. Newson, *Infant Care in an Urban Community* (London, 1963), ch. 13. To counteract any tendency towards romanticising family relationships in traditional working-class life, see E. Slater and M. Woodside, *Patterns of Working Class Marriage* (London, 1951); and M. Spring Rice, *Working Class Wives* (London, 1937).

needs through family relationships, it may be anticipated that those men at least who enjoy no special occupational skills or responsibilities will less commonly regard their workplace as a *milieu* in which they are in search of satisfactions of this kind. Rather, time spent in work-based association will more probably be seen as detracting from time available for family life and thus as representing a social cost. Correspondingly, work-linked obligations or social attachments, beyond those essential to retaining employment, will tend to be avoided. Furthermore, as we have already suggested, workers of the kind in question are likely to be subject to increasing pressure to give priority in their employment to maximising economic returns; that is, to define their work as a means of gaining resources for the pursuit of extrinsic—largely familial—ends. Finally, so far as the enterprise itself is concerned, it must be remembered that, independently to some extent of the pattern of technological change, the *scale* of plants and establishments is likely to increase further, and also the degree of bureaucratic control and administration to which employees are exposed. Thus, the continuing rationalisation of work in these ways is yet another factor which may be expected to inhibit workers' identification with, and commitment to, the enterprise in any moral sense.

(iii) As regards trade unionism, it is clear that in one respect at least our affluent workers[1] merely reveal—though in extreme form—a pattern of behaviour which is very general and in no way recent; that is, in their low participation in branch affairs. However, of greater interest is the question of whether they may be regarded as indicative of newer trends in their *concurrent* relatively high involvement in unionism at workplace level; that is, in union activity focused on the particular, largely economic, issues of their own shop and factory. In our view, the almost complete divorce between the unionism of the branch and of the workplace which is manifest here *is* likely to develop on a much wider scale, as also may associated views of the functions of trade unions of a distinctively limited and instrumental kind. Such a trend in unionism we would see as the most probable concomitant of the trends in orientations to work and to family and community life to which we have already referred. To the extent that wants and expectations from work are confined to high-level economic returns, so the meaning of trade unionism will tend to be interpreted in a similarly instrumental way. And to the extent that individuals' central life interests are to be found in the cultivation and enjoyment of their private, domestic lives, commitment to trade unionism, understood as a social movement or as an expression of class or occupational solidarity, is unlikely

---

[1] The craftsmen excepted.

to be widespread. On the other hand, where there is a strong drive to increase the material rewards of work, and thus consumer power, then involvement in union activity concerned with matters of wages and conditions of service of immediate interest to workers may, of course, be expected—and involvement, perhaps, of some intensity. While militancy directed towards such ends as greater worker control may well become more difficult to sustain among home-centred employees, we would regard greater aggressiveness in the field of 'cash-based' bargaining as a very probable development.[1]

(iv) Finally, on the question of aspirations for the future, we would think that there is at least one general characteristic of our affluent workers which will become increasingly common; namely, their awareness of themselves as carrying through some individual, or more probably family, project—their awareness of being engaged in a course of action aimed at effecting some basic change in their life situation and, perhaps, in their social identity. As we noted earlier, such an outlook is in marked contrast to the fatalistic social philosophy which was frequently encountered among the inhabitants of the traditional working-class community. However, as the proportion of manual workers with personal experience of long-term economic insecurity diminishes, more optimistic attitudes towards the future may be expected to develop more widely. And as the normative force of traditional ways of life is weakened, through both their physical disruption and the presentation of attractive alternatives, it may be anticipated that to an increasing extent manual workers and their families will pursue new goals and standards in a relatively purposive and planful fashion. In this respect, we would suggest, the workers we studied can be regarded as being in some sense both pioneers and exemplars. The life-styles which they are now creating for themselves may well set the patterns and the norms for subsequent recruits to the 'new' working class and at the same time stand as inducements to others still to seek in their turn a road which leads to affluence.

In these several ways it is our view that the subjects of our Luton enquiry will prove to be more typical of the future than they are of the present time. But it need scarcely be added that the foregoing paragraphs should in no way be understood as implying unconditional predictions about the future course of events. They are intended rather as an attempt at outlining, in the light of our research, some probable consequences for working-class economic life of already observable trends of change within

---

[1] For a broadly similar view to the above, see Political and Economic Planning, *Trade Unions in a Changing Society* (London, 1963), pp. 196–204 esp.

British society at large. Such trends may, of course, be checked or reversed in ways which cannot be foreseen; and it is only on the condition that they continue that our analysis can stand.

Turning now to the main theoretical considerations which arise from our research, we may usefully recapitulate the discussion of earlier chapters by referring first to 'human relations' theory and secondly to what we have termed the 'technological implications' approach. In both these respects, as we have seen, our findings provide a basis for some critical comment.

As regards 'human relations', in both its earlier and later versions, the main point to be raised concerns the nature of the satisfactions which industrial workers require from their employment. It is fundamental both to the position of Mayo and his associates and to that of exponents of 'neo-human-relations' that men seek to satisfy in their work not only economic needs but also needs of a 'social' kind—for acceptance, approval, recognition, status, and so on. Where these latter 'higher level' needs are not met, then, it is claimed, in some form or other a pathological situation is likely; that is to say, a situation in which individuals will suffer psychologically or in which the industrial organisation will lose in effectiveness or, most probably, a situation in which both of these negative effects will be experienced. However, in view of the data which emerge from our research, it would appear that the above argument is one which calls for modification in several respects.

To begin with, it appears essential to recognise that while from a psychological standpoint the attempt to specify the range and structure of individual human needs may be legitimate and relevant,[1] one cannot proceed directly from this to specify the wants and expectations of particular individuals in regard to some given aspect of their social lives. For wants and expectations are culturally determined *variables*, not psychological constants; and from a sociological standpoint what is in fact of major interest *is* the variation in the ways in which groups differently located in the social structure actually experience and attempt to meet the needs which at a different level of analysis may be attributed to them all.

As we have argued from the first, a wide range of possible orientations exists in regard to work. In some cases, workers may look to their employment to provide a variety of rewards of an intrinsic kind as well as extrinsic, economic rewards; they may even be prepared to sacrifice the latter to some extent in preserving or enhancing the former. In other cases,

---

[1] As, for example, in the work of Maslow—which has been an important influence on 'neo-human-relations' theory. See A. H. Maslow, *Motivation and Personality* (New York, 1954).

workers may concentrate very heavily on economic returns and largely restrict their pursuit of satisfactions of an expressive or affective nature to their out-of-work lives. Moreover, it must be stressed that such differing orientations cannot be taken simply as representing reactions or adaptations to given types of employment—as being brought about by the fitting of wants and expectations to what in fact particular jobs have to offer. It may well be the case, as we have shown, that a given orientation to work will lead to a man taking up a certain type of job—one, that is, which he sees as being of a kind best suited to meeting the priorities he holds in regard to work, at least for the time being.

Consequently, in seeking to explain and to understand attitudes, behaviour and social relationships within a particular work situation, analysis will more usefully begin with the orientations to work which are found to prevail, rather than with quite general assumptions about the needs which all workers have. For example, as we have seen, where men are oriented towards their employment in an essentially instrumental way, situations which from the point of view of 'human relations' theory would appear potentially pathological do not necessarily prove to be so. In such a case, therefore, the explanatory value of this theory cannot be very great. The absence of solidary work groups or of 'employee-centred' supervision is unlikely to produce any marked degree of frustration or discontent on the part of employees; and the fact that they do not identify very closely with the enterprise or feel any sense of moral commitment towards it need in no way betoken a breakdown in organisational coherence or effectiveness. On the contrary, workers may strongly approve of their firm as an employer and believe that it gives them definite employment advantages—that is, in the form of the high-level economic returns which represent their main objective in work. And on this basis they may be attached to the enterprise no less firmly than through the normative integration which is the ultimate goal of 'human relations' practice.

As Landsberger has pointed out, the 'human relations' approach must be understood in part as a reaction against the strongly individualistic emphases of classical economics and of early industrial psychology.[1] In addition it was also powerfully influenced by Mayo's vision of modern society as lapsing into a disorganised and anomic state. Hence the importance given—both theoretically and prescriptively—to man's need for solidary relationships with his fellows and for opportunities to work with others towards common ends; hence too the stress on the part that must be played by the industrial enterprise in providing a basis for such

[1] H. Landsberger, *Hawthorne Revisited* (Ithaca, 1958), pp. 86–8.

7-2

'belongingness' and social co-operation in a society in which the extended family and local community were in decline.[1] However, it is now apparent that both modern man and modern society are in fact a good deal more 'adaptive' than Mayo and his followers supposed. It is possible for work not to be a central life interest and to be given largely instrumental meaning without the individual being thereby virtually deprived of all social activities and relationships which are rewarding in themselves. Rather, as we have seen, the readiness to adopt an orientation to work of the kind in question would appear often to indicate a commitment to the interest of one primary group—the conjugal family—which is of an overriding kind.[2]

In the case of the 'technological implications' approach, the observations which the findings of our research suggest are again ones that touch upon fundamental issues. Here, however, these are ones which relate not to basic psychological assumptions but rather to a certain mode of sociological explanation.

As we have earlier suggested, the approach in question represents in effect an attempt to apply to the study of the industrial enterprise a form of

[1] See in particular Elton Mayo, *The Social Problems of an Industrial Civilization* (Boston, 1947); also, Reinhard Bendix and Lloyd Fisher, 'The Perspectives of Elton Mayo', *The Review of Economics and Statistics*, vol. 31 (1949), and Clark Kerr and Lloyd Fisher, 'Plant Sociology: the Elite and the Aborigines' in M. Komarovsky (ed.), *Common Frontiers of the Social Sciences* (Glencoe, 1957).

[2] We would not wish it to be thought here that we believe it either desirable or possible to discard entirely all conceptions of human needs in the study of industrial life. As we have said, our concern is rather with the degree of variation that is possible in the ways in which such needs are actually felt and their satisfaction pursued. Moreover, in one respect—largely neglected by 'human relations' exponents—we would in fact accept that the limits to this variation may be relatively narrow; that is, in the relationship between workers and the actual work-tasks they are required to perform. Even here, it should be noted, recent research has indicated that over quite a wide range of industrial jobs the degree of satisfaction experienced is likely to be determined more by the culturally shaped wants and expectations which men *bring to* their employment than by objective aspects of the jobs themselves, so that workers with certain social and cultural characteristics may be more satisfied with simple, undemanding jobs than with more complex and challenging ones. (See A. N. Turner and P. Lawrence, *Industrial Jobs and the Worker*, Cambridge, Mass., 1966.) Nevertheless, there now also exists ample evidence—to which we have here contributed further—that certain types of work in modern industry, of an *extremely* repetitive, fragmented, and 'meaningless' kind, are very regularly a source of *deprivation* to those who carry them out, even if their wants and expectations from work are strictly limited. And, furthermore, it is certainly possible that the continuous exposure to stress and frustration which is in question here may be in some way psychologically damaging to the individuals involved. (See, for example, Arthur Kornhauser, *Mental Health of the Industrial Worker*, New York, 1965.) As we have argued, workers may define their work situation in such a way that they do not look to this *milieu* as one in which 'social' satisfactions are likely to be gained and do not, therefore, feel greatly deprived in their absence. But beyond a certain point, it would seem, the (in part physical) strains and pressures of some forms of industrial work, and their attendant detrimental consequences for the individual, cannot be 'defined away'.

structural-functional analysis. Technology is regarded as the set of means through which the enterprise seeks to achieve its business objectives and thus to 'survive' in its economic environment. Any given form of technology, if it is to operate effectively, can then be seen as having certain organisational requirements or 'imperatives' (although there may be alternative sets of these) which will be reflected in the pattern of work-tasks and -roles existing throughout the enterprise. This pattern can then in turn be taken, it is argued, as a crucial determinant of work attitudes and behaviour and of the structure of in-plant social relationships in general—not only between men on the shop floor but between workers and supervisors, workers and management, supervisors and management, and so on. Accepting this approach, it therefore becomes possible to offer explanations of *observed* attitudes, behaviour and relationships within an industrial context by relating these to the exigencies and constraints which stem from the functioning of the enterprise, understood as a social system 'geared', as it were, for economic production.

However, this entire theoretical position must of course depend for its validity upon the extent to which, in Woodward's formulation, 'industrial behaviour at all levels is a function of the work situation itself';[1] in other words, upon the extent to which employees' performance and experience of their technologically determined work-tasks and -roles is correlated with the ways in which they are disposed to act towards their mates, their superiors, their employer, etc. And in this respect, the main significance of the findings presented in this study is to indicate that no such correlation need exist.

As we have shown, technology was clearly the major factor in determining the level of intrinsic satisfaction which our respondents were able to derive from their jobs. It was also evident that technical organisation importantly influenced the pattern of social interaction in work in the shops and departments with which we were concerned, and could thus, for instance, inhibit the formation of solidary work groups or restrict the amount of contact which was possible between supervisors and the men in their charge. But, nonetheless, little systematic association was revealed among the workers we studied between their immediate experience of their work situations as technologically conditioned, and the range of attitudes and behaviour which they more generally displayed as industrial employees. If, for example, we consider the semi-skilled men—the machinists, process workers and assemblers—what is perhaps most striking

[1] 'Industrial Behaviour—Is there a Science?', p. 13. Woodward is, of course, in this instance using the word 'function' in its mathematical, not sociological, sense.

is the similarity of their attitudinal and behavioural patterns, despite the very different technological environments in which men in these groups work. Consequently, our findings could lend little support to the idea that because of the considerable strains and pressures that it imposes, mass production technology—and notably assembly-line technology—tends to generate more antagonistic attitudes on the part of workers and more conflict-laden work relationships than does, say, the technology of batch or of process production. The experience of some form of physical or psychological stress in work, even though most marked with the assemblers, was in fact fairly general among the semi-skilled men in our sample, and few gained any high level of satisfaction directly from their jobs. Yet it was also the case that a majority reported reasonably harmonious relations with their first-line supervisors, saw their relationship with their employer as being, at least within limits, one of collaboration and interdependence, regarded their firm's record of industrial peace in a favourable light and had never thought of leaving their employment.

This absence of any direct association between technologically conditioned experience within the work situation and attitudes and behaviour that are of wider reference represents a serious difficulty for a theoretical approach which takes as its starting point the enterprise as a 'socio-technical' system.[1] The fact that such a lack of association may be found points to a definite limitation on the explanatory value of such an approach, and one which its exponents do not in general appear to have recognised.[2] On the other hand, the explanatory relevance of the wants and expectations which men *bring to* their work is in this way underlined. For the orientation which workers have to their employment and the manner, thus, in which they define their work situation can be regarded as *mediating* between features of the work situation objectively considered and the nature of workers' response. And as orientations to work vary, so too may variations be expected in the attitudinal and behavioural implications of any given technological environment. For instance, technological constraints on collaboration in work-tasks or on work-group formation generally will be far less likely to lead to frustration and pervasive discontent among workers for whom work is an essentially instrumental activity

---

[1] This particular term is, of course, one specific to the Tavistock Institute group. However, the basic ideas involved appear to be shared by all exponents of the 'technological implications' approach, even if they have not always been applied with the sophistication of their originators. Cf. Walker, Guest and Turner, *The Foreman on the Assembly Line*, pp. 147–8.

[2] The one attempt of which we are aware to consider some of the basic problems of the approach in question is in an unfortunately unpublished paper by a member of the Tavistock Institute: F. E. Emery, 'Characteristics of Socio-Technical Systems', The Tavistock Institute of Human Relations (1959).

than among men who are in fact seeking for 'social' satisfactions in their employment in addition to economic returns. And, similarly, technologically necessitated methods of control of a bureaucratic and impersonal kind will tend to have far more disturbing and dysfunctional consequences for the latter type of worker than they will for the former.

In the case of the men in our sample, the particularly sharp contrast between their largely negative experience of their work-tasks and -roles and their largely positive dispositions towards their employing organisations must clearly be related to the fact that to an outstanding degree they shared in the same orientation to work and one which was of an exceptionally instrumental kind. But lest this state of affairs should be regarded as being quite atypical, the two following points should be noted. First, as we have argued above, there are grounds for believing that a markedly instrumental view of work may well become more widespread, at least among semi-skilled men. And, secondly, it may be assumed that under conditions of full or near-full employment, the taking or retaining of industrial jobs will regularly involve some form of *choice* as between different patterns of reward. Thus it is likely that there is a fairly general tendency in operation for the labour forces of particular enterprises to become to some degree homogeneous, in terms of their members' orientation to work, as a result simply of processes of self-selection. Men with a certain order of priorities in regard to work will tend to be found together in employments which offer the best opportunities for achieving the returns to which they have given highest value. It may then be argued that in *any* attempt at explaining and understanding attitudes and behaviour within modern industry, the probability at least must be recognised that orientations to work which employees hold in common will need to be treated as an important *independent* variable relative to the in-plant situation.[1]

The basic shortcoming of the 'technological implications' approach is that the attempt to provide explanations from the point of view of the 'system' entails the neglect of the point of view of the actors involved.

[1] There is an interesting parallel between our argument here and that advanced by critics of 'ecological' explanations of the social life of local communities. To the extent that choice in area of residence is possible, it has been pointed out, the applicability of ecological explanations declines. For patterns of choice and the relative cultural and social homogeneity of community populations which results then become central to the analysis of life-styles and social relationships, and ecology is reduced to the status of a set of limiting conditions. Moreover, the two factors which have been regarded as most important in determining choice of area of residence are also ones we have emphasised in regard to orientations to work: position in the life-cycle and class and status situation. See, for example, Herbert J. Gans, 'Urbanism and Surburbanism as Ways of Life: a Re-evaluation of Definitions' in A. M. Rose (ed.), *Human Behaviour and Social Processes* (London, 1962).

Where the dispositions of actors are in fact considered, then the logic of the analysis permits only that these be regarded as epiphenomena of the functioning of the system. The inadequacies of such an approach therefore become most marked when it is *empirically the case* that the individuals in the enterprise under analysis are not simply a random collection but share rather in certain values and goals to which their involvement may be attributed in the first place, and whose sources must then clearly be sought externally to the enterprise.

In using our research data as a basis for the foregoing criticism of certain 'established' positions in industrial sociology, it has not been our intention to be merely destructive. It is manifest that both the approaches with which we have been concerned offer valuable insights and have some explanatory contribution to make. Our aim has not been to dismiss them but to try to identify their doubtful assumptions and analytical weaknesses. At the same time we have also sought to be somewhat more positive by giving at least an indication of the lines on which, in our view, theoretical development should proceed if the gaps which presently exist are to be made good.

As should be evident from the style of analysis which we have followed throughout this monograph, we believe that in industrial sociology what may be termed an action frame of reference could, with advantage, be more widely adopted; that is to say, a frame of reference within which actors' own definitions of the situations in which they are engaged are taken as an initial basis for the explanation of their social behaviour and relationships. In contrast with approaches which begin with some general and normative psychology (or philosophy) of individual needs in work, or with some conception of the 'needs' of the efficiently operating industrial enterprise, an action frame of reference would direct attention systematically to the *variety of meanings* which work may come to have for industrial employees. And this in turn would then compel recognition of the fact that in modern society the members of the industrial labour force form a highly differentiated collectivity—in terms, for example, of the positions and roles they occupy in their non-working lives, in their subcultural characteristics, and in the pattern of their life histories and objectives for the future.

Operating from such a position, the first step must be that of establishing empirically the way in which, in any given case, the wants and expectations which men bring to their employment, and the interpretation which they thus give to their work, shape the attitudinal and behavioural patterns of their working lives as a whole. And to be included here are not only their relationships with their mates, supervisors and managers in the immediate work situation but also, for example, their stance towards their firm as an employer, their 'image' of the industrial enterprise, their style of trade unionism and the manner in which they envisage, and plan for, the lives ahead of them. To have shown the nature of this patterning in the case of our sample of affluent workers we would see as being the main contribution of the present study.

The second step—which we have ourselves been able to take in only a tentative fashion—is that of demonstrating how any orientation to work which is in question is in fact socially generated and sustained. The values and motivations that lead workers to the view of work they have adopted must be traced back, so far as this is possible, to typical life situations and experiences. In this way, therefore, the possibility—indeed, the necessity —arises, as it does not with the other approaches we have considered, of explaining and understanding the social life which goes on within the enterprise by reference ultimately to the structure and processes of the wider society in which the enterprise exists.[1] And this, in our view, is an essential development if industrial sociology is to vindicate itself from the charges that its horizons are restricted to the enterprise and that its perspectives, if not its prejudices, are those of management.

More importantly, an approach of the kind outlined would also seem to us necessary if industrial sociology is to accommodate to what we would regard as an increasingly well-attested *fact*—and one which our own findings serve to illustrate: namely, that in modern, 'mass' society, the enterprise is often not an organisation of any great normative influence in the lives of its manual labour force. Following Etzioni, it is an organisation which, in normative terms, could be said to be 'more pervaded than pervasive'.[2] In consequence of this fact, it may well be that the attitudes and behaviour of industrial workers will in many respects be more intelligible in relation to the roles they occupy—and the values they accept and the goals they pursue—within, say, familial or community contexts than in relation to the tasks they perform and the roles they fulfil actually as employees.[3] The possibility must at all events be recognised and allowed for that where workers are involved in their employing organisations in only a limited, calculative way, the influence exerted on them by aspects of the

[1] To achieve this fully, would, of course, require investigation of the orientations to work and associated attitudes and behaviour not only of rank-and-file employees but also of all other groups involved in the enterprise. Most studies thus far made of administrative, technical and managerial grades have unfortunately 'stopped at the office door'.

[2] See *A Comparative Analysis of Complex Organizations*, pp. 160–8.

[3] For some recent studies which document this point, see the following: in regard to job satisfaction, Turner and Lawrence, *Industrial Jobs and the Worker*, L. Karpik, 'Urbanisation et Satisfactions au Travail', *Sociologie du Travail*, no. 2 (1966), and 'Attentes et Satisfactions au

in-plant situation may be primarily through physical and economic constraints, and that so far as they are concerned the enterprise may not be to any significant extent a 'moral' community.

In sum, therefore, we would argue that if industrial sociology is to remain a viable field of enquiry, it cannot be limited to the investigation of interpersonal or 'small group' relations within the work situation, nor yet to the study of industrial organisations conceptualised as social systems. It must rather be understood, in the manner of our French colleagues, as *sociologie du travail*. This is not to say, of course, that such general regularities as may be established in the dynamics of work-group relations or in the structure and functioning of industrial organisations are to be regarded as of no interest. But in the perspective we adopt in this study, they cannot be seen as analytically central: they are to be thought of, rather, as limiting factors on a range of variation in industrial attitudes and behaviour that derives from the differing ways in which men may be oriented to their work.

travail', *Sociologie du Travail*, no. 4 (1966); in regard to output and earnings, Sheila Cunnison, *Wages and Work Allocation* (London, 1966); and in regard to relations with fellow workers, Michel Crozier, *Le Monde des Employés de Bureau* (Paris, 1965).

Appendix A. Additional tables

TABLE A1. *Response rates by firm and type of work*

Firm and type of work	Number in original sample	Number interviewed (work)	Response percentage	Number interviewed (home)	Overall response percentage
Vauxhall					
assembly	127	100	79	86	68
Skefko					
machining	65	45	69	41	63
machine setting	31	23	74	23	74
maintenance etc.	58	46	79	45	78
All Skefko	154	114	74	109	71
Laporte					
process work	31	23	74	23	74
maintenance	14	13	93	11	79
All Laporte	45	36	80	34	76
TOTALS	326	250	77	229	70

TABLE A2. *Reported average take-home pay*

Amount of take-home pay	Craftsmen (N = 56)	Setters (N = 23)	Process workers (N = 23)	Machinists (N = 41)	Assemblers (N = 86)	All (N = 229)
	Percentage					
Under £18	27	13	74	44	63	47
£18–£20 19s.	32	52	13	37	31	33
£21–£23 19s.	30	26	13	17	5	16
£24 and over	11	4	0	2	1	4
No information	0	4	0	0	0	(1)
TOTALS	100	99	100	100	100	100

TABLE A3. *Estimated average overtime*

Hours overtime per week	Craftsmen (N = 56)	Setters (N = 23)	Process workers (N = 23)	Machinists (N = 41)	Assemblers (N = 86)	All (N = 229)
	Percentage					
0–3	29	0	66	17	83	48
Over 3–10	57	44	17	39	14	32
Over 10	13	52	17	44	3	19
No information	2	4	0	0	0	1
TOTALS	101	100	100	100	100	100

TABLE A4. *Number of jobs held in course of working life**

Number of jobs	Craftsmen (N = 56)	Setters (N = 23)	Process workers (N = 23)	Machinists (N = 41)	Assemblers (N = 86)	All (N = 229)
	Percentage					
1, i.e. always in present job	2	0	0	0	0	(1)
2	25	0	17	10	5	11
3 to 5	52	48	35	56	64	55
6 to 10	18	39	35	32	27	28
More than 10	4	13	13	2	5	6
TOTALS	101	100	100	100	101	100

* I.e. including present one.

TABLE A5. *Reasons given for staying in present firm: white-collar sample*

Class of reason	Times mentioned	Percentage mentioning (N = 54)
Nature of work	21	39
Good security	19	35
Level of pay	16	30
Fair employer, good industrial relations, good management	15	28
Good colleagues	10	19
Good fringe benefits, welfare provisions	10	19
Lives near place of work	7	13
Too old to move	7	13
Other reasons	8	15
ALL REASONS	113	

TABLE A6. *Assessment of comparable employment advantages in other firms by advantages seen in present employment (i.e. reasons given for staying in present job)*

Occupational group	Firms seen as giving same advantages as present one	Reasons for staying in present job: percentage mentioning				
		Level of pay and/or other economic factors*	Non-economic aspects of work or employment	Other reasons	N	Percentage of occupational group
Craftsmen and	Not many	82	70	32	44	56
Setters	Many	100	27	41	22	28
	Other, D.K.	*100*	*60*	*20*	*5*	*6*
	D.N.A.	*75*	*13*	*25*	*8*	*10*
TOTAL		87	52	33	79	100
Process workers,	Not many	85	40	26	88	59
Machinists and	Many	87	30	37	30	20
Assemblers	Other, D.K.	78	50	17	18	12
	D.N.A.	57	21	43	14	9
TOTALS		82	37	28	150	100

* I.e. security of employment and social welfare and other 'fringe' benefits.

TABLE A7. *Trade union experience in relation to present firm by length of service*

Union experience	Length of service (years)	Craftsmen	Setters	Process workers	Machinists	Assemblers	All
Became unionists on	0–5	5	1	4	3	15	28
or after joining	5–15	4	10	2	7	11	34
present firm	15+	8	4	3	4	5	24
TOTAL		17	15	9	14	31	86
Were unionists on	0–5	20	2	3	21	21	67
joining present firm	5–15	8	5	6	5	11	35
and remained unionists*	15+	4	1	0	1	5	11
TOTALS		32	8	9	27	37	113
GRAND TOTALS		49	23	18	41	68	199

* Though possibly changing unions.

TABLE A8. *Attitude towards idea of becoming a foreman by action taken in regard to promotion*

	Action taken†			
Attitude towards idea of promotion*	Has never thought seriously of becoming a foreman	Has thought seriously but has taken no action	Has thought seriously and has taken some action	Total
	Percentage of total sample			
Positive	32	9	8	49
Negative	41	6‡	2‡	48
Other, D.K.	2	1	0	3
TOTALS	75	16	10	101/100

* Based on categories of table 54.
† Based on categories of table 55.
‡ These were cases of men who had thought seriously or taken action about promotion in the past but who were now not favourably disposed to the idea.

Appendix B. A note on the sample

The 'population' of the critical case with which our study was concerned is described on p. 4 of the text. The sample interviewed is not a simple random one of this population. In regard to each of the occupational categories in question—assemblers at Vauxhall, machinists, craftsmen and setters at Skefko, and process workers and craftsmen at Laporte—the sample is based on men in these categories who worked in certain selected departments. In Vauxhall, our assemblers were drawn from six of the major assembly divisions in the plant: the four- and six-cylinder engine assembly lines, the body and trim shops on the car line, and the body and trim shops on the van or 'commercial' line. In Skefko, our machine operators and setters came from a number of the largest machine shops covering heavy grinding, turret-lathe turning and 'automatic' turning; and the craftsmen were taken from the plant's two millwrights' shops and from the toolroom. In Laporte, the process workers and maintenance craftsmen came from all process departments which were in full production—that is, which were not engaged on pilot schemes.

The difficulty of such a sample is obvious: one cannot generalise from it to the population except on the assumption that the respondents from the departments which were taken were in each case representative of all the men in the occupational category concerned. However, while this was recognised, the course which was actually pursued commended itself for the following reasons: (i) in some cases the administrative problems which would have been involved in covering all relevant departments would have exceeded management's willingness to co-operate; (ii) for each department included, some appreciable time had to be spent with the managers, supervisors and union officials concerned explaining, and securing agreement to, our interviewing procedures; (iii) in each department, too, a still greater amount of time was required to discover 'how things worked', so that intelligent interviewing could be carried out, and to make an adequate observational survey; (iv) with every occupational category it appeared—and proved—possible to take in most of the larger departments in which men who met our specifications on age, marital status, earnings and residence were concentrated, with the result that within each category an estimated 60–70% of our population was in fact covered. On this basis, and since we could find no grounds for supposing that the men left out differed widely from those included, we feel that the assumption may reasonably be made that in this respect our sample will not be seriously misleading.

Within the departments we selected, our aim was—in principle—to invite for interview *all* those men who came within our population. This was desirable in most cases in order to secure a sufficiently large number of respondents to permit useful statistical analysis of our interview material. This policy proved feasible, and was in fact implemented, in all the departments in question with the exception of the two largest of the Vauxhall assembly divisions—the body and trim shops on the car line. Here, the number involved made further sampling necessary and this was carried out on a random basis from personnel records. This complication meant, of course, both that the assemblers in the two departments in question were under-represented within their occupational category and that the assemblers generally were under-represented in our sample. To correct these imbalances, some form of appropriate 'weighting' could, and strictly speaking should, have been introduced. However, in the first respect, there proved to be little point in doing this since a careful check on the interview material revealed no systematic differences in the pattern of response of the men from the car-line divisions and that of the rest of the assemblers. Thus, weighted results would not in the main have differed sufficiently to affect the interpretation of the data from the percentage figures produced by taking all the assemblers together on an equal basis.[1] In the second respect, the under-representation might appear more serious and would indeed be so if in our discussion of the interview material we had wished at all points to give great importance to the pattern of response of the sample as a whole. However, as is emphasised in the Introduction, this is not the case and our discussion is largely organised around comparisons between the various occupational groups which the sample comprises, other than where the similarity in the response of all groups is the notable feature.

[1] In the one or two particular instances where the pattern of response of the car line men does differ notably from that of the other assemblers, this has been noted in the text.

Appendix C. The occupational classification used in the study

The occupational classification set out below was constructed on the basis of previous efforts by British sociologists, notably that of Hall and Caradog Jones.[1] Each particular occupational classification used in this and other reports on our research has been derived from this more comprehensive classification through collapsing categories in whatever ways appeared most useful from case to case. For example, in our tables 15 and 16, occupational category 1 corresponds in the following classification to 1(*a*), 2(*a*) and 3(*a*); category 2 to 1(*b*), 2(*b*), 3(*b*) and 4(*b*); and category 3 to 4(*a*); categories 5 to 8 are taken over unchanged. In tables 70 and 71, 'white-collar' corresponds to 1(*a*) and (*b*), 2(*a*) and (*b*), and 3(*a*) and (*b*); 'intermediate' to 4(*a*) and (*b*); and 'manual' to 5, 6, 7 and 8.

In allocating occupations to classes we followed the general rule of choosing the 'lower' alternative in all borderline cases or cases where our information was incomplete or ambiguous. The examples given below are selected in order to give some idea of the range of occupations included in particular categories as well as of 'typical' occupations.

Occupational Status Level	*Examples*
1(*a*) Higher professional, managerial and other white-collar employees	Chartered accountant, business executive, senior civil servant, graduate teacher
(*b*) Large industrial or commercial employers, landed proprietors	—
2(*a*) Intermediate professional, managerial and other white-collar employees	Pharmacist, non-graduate teacher, departmental manager, bank cashier
(*b*) Medium industrial or commercial employers, substantial farmers	—
3(*a*) Lower professional, managerial and other white-collar employees	Chiropodist, bar manager, commercial traveller, draughtsman, accounts or wages clerk
(*b*) Small industrial or commercial employers, small proprietors, small farmers	Jobbing builder, taxi owner-driver, tobacconist

[1] J. Hall and D. Caradog Jones, 'The Social Grading of Occupations', *British Journal of Sociology*, vol. 1 (January 1950).

Occupational Status Level	*Examples*
4(*a*) Supervisory, inspectional, minor official and service employees	Foreman, meter-reader, shop assistant, door-to-door salesman
(*b*) Self-employed men (no employees or expensive capital equipment)	Window-cleaner, jobbing gardener
5 Skilled manual workers (with apprenticeship or equivalent)	—
6 Other relatively skilled manual workers	Unapprenticed mechanics and fitters, skilled miners, painters and decorators, p.s.v. drivers
7 Semi-skilled manual workers	Machine operator, assembler, storeman
8 Unskilled manual workers	Farm labourer, builder's labourer, dustman

Appendix D. Labour disputes at Vauxhall 1965–67

During the period in which this monograph was being prepared, a number of labour disputes occurred at Vauxhall's Luton plant, thus ending the firm's long record of success in avoiding overt industrial conflict. At least one writer has regarded these outbursts of unrest as invalidating the argument (pp. 73–8 above) that Vauxhall workers, rather than interpreting their relationship with their firm in fundamentally 'oppositional' terms in the manner of more class conscious workers, see in this relationship important elements of interdependence and reciprocity. The Vauxhall disputes, it has been suggested, demonstrate the long-run inevitability of the emergence of class consciousness and of generalised discontent among men who are condemned to perform inherently unrewarding work-tasks and who are systematically exploited under a capitalist system.[1]

The following observations appear pertinent.

(i) Vauxhall is still very far from being a centre of industrial unrest—and most obviously so if judged by the standards of the car industry itself. In 1965, the year in which Vauxhall had its first official and complete stoppage in nearly half a century, the total number of man days lost through disputes was less than 1% of the total for the industry as a whole. This figure will no doubt be higher for 1967—when production at Luton was disrupted over a period of two weeks —but will still remain small. Apart from the last mentioned stoppage, all others have been short-lived.

(ii) On the basis of press reports and comment, there seems little doubt that the Vauxhall disputes have been decisively centred on *pay*. Whenever other issues have been raised—working conditions, work rules, job transfers, shift-work etc.—these have been more or less quickly revealed as primarily bargaining counters in a struggle over wage levels. For example, in the 1967 dispute, all observers were agreed that at the root of discontent was the 'lag' of wages at Vauxhall behind those being paid at the Midlands car plants, and that the production workers' essential demand was for a basic £20 a week pay-packet. The settlement of the dispute followed an improved cash offer by the firm. Dissatisfaction, therefore, rather than being generalised, has been *highly focused* on the matter of remuneration.[2]

---

[1] See Robin Blackburn, 'The Unequal Society' in Blackburn and Alexander Cockburn (eds. *The Incompatibles: Trade Union Militancy and the Consensus* (London, 1967). Blackburn's remarks refer to Goldthorpe, 'Attitudes and Behaviour of Assembly Line Workers'.

[2] This is not to deny that such dissatisfaction was in some instances aggravated by unusual clumsiness on the part of management. However from autumn, 1966, the major factor creating

(iii) The pattern that disputes have followed at Vauxhall and the tactics used on the side of labour have been distinctive. Although sometimes beginning with angry walk-outs and even demonstrations, disputes, if protracted, have been chiefly waged through banning overtime and working to rule. Occasional attempts to put pressure on management by organised 'early leaving' have petered out unsuccessfully; and despite calls from militants, there has been conspicuously little enthusiasm for the strike weapon. During the 1967 dispute, local union officials repeatedly disowned the idea of striking and, as in earlier cases, the eventual stoppage of production resulted from a decision by management. What is indicated here, then, is clearly nothing so dramatic as 'an explosion of consciousness': rather, it would seem, one has a situation in which workers feel a strong sense of grievance over pay and are anxious to press their claims, but only in ways designed to cause the minimum loss of earnings. Closure of the plant until men are prepared to resume normal working is, of course, the obvious counter-tactic for management to adopt.

(iv) That conflict of the kind in question should occur is in no way contrary to our understanding of the orientation of Vauxhall workers towards their firm and towards their employment generally. We stress (pp. 84–9) that the 'teamwork' image of the enterprise, although dominant, has definite limits, and that in regard to the conditions on which 'teamwork' shall take place, the interests of employer and employees are often seen as divergent. For example, we note (p. 87) that four-fifths of the Vauxhall men in our sample were of the opinion that their firm could afford to pay them more.[1] Finally, we specifically argue, following our previous analysis, that among workers with a markedly instrumental approach to work 'we would regard greater aggressiveness in the field of 'cash-based' bargaining as a very probable development' (p. 177). At the same time, the point remains that industrial conflict which *is* largely restricted to economic issues can go together with a strong awareness on the part of workers of their interdependence with their employer and of the possibility of mutually beneficial 'accommodation'. Indeed such a co-existence of conflict and co-operation we would see as implicit in any economic association.

a tense situation within the plant was the sales slump. Within Vauxhall the Luton plant bore the full brunt of this since the Viva, the firm's most successful car, was made entirely at Ellesmere. Prolonged short-time working and fluctuating earnings were experiences to which most workers at Luton were unaccustomed.

[1] These points were also made in Goldthorpe, 'Attitudes and Behaviour of Assembly Line Workers' but are entirely ignored by Blackburn in his comments.

References

Acton Society Trust, *Management Succession* (London, 1956).
  The Worker's Point of View (London, 1962).
Adams, Stuart, 'Status Congruency as a variable in Small Group Performance',
  Social Forces, vol. 32 (1953).
Argyle, M., *et al.*, 'The Measurement of Supervisory Methods', *Human
  Relations*, vol. 10, no. 4 (1957).
Argyris, Chris, 'The Organisation—What makes it Healthy?', *Harvard Business
  Review*, vol. XXXVII, no. 5 (1958).
  'Understanding Human Behaviour in Organizations: One Viewpoint', in M.
  Haire (ed.), *Modern Organization Theory* (New York, 1959).
  Integrating the Individual and the Organization (New York, 1964).
Bain, G. S., 'The Growth of White-Collar Unionism in Great Britain', *British
  Journal of Industrial Relations*, vol. IV, no. 3 (1966).
Baldamus, W., *Efficiency and Effort* (London, 1961).
Banks, J. A., *Industrial Participation* (Liverpool, 1963).
Barber, Bernard, 'Participation and Mass Apathy in Associations', in A. W.
  Gouldner (ed.), *Studies in Leadership* (New York, 1950).
Behrend, H., *Absence under Full Employment* (Birmingham, 1951).
Bendix, R. and Fisher, Lloyd, 'The Perspectives of Elton Mayo', *The Review of
  Economics and Statistics*, vol. 31 (November 1949).
Blackburn, Robin, 'The Unequal Society' in Blackburn and Alexander Cockburn
  (eds.), *The Incompatibles: Trade Union Militancy and the Consensus* (London,
  1967).
Blau, Peter M. and Scott, W. Richard, *Formal Organisations* (London, 1963).
Blauner, Robert, 'Work Satisfaction and Industrial Trends in Modern Society',
  in W. Galenson and S. M. Lipset (eds.), *Labor and Trade Unionism* (New
  York, 1960).
  Alienation and Freedom: the Factory Worker and his Industry (Chicago,
  1964).
British Institute of Management, *Absence from Work* (London, 1963).
Cannon, I. C., *The Social Situation of the Skilled Worker*, University of London
  Ph.D. thesis, 1961.
  'Ideology and Occupation', paper presented to the Sixth World Congress of
  Sociology (Evian, 1966).
Carter, Michael, *Into Work* (London, 1966).
Chinoy, Ely, *Automobile Workers and the American Dream* (New York, 1935).
Cottrell, W. F. *The Railroader* (Palo Alto, 1940).
Crozier, Michel, *Le Monde des Employés de Bureau* (Paris, 1965).

References

Cunnison, Sheila, *Wages and Work Allocation* (London, 1966).

Cyriax, George and Oakeshott, Robert, *The Bargainers* (London, 1960).

Dale, J. R., *The Clerk in Industry* (Liverpool, 1962).

Dean, Lois R., 'Social Integration, Attitudes and Union Activity', *Industrial and Labor Relations Review*, vol. 8, no. 1 (October 1954).

Dean, Lois R., 'Interaction, reported and observed: the case of one local union', *Human Organization*, vol. 17, no. 3 (Autumn, 1956).

Dennis, N., Henriques, F. and Slaughter, C., *Coal is Our Life* (London, 1956).

Department of Scientific and Industrial Research, *Automation*, H.M.S.O. (London, 1956).

Dubin, Robert, 'Industrial Workers' Worlds: a Study of the "Central Life Interests" of Industrial Workers', *Social Problems*, vol. 3 (January 1956).
The World of Work (Englewood Cliffs, 1958).

Duncan, P., 'Conflict and Co-operation among Trawlermen', *British Journal of Industrial Relations*, vol. 1, no. 3 (1963).

Emery, F. E., 'Characteristics of Socio-Technical Systems' (cyclostyled), The Tavistock Institute of Human Relations (1959).

Emery, F. E. and Trist, E. L., 'Socio-Technical Systems', in *Management Sciences: Models and Techniques*, vol. II (London, 1960).

Etzioni, Amitai, *A Comparative Analysis of Complex Organizations* (Glencoe, 1961).

Form, William H. and Geschwender, James A., 'The Social Reference Basis of Job Satisfaction: the Case of Manual Workers', *American Sociological Review*, vol. 27, no. 2 (1962).

Friedmann, Eugene A. and Havighurst, Robert J., *The Meaning of Work and Retirement* (Chicago, 1954).

Friedmann, Georges, *Où va le Travail Humain?* (Paris, 1953).
Le Travail en Miettes, 2nd ed. (Paris, 1964).

Frisch-Gauthier, Jacqueline, 'Moral et Satisfaction au Travail', in Georges Friedmann and Pierre Naville (eds.), *Traité de Sociologie du Travail*, vol. 2 (Paris, 1962).

Gans, Herbert J., 'Urbanism and Suburbanism as Ways of Life: a Re-evaluation of Definitions' in A. M. Rose (ed.), *Human Behaviour and Social Processes* (London, 1962).

Gerth, H. H. and Wright Mills, C. (eds.), *From Max Weber: Essays in Sociology* (London, 1948).

Glass, D. V. (ed.), *Social Mobility in Britain* (London, 1954).

Goldstein, Joseph, *The Government of British Trade Unions* (London, 1952).

Goldthorpe, John H., 'Technical Organisation as a Factor in Supervisor–Worker Conflict', *British Journal of Sociology*, vol. X, no. 3 (1959).
'La Conception des Conflits du Travail dans l'Enseignement des Relations Humaines', *Sociologie du Travail*, no. 3 (1961).
'Attitudes and Behaviour of Car Assembly Workers: a deviant case and a theoretical critique', *British Journal of Sociology*, vol. XVII, no. 3 (September 1966).

Goldthorpe, John H. and Lockwood, D., 'Affluence and the British Class Structure', *Sociological Review*, vol. 11, no. 2 (July 1963).

Goldthorpe, John H., Lockwood, D., Bechhofer, F. and Platt, J., *The Affluent Worker: Political Attitudes and Behaviour* (Cambridge, 1968).

The Affluent Worker in the Class Structure (Cambridge, 1969).

Goodman, L. Landon, *Man and Automation* (London, 1957).

Goodrich, Carter L., *The Frontier of Control: a Study in British Workshop Politics* (London, 1920).

Gouldner, Alvin W., *Patterns of Industrial Bureaucracy* (London, 1954).

Greystoke, J. R., Thomason, G. F. and Murphy, T. S., 'Labour Turnover Surveys', *Personnel Management*, vol. XXXIV, no. 321 (September 1952).

Hall, J. and Caradog Jones, D., 'The Social Grading of Occupations', *British Journal of Sociology*, vol. I, no. 1 (January, 1950).

Hardie, D. W. F. and Pratt, J. D., *A History of the Modern British Chemical Industry* (Oxford, 1966).

Harrison, Martin, *Trade Unions and the Labour Party since 1945* (London, 1960).

Hoggart, Richard, *The Uses of Literacy* (London, 1958).

Homans, G. C., *Sentiments and Activities* (Glencoe, 1962).

Horobin, G., 'Community and Occupation in the Hull Fishing Industry', *British Journal of Sociology*, vol. III, no. 4 (1957).

Jasinski, Frank J., 'Technological Delimitation of Reciprocal Relationships', *Human Organization*, vol. 15, no. 2 (1956).

Jefferys, Margot, *Mobility in the Labour Market* (London, 1954).

Kahn, Hilda, *Repercussions of Redundancy* (London, 1964).

Karpik, L., 'Urbanisation et Satisfactions au Travail', *Sociologie du Travail*, no. 2 (1966).

'Attentes et Satisfactions au Travail', *Sociologie du Travail*, no. 4 (1966).

Kerr, Clark, 'What became of the Independent Spirit?' *Fortune* (June 1953).

Labor and Management in Industrial Society (New York, 1964).

Kerr, Clark and Fisher, Lloyd, 'Plant Sociology: the Elite and the Aborigines', in M. Komarovsky (ed.), *Common Frontiers of the Social Sciences* (Glencoe, 1957).

Klein, Josephine, *Samples from English Cultures* (London, 1965).

Klein, Lisl, *Multiproducts Ltd* (London, 1964).

Kornhauser, Arthur, *Mental Health of the Industrial Worker* (New York, 1965).

Kovner, Joseph and Lahne, Herbert J., 'Shop Society and the Union', *Industrial and Labor Relations Review*, vol. 7, no. 1 (October 1953).

Landsberger, H., *Hawthorne Revisited* (Ithaca, 1958).

Lenski, Gerhard, 'Status Crystallization: a non-vertical dimension of social status', *American Sociological Review*, vol. 19 (1954).

Likert, Rensis, 'A Motivation Approach to a Modified Theory of Organization and Management', in M. Haire (ed.), *Modern Organization Theory* (New York, 1959).

New Patterns of Management (New York, 1961).

Lipset, S. M., *The First New Nation* (London, 1963).

References

Lipset, S. M. and Gordon, Joan, 'Mobility and Trade Union Membership', in S. M. Lipset and R. Bendix (eds.), *Class, Status and Power*, 1st ed. (London, 1954).

Lipset, S. M., Trow, M. A. and Coleman, J. S., *Union Democracy* (Glencoe, 1956).

Liverpool, University of, Department of Social Science, *The Dock Worker* (Liverpool, 1954).

Lockwood, D., 'The "New Working Class"', *European Journal of Sociology*, vol. 1, no. 2 (1960).

Lockwood, D. and Goldthorpe, John H., 'The Manual Worker: Affluence, Aspirations and Assimilation', paper presented to the Annual Conference of the British Sociological Association, 1962.

Long, P., *Labour Turnover under Full Employment* (Birmingham, 1951).

Lupton, T., *On the Shop Floor* (London, 1963).

McGregor, Douglas, *The Human Side of Enterprise* (New York, 1960).

Maier, N. R. F., *Psychology in Industry* (Boston, 1955).

Maslow, A. H., *Motivation and Personality* (New York, 1954).

Mayo, Elton, *The Social Problems of an Industrial Civilisation* (Boston, 1947).

Merton, R. K., *Social Theory and Social Structure* (Glencoe, 1957).

Miller, S. M., 'Comparative Social Mobility', *Current Sociology*, vol. IX, no. 1 (1960).

Morse, Nancy, *Satisfactions in the White-Collar Job* (Michigan, 1953).

Moser, C. A. and Scott, Wolf, *British Towns* (Edinburgh and London, 1961).

Newson, J. and E., *Infant Care in an Urban Community* (London, 1963).

Parker, S. R., 'Type of Work, Friendship Pattern and Leisure', *Human Relations*, vol. 17, no. 3 (August 1964).

'Work and Non-Work in Three Occupations', *Sociological Review*, vol. 13, no. 1 (1965).

Parsons, Talcott, *Essays in Sociological Theory* (revised ed.) (Glencoe, 1954).

Political and Economic Planning, *British Trade Unionism* (London, 1948).

Trade Unions in a Changing Society (London, 1963).

Roberts, B. C., *Trade Union Government and Administration in Great Britain* (London, 1956).

Rowntree, B. S., *Poverty: a study of town life* (London, 1901).

Roy, Donald F., 'Quota Restriction and Goldbricking in a Machine Shop', *American Journal of Sociology*, vol. 57 (March 1952).

'Efficiency and the "Fix"', *American Journal of Sociology*, vol. 60 (1954-5).

Sayles, Leonard R., *Behavior of Industrial Work Groups* (New York, 1958).

Scott, W. H., Halsey, A. H., Banks, J. A. and Lupton, T., *Technical Change and Industrial Relations* (Liverpool, 1956).

Seidman, Joel, London, Jack, Karsh, Bernard and Tagliacozzo, Daisy L., *The Worker Views his Union* (Chicago, 1958).

Shimmin, Sylvia, 'Extra-Mural Factors influencing Behaviour at Work', *Occupational Psychology*, vol. 36 (July 1962).

Silberston, Aubrey, 'The Motor Industry, 1955-1964', *Bulletin of the Oxford University Institute of Economics and Statistics*, vol. 27, no. 4 (1965).

Slater, E. and Woodside, M., *Patterns of Working Class Marriage* (London, 1951).

Spinrad, W., 'Correlates of Trade Union Participation: a summary of the literature', *American Sociological Review*, vol. 25, no. 2 (1960).

Spring Rice, M., *Working Class Wives* (London, 1937).

Sykes, A. J. M., 'Some Differences in the Attitudes of Clerical and of Manual Workers', *Sociological Review*, vol. 13, no. 1 (1965).

'The Cohesion of Trade Union Workshop Organization', *Sociology*, vol. 1, no. 2 (1967).

'Trade Union Workshop Organisation in the Printing Industry', *Human Relations*, vol. 13, no. 1 (1960).

Thomas, G., *Labour Mobility in Great Britain, 1945–1949*, Ministry of Labour and National Service (London, 1951).

Touraine, A. and Mottez, B., 'Classe Ouvrière et Société Globale', in Georges Friedmann and Pierre Naville (eds.), *Traité de Sociologie du Travail*, vol. 2 (Paris, 1962).

Touraine, A. and Ragazzi, O., *Ouvriers d'Origine Agricole* (Paris, 1961).

Tréanton, J.-R. and Reynaud, J.-D., 'La Sociologie Industrielle, 1951–62', *Current Sociology*, vol. XII, no. 2 (1963–4).

Trist, E. L. and Bamforth, K. W., 'Some Social and Psychological Consequences of the Longwall Method of Coal-getting', *Human Relations*, vol. 4, no. 1 (1951).

Trist, E. L., Higgin, J. W., Murray, H. and Pollock, A. B., *Organizational Choice* (London, 1963).

Tunstall, J., *The Fishermen* (London, 1962).

Turner, A. N., 'Interaction and Sentiment in the Foreman-Worker Relationship', *Human Organization*, vol. 14, no. 1 (1955).

'Foreman, Job and Company', *Human Relations*, vol. X, no. 2 (1957).

Turner, A. N. and Lawrence, P., *Industrial Jobs and the Worker* (Cambridge, Mass., 1966).

Viteles, Morris S. *Motivation and Morale in Industry* (New York, 1953).

Walker, Charles R., *Steeltown* (New York, 1950).

Walker, Charles R. and Guest, Robert H., *The Man on the Assembly Line* (Cambridge, Mass., 1952).

Walker, Charles R., Guest, R. H. and Turner, A. N., *The Foreman on the Assembly Line* (Cambridge, Mass., 1956).

Webb, Sidney and Beatrice, *The History of British Trade Unionism* (London, 1911).

Weber, Max, *The Protestant Ethic and the Spirit of Capitalism* (trans. T. Parsons) (London, 1947).

Wilensky, H. 'Life Cycle, Work Situation and Participation in Formal Associations' in R. W. Kleemeier (ed.), *Aging and Leisure* (New York, 1961).

'The Moonlighter: a Product of Relative Deprivation', *Industrial Relations*, vol. 3, no. 1 (1963).

References

Willener, Alfred, 'L'Ouvrier et l'Organisation', *Sociologie du Travail*, no. 4 (1962).

 'Payment Systems in the French Steel and Iron Mining Industry', in George K. Zollschan and W. Hirsch (eds.), *Explorations in Social Change* (Boston, 1964).

Willmott, Peter, *The Evolution of a Community* (London, 1963).

Wilson, A. T. M., 'Some Aspects of Social Process', *Journal of Social Issues*, vol. 7, no. 5 (1951).

Woodward, Joan, *Management and Technology*, H.M.S.O. (London, 1958).

 'Industrial Behaviour—Is there a Science?' *New Society*, 8 October 1964.

Wyatt, S. and Marriott, R., *A Study of Attitudes to Factory Work*, H.M.S.O. (London, 1956).

Zweig, F., *The British Worker* (London, 1952).

 The Worker in an Affluent Society (London, 1961).

Index

Index

Index

Cambridge studies in sociology

Cambridge papers in sociology

Cambridge studies in sociology 1

THE AFFLUENT WORKER:
INDUSTRIAL ATTITUDES AND
BEHAVIOUR